EVERYMAN, *I will go with thee,*
and be thy guide,
In thy most need to go by thy side

PERCY BYSSHE SHELLEY

Selected Poems

Edited, with an introduction and notes, by Timothy Webb
Reader in the Department of English and Related Literature
University of York

Dent: London and Melbourne
EVERYMAN'S LIBRARY

© Introduction and notes,
J. M. Dent & Sons Ltd, 1977

All rights reserved
Made in Great Britain by
The Guernsey Press Co. Ltd, Guernsey, C.I. for
J. M. Dent & Sons Ltd
Aldine House, 33 Welbeck Street, London W1M 8LX
First published 1977
Reprinted, with corrections and minor revisions, 1983
Last reprinted 1984

British Library Cataloguing in Publication Data
Shelley, Percy Bysshe
  Shelley: selected poems. – (Everyman's
  university library).
  1. English poetry
  I. Webb, Timothy II. Series
  821'.7   PR5402
  ISBN 0-460-10186-1
  ISBN 0-460-11186-8 Pbk

CONTENTS

Shelley's Life in Context   viii
Note on the Text and Acknowledgments   xii
Introduction   xvi
Select Bibliography   xxxii
Hymn to Intellectual Beauty   1
Mont Blanc   3
Verses Written on Receiving a Celandine in a Letter
   from England   7
To the Lord Chancellor   9
Ozymandias   11
Stanzas Written in Dejection, December 1818, near
   Naples   11
Julian and Maddalo   12
From Prometheus Unbound   29
   Act I   33
   Act II Scene iv   57
   From Act III Scene iv   61
   From Act IV   64
The Mask of Anarchy written on the Occasion of
   the Massacre at Manchester   65
Ode to the West Wind   76
From Peter Bell the Third   79
Ode to Heaven   88
England in 1819   90
Lines to a Critic   90
Ode to Liberty   91
The Cloud   98
From The Sensitive Plant   100
An Exhortation   101

Song (Rarely, rarely comest thou)   102
To a Sky-lark   104
Letter to Maria Gisborne   107
From Homer's Hymn to Mercury   115
Two Songs for *Midas*   120
The Two Spirits: An Allegory   122
Sonnet to the Republic of Benevento   123
Goodnight   124
Fragment: To the Moon   124
Epipsychidion   125
Lines Written on Hearing the News of the Death of
    Napoleon   141
Adonais   142
The Aziola   158
From Hellas: Two Choruses   158
The flower that smiles today   161
To Night   161
Fragment: Rose leaves, when the rose is dead   162
O World, O Life, O Time   163
When passion's trance is overpast   163
One word is too often profaned   164
To Edward Williams   164
To Jane: The Recollection   166
From Goethe's Faust: Prologue in Heaven   168
Fragment: The Triumph of Life   171
To Jane (The keen stars were twinkling)   188
Fragment: Lines Written in the Bay of Lerici   189
Notes   191
Index of first lines   231

FOR RUTH

1792　Born 4 August at Field Place, Horsham, Sussex; eldest child of Timothy Shelley, landowning Whig M.P., later a Baronet.

1802-4　At Syon House Academy, Isleworth, near London.

1804-10　At Eton where he is bullied, develops scientific interests and writes two Gothic novels, *Zastrozzi* and *St. Irvyne* (both published 1810). With his sister writes and publishes *Original Poetry by Victor and Cazire* (published and withdrawn 1810).

1810　Goes up to University College, Oxford (October). *Posthumous Fragments of Margaret Nicholson* published (November).

1811　Meets sixteen-year-old Harriet Westbrook, whose father is the proprietor of a London coffee-house (January). Expelled from his college (25 March) with his friend T. J. Hogg for refusing to answer questions concerning their pamphlet *The Necessity of Atheism* (published February). Elopes with Harriet and marries her in Edinburgh (29 August). In December visits Lake District and meets Southey.

1812　Working on lost novel *Hubert Cauvin*. Visits Dublin; speaks, writes and distributes pamphlets on behalf of Catholic emancipation and Repeal of the Union (February-March). *Address to the Irish People* and *Proposals for an Association of . . . Philanthropists* published (February). *Declaration of Rights* printed. Becomes a vegetarian (March). Lives in Wales, then Lynmouth, Devon where he is watched by government spies and his servant is imprisoned for distributing *Declaration of Rights*. 950 copies out of 1,000 of *Letter to Lord Ellenborough* burnt by printer. Moves to Tremadoc (North Wales) in September; assists in creation of model village and embankment. Meets T. L. Peacock and William Godwin. Writing *Queen Mab*.

1813　Unexplained nocturnal incident, possibly designed to scare Shelley away (26 February). Visits Dublin and

Killarney, returning to London early in April. *Queen Mab* privately issued (May). Daughter Ianthe born (23 June). Settles at Bracknell (July), where he sees much of Peacock.

1814   *A Refutation of Deism* printed. Ferdinand of Spain annuls Constitution of the Cortes (4 May). Elopes with Mary Godwin (27 July); together with Claire Clairmont they tour Continent newly opened after end of war in April and return on 13 September. Congress of Vienna opens (1 November). Charles born to Harriet (30 November). Financial difficulties.

1815   Mary's first child born (22 February); dies two weeks later. Battle of Waterloo (18 June). Receives annual income of £1,000 on death of grandfather (June). Moves to Bishopsgate near Windsor (August), where he writes *Alastor.*

1816   Son William born to Mary (24 January). *Alastor* published (February). Summer tour brings him together with recently exiled Byron at Lake of Geneva, where he writes 'Hymn to Intellectual Beauty' (late June) and 'Mont Blanc' (late July) and Mary is inspired to begin *Frankenstein* (published 1818). Returns to England (8 September) and settles at Marlow (autumn); becomes friendly with Leigh Hunt. Suicide of Mary's half-sister Fanny Imlay (9 October). Suicide of Harriet (9 November; discovered 10 December). Spa Fields Riots in London (2 December). Marries Mary (30 December).

1817   Birth of Allegra, Byron's daughter by Claire (12 January). Meets Keats (February). Habeas Corpus suspended (17 March-31 January 1818); various measures against sedition. Loses Ianthe and Charles through judgment of Lord Eldon (27 March). Settles at Marlow (March), where he remains friendly with Peacock, the Hunts and Hogg and gives help to distressed lace-workers. *A Proposal for Putting Reform to the Vote* published (March). Finishes *Laon and Cythna* and begins *Rosalind and Helen* (September). Daughter Clara born (2 September). *History of a Six Weeks' Tour* published. In bad health. *An Address to the People on the Death of the Princess Charlotte* published (written 11-12 November); this concerns the fate of the Derby rioters (executed 7 November through the offices of an *agent provocateur*). *Laon and Cythna* published and withdrawn (December).

1818   A more discreet version of *Laon and Cythna* published as
        The Revolt of Islam (January). Departs for Italy
        (11 March) intending perhaps to return, but never does
        so. Sends Allegra to Byron (28 April). At Leghorn (from
        9 May) where he meets the Gisbornes; at Bagni di Lucca
        (from 11 June) where he completes *Rosalind and Helen*,
        translates Plato's *Symposium* (July) and begins essay on
        the manners of the Greeks (August). Burdett's motion
        for parliamentary reform heavily defeated (2 June).
        Visits Byron in Venice (late August), the inspiration for
        Julian and Maddalo; settles at nearby Este till 5 November. Clara dies (24 September). Begins *Prometheus
        Unbound, Julian and Maddalo* and 'Lines Written among
        the Euganean Hills' (autumn). Visits Ferrara, Bologna,
        Rome (20-27 November) and settles in Naples (11 December). Visits Vesuvius, Bay of Baiae and writes 'Stanzas
        Written in Dejection' (December).

1819   Visits Paestum and Pompeii (24-25 February). Leaves
        Naples (28 February). Settles at Rome (5 March) where
        he finishes Acts II and III of *Prometheus Unbound*
        (March-April) and perhaps *Julian and Maddalo*.
        Rosalind and Helen published (spring). William dies
        (7 June). Leaves Rome (10 June) and settles at Leghorn
        (17 June) where he works on *The Cenci*. 'Peterloo'
        Massacre in Manchester (16 August); writes *The Mask of
        Anarchy* (September; not published till 1832). Moves to
        Florence (2 October); writes *Peter Bell the Third*, 'Ode
        to the West Wind' (October) and long public letter on
        trial of radical printer, Richard Carlile (early November);
        finishes *Prometheus Unbound*. Begins *A Philosophical
        View of Reform* (not published till 1920). Son Percy
        Florence born (12 November). 'England in 1819' (December). The 'Six Acts', a series of strongly repressive
        measures, passed in England (December).

1820   Beginnings of Revolution in Spain (1 January). Moves to
        Pisa (26 January). Death of George III (29 January).
        Discovery of 'Cato Street Conspiracy' (23 February).
        The Cenci published (spring). Ferdinand VII restores
        Constitution and abolishes Inquisition (7 March). Moves
        to Leghorn (15 June-4 August). Writes 'The Sensitive

Plant', 'Ode to Liberty' and 'The Cloud' (possibly at
Pisa), 'To a Sky-lark' (probably June), *Letter to Maria
Gisborne* (July), translates Homeric *Hymn to Mercury*
(early July). Revolt in Naples and promise of Consti-
tution (2-7 July). Bill of Pains and Penalties against
Princess Caroline whom George IV wishes to divorce
introduced in Parliament (5 July) but dropped together
with inquiry into her conduct (10 November). At Baths of
San Giuliano, near Pisa (August-October). Writes *The
Witch of Atlas* (14-16 August) and 'Ode to Naples' (17-
25 August). *Promethus Unbound* published (August).
Writes *Swellfoot the Tyrant* on the Caroline affair
(August-September; published and suppressed in Dec-
ember). Conference at Troppau to discuss policy against
revolutionary   tendencies   in   Europe   (23 October-
17 December;   12 January-12 May 1821 at Laibach).
Returns to Pisa (31 October). Friendship with Emilia
Viviani (December).

1821   Pirated edition of *Queen Mab* published in London by
William Clarke; it is seized and he is later imprisoned
because of the contents. Arrival of Edward and Jane
Williams (13 January). Working on *Epipsychidion* (fin-
ished 16 February). Begins *A Defence of Poetry* in
response to Peacock (February-March; not published till
1840). Greek War of Independence begins (6 March;
Shelley hears news 1 April). Neapolitan rising crushed
by Austrians and Ferdinand IV restored (7-23 March).
Hears of Keats' death in Rome on 23 February
(11 April); writes *Adonais* (finished June; printed July).
Death of Napoleon (5 May). Rejection of Lord John
Russell's motion for parliamentary reform (9 May).
Anonymous publication of *Epipsychidion* (May). Cor-
onation of George IV (19 July); death of Queen Carol-
ine (7 August). Visits Byron at Ravenna (August). Writes
Hellas (October). Byron arrives at Pisa (November).

1822   Working on *Charles the First*. Trelawny arrives (14 Jan-
uary). Greek independence proclaimed (27 January).
Hellas published (February). Writes poems to Jane;
translates scenes from Goethe's *Faust* and Calderón
(spring). Allegra Byron dies (20 April). With the
Williamses moves to Casa Magni at San Terenzo near
Lerici (30 April). Sailing on the *Don Juan* (delivered

12 May). Writing *The Triumph of Life* (? late May-June; unfinished). Drowned with Williams when sailing back from Leghorn to Lerici after welcoming the Hunts (8 July).

1824   *Posthumous Poems* (collected by Mary from Shelley's papers).

NOTE ON THE TEXT

The textual history of Shelley's poetry has been highly unfortunate. Many of the poems by which he is best known were published after his death and without his final authority. Some of these poems (e.g. *The Mask of Anarchy*) had not been published because his publishers feared prosecution; others were less dangerous but had not yet found an appropriate home. Others, such as *Letter to Maria Gisborne*, were essentially private and not intended for publication. A significant number of fragments and lyrics were discovered among the manuscript drafts; these were often rough, sparsely punctuated, and sometimes illegible. Nearly all of these poems, representing so many different stages of authorial intention, were published but with little indication of the significant variations in their status. Although his wife and the later nineteenth-century editors deserve great credit for their dedication to an extremely difficult undertaking, they must also take the blame for distorting and sometimes misrepresenting Shelley's achievement. Not infrequently they misread his handwriting, misunderstood his intentions, published lines and even stanzas in the wrong order (as in 'The Boat on the Serchio', and 'Rose leaves, when the rose is dead'), tidied up his grammar and occasionally rewrote his poems according to their own notions of how Shelley might or ought to have written them.

The present edition attempts to be as faithful as possible to Shelley's texts and his intentions, while keeping in mind the claims of legibility. I have modernized spellings where there seemed little point in retaining the old form (e.g. *thro'* or most past tenses ending *-st*) but I have retained any spellings which might have special significance either for sound or meaning (e.g. *sate, phantasy, leapt*). Shelley's frequent misspellings have been corrected and his ampersands amplified to *and*. In his drafts and fair copies Shelley was liberal and often erratic in his use of capitals; many of these did not appear in the printed versions. I have on occasions ignored Shelley's capitals where they seem unduly obtrusive and where it seems unlikely that he would have retained them in a printed version; in these cases the editions of Mrs Shelley have provided an invaluable guide. Conversely, there have been a number of cases where Shelley did not see his own work through the press and the capitalization of the printed version has had to be checked against the remaining drafts and fair copies.

Where possible I have followed first editions or fair copies, though in both cases I have found it necessary to emend both substantively and in matters of punctuation. Notoriously, Shelley was displeased with the *Prometheus Unbound* collection (1820) published in England while he was in Italy. In this instance particularly I have made use of his own fair copies to correct the first edition. Fair copies by Mary have been checked against manuscript drafts where these are available; fair copies by Shelley have been followed as meticulously as possible in every detail, though it has sometimes been necessary to add punctuation, usually at line endings, if the poem is to make any sense. Such additions have been made with great caution and, where possible, after a consultation of the manuscript draft. *Julian and Maddalo* is a good example: Shelley sent it to Hunt with instructions that it was to be published as it stood, yet even here a few commas have proved absolutely necessary. Here as elsewhere I have followed Shelley's idiosyncratic system of dashes and dots and his characteristic use of the semicolon. In the case of rough drafts such as *The Triumph of Life* I have followed the same principle of minimum intervention: Shelley, of course, would have improved these poems had he lived. The notes indicate whether a poem was published before or after Shelley's death; unfinished poems are marked *Fragment*; an attempt has been made to indicate the general context of publication.

All texts (published and unpublished) have been checked against drafts and/or fair copies where this is possible. My main sources are as follows: 'Hymn to Intellectual Beauty' (*The Examiner*, 19 January 1817); 'Mont Blanc' (*History of a Six Weeks' Tour*, 1817); 'Verses Written on Receiving a Celandine' (Mary Shelley's fair copy, Houghton Library); 'To the Lord Chancellor' (Shelley's fair copy, Houghton Library); 'Ozymandiaş' (*The Examiner*, 11 January 1818); 'Stanzas Written in Dejection, near Naples' (Shelley's fair copy, Bodleian Library, supplemented by fair copy in Pierpont Morgan Library); *Julian and Maddalo* (Shelley's fair copy, Pierpont Morgan Library); *Prometheus Unbound*, 'Ode to the West Wind', 'Ode to Heaven', 'Ode to Liberty', 'The Cloud', 'The Sensitive Plant', 'An Exhortation', 'To a Sky-lark' (all from *Prometheus Unbound*, 1820, corrected against fair copies in the Bodleian and Houghton Libraries); *The Mask of Anarchy* (Shelley's fair copy, British Library, supplemented by Mary Shelley's corrected fair copy, Library of Congress, Washington); *Peter Bell the Third* (Mary Shelley's fair copy, Bodleian Library, supplemented by her edition of 1839); 'England in 1819' (Shelley's fair copy, Bodleian Library); 'Rarely, rarely, comest thou' (Shelley's fair copy, Houghton Library); *Letter to Maria Gisborne* (John Gisborne's annotated copy of Posthumous Poems, supplemented by Mary Shelley's fair copy, Huntington Library); 'Lines to a Critic' (Shelley's fair copy, Bodleian Library); *Hymn to Mercury* (Shelley's fair copy, Houghton Library); Two Songs for *Midas* (Shelley's holograph draft, Bodleian Library); 'The Two Spirits' (Shelley's holograph draft, Bodleian Library); 'Sonnet to the Republic of Benevento' (Shelley's fair copy, Bodleian Library, supplemented by fair copy, Houghton Library); 'Goodnight' (Shelley's fair copy, Pierpont Morgan Library); 'To the Moon' (Shelley's unfinished holograph draft, Bodleian Library); *Epipsychidion* (1821); 'Lines Written on Hearing the News of the Death of Napoleon' (*Hellas*, 1822); *Adonais* (1821); 'The Aziola' (Shelley's holograph draft of ll. 1-12, Bodleian Library, supplemented by Mary Shelley's fair copy, Pierpont Morgan Library); Two Choruses from *Hellas* (first edition, 1822, supplemented by fair copy by Edward Williams, Huntington Library); 'The flower that smiles today' (Shelley's fair copy, Bodleian Library); 'To Night' (Shelley's fair copy, Houghton Library); 'Rose leaves, when the rose is dead' (Shelley's unfinished holograph draft, Bodleian Library); 'O World, O Life, O Time' (Shelley's fair copy, Bodleian Library); 'When passion's trance is overpast' (Shelley's holograph draft, Bodleian Library); 'One word is too often profaned' (Mary Shelley's fair copy, Bodleian Library); 'To Edward Williams' (Shelley's fair copy, Edinburgh University Library); 'To Jane: The Recollection' (Shelley's fair copy, British Library); *Prologue in Heaven* (Shelley's fair copy, Bodleian Library); *The Triumph of Life* (Shelley's unfinished holograph draft, Bodleian Library); 'The keen stars were twinkling' (Shelley's fair copy, John Rylands Library, Manchester); 'Lines Written in the Bay of Lerici' (Shelley's holograph draft, Bodleian Library). Shelley's letters are quoted from *The Letters of Percy Bysshe Shelley*, ed. F. L. Jones, Oxford, 1964.

I should like to acknowledge the following debts for permission to consult and quote from manuscript material: to the Delegates of the Clarendon Press, Oxford for the rich collection of Shelley MSS. in the Bodleian Library, Oxford (and the *Letters of Percy Bysshe Shelley*, ed. F. L. Jones); to the Houghton Library, Harvard for 'Verses Written on Receiving a Celandine' and for the fair copies reproduced in facsimile in the *Harvard Shelley Notebook*, ed. G. E. Woodberry, 1929; to the Pierpont Morgan Library, New York for *Julian and Maddalo*, 'Stanzas Written in Dejection', 'Good Night' and 'The Aziola'; to the Henry Huntington Library, San Marino, California for *Letter to Maria Gisborne* and for Edward Williams' fair copy of choruses from *Hellas*; to the Library of Congress, Washington for Mary Shelley's fair copy of *The Mask of Anarchy*; to the British Library, London for the Wise MS. of *The Mask of Anarchy* and for 'To Jane: The Recollection'; to the John Rylands University Library, Manchester for 'The keen stars were twinkling'; to Edinburgh University Library for 'To Edward Williams'.

I should also like to express my gratitude to previous editors of Shelley — notably to Geoffrey Matthews and Judith Chernaik; to Donald Reiman both for his edition of *The Triumph of Life* (which together with that of Geoffrey Matthews has been a milestone in the recovery of Shelley's texts) and for his constant encouragement and interest; to Peter Butter for his annotated edition; to Neville Rogers, who kindly offered to read the TS. and made some valuable suggestions; to L. J. Zillman and to the late C. D. Locock. To all of these I owe a great deal. This edition could not have been produced without the inspiration and example of Kenneth Neill Cameron, the late Earl Wasserman, Harold Bloom and M. H. Abrams, who have all done much to establish Shelley as a serious poet and to set him in context. My thanks are also due to Robert Casto. The greatest help came from my wife, Ruth, whose advice, interest, encouragement and forbearance have been invaluable.

INTRODUCTION

I

On 16 August 1822 the body of Percy Bysshe Shelley was cremated on a funeral pyre: the chosen spot was a beach not far from Via Reggio in Italy where his boat had gone down in a storm. Frankincense and salt were thrown into the furnace, wine and oil over the body; Shelley's friends desired that at the last he should be honoured like a Greek hero. Symbolically, or so it seemed, his heart was not consumed by the flames, so that Edward Trelawny was able to rescue it at the last moment. Later, it became the object of an unseemly squabble betw:en the poet's widow and Leigh Hunt; when she was finally granted custody, Mary Shelley secreted it in a copy of *Adonais*, which she kept inside her pillow. Medical evidence suggests that her affections may have been misplaced; in all probability, the organ which survived the fiery furnace was not Shelley's heart but his liver.

The whole episode is highly instructive not only for Shelley's biographers but for those who are concerned with the value of his poetry. It was Shelley's misfortune that he lived (and died) in dramatic and often exotic circumstances which have attracted more interest than his genuine poetic achievements and which have influenced the responses even of critics who claim an antiseptic indifference to the facts of biography. Even more damaging is the fact that the popular version of Shelley's life presents an idealized and seriously distorted picture of a personality which was richly complex. It is difficult to escape from the legend so potently created by Trelawny, Thomas Jefferson Hogg, Peacock, Mary Shelley and the other early biographers, all of whom had personal reasons for exaggerating Shelley's ethereality, his effeminacy, his weakness, his ignorance of the facts of life, his being a Poet with a capital P. It is also difficult not to make a simple equation between the poetry and the life, not to assume that the poet-hero of *Alastor* is Shelley himself or that *Julian and Maddalo* is a direct transcription from the life. Yet, although many of Shelley's poems do relate very closely to his own experience, Shelley took great care to alchemize them, to purify them of the dross of what was merely personal. He insisted that the limited facts of personal biography should always be avoided or transcended: 'A story of particular facts is as a mirror which obscures and distorts that which should be beautiful: poetry is a mirror which makes beautiful that which is distorted.' Or, to approach it from a different angle: 'The poet and the man are two different natures.'[1]

Shelley had a sense of poetic decorum which would not have been out of place in the eighteenth century. In 'To a Sky-lark' he speaks of the poet 'hidden / In the light of thought', his identity subsumed in the radiance of inspiration. The majority of his most personal poems, notably his lyrics, were not published during his lifetime: some (such as 'To Edward Williams') were sent to friends with strict instructions that they were to be kept private, while others (such as 'To the Moon') were left unfinished and might have had a rather different bearing had they been completed. Some of Shelley's most celebrated and seemingly personal lyrics were intended in all probability as songs for plays such as *Hellas* and *Charles the First*. Of course, these poems are informed by Shelley's own experiences and fuelled by his own emotions but they are not mere spontaneous effusions or over-flowings of the heart: instead they offer what T. S. Eliot described as *'significant* emotion, emotion which has its life in the poem and not in the history of the poet'.[2] To interpret them biographically is as crude and pointless as to equate Shakespeare's 'Mistress mine' with Anne Hathaway.

It is also important to recognize the shaping influence of genre and convention. 'The Indian Serenade' (not included here) was regularly interpreted as a directly autobiographical piece until recent researches showed that it was also called 'The Indian Girl's Song', was intended to be sung by a woman and belongs to the tradition of the oriental lyric which typically relies on a certain emotional extravagance.[3] Again, many of what Cleanth Brooks once described as 'Shelley's sometimes embarrassing declarations'[4] can now be traced to the tradition of prophetic poetry, as found for example in the Psalms. Thus, the exaltations and despairs of poems like 'Ode to the West Wind' should be approached in the context of religious experience and the conventions of religious literature rather than with reference to Shelley's habit of dining on bread and raisins.[5] Again, the poetic collapses of poems like *Epipsychidion* are highly stylized and carefully staged developments of the prophetic tradition, for which Pindar, Dante and the Bible provide many of the clues.[6] Shelley insists on the evanescence of inspiration and the inadequacy of language; the profuse similes of 'To a Sky-lark' arise from a deep sense of this inadequacy, while *Epipsychidion* very boldly attempts to enact the kindlings and dwindlings of the poetic

process. Some may consider these emphases debilitating or un-
healthy; nobody should continue to claim that Shelley was simply
indulging in 'self-expression'. All of these poems are characterized
by extreme artistic self-consciousness.

Shelley had strict notions about the need for the poet to
transcend the temptations to self-indulgence and emotional ex-
hibitionism. In *The Triumph of Life* he makes an important
distinction between those poets who achieved this moral equilib-
rium and Rousseau who, by his own admission, did not:

> See the great bards of old, who inly quelled
>
> The passions which they sung, as by their strain
>   May well be known: their living melody
> Tempers its own contagion to the vein
>
>   Of those who are infected with it — I
> Have suffered what I wrote, or viler pain! —
>
>   And so my words were seeds of misery,
> Even as the deeds of others (274-81).

The manuscript reveals that Rousseau is pointing here to 'Homer
and his brethren', who may be identified as the Greek tragedians,
Lucretius, Virgil, Dante, Petrarch, Chaucer, Shakespeare, Cal-
deron and Milton, all of whom attained the self-control which is
necessary for great artistic achievement.[7] If their poetry has had
unfortunate effects, that may be attributed not to any weakness
which is inherent in the poetry but to the weakness of their readers,
since 'of such truths / Each to itself must be the oracle' (*P.U.*, II.
iv. 122-3). If the *Iliad* encourages the wrong kind of militaristic
valour or *Paradise Lost* seems to sanction a vindictive dispensation
of justice, it is not because Homer thirsted for blood or Milton for
vengeance but because we impose our own selfishness and our own
limitations on what they have written. Homer and his brethren
provide the potentially dangerous emotions of their poetry with the
antidote of moral and artistic control (they temper their own
contagion). Rousseau, on the other hand, did not succeed in
mastering his own emotions: he was not able to repress 'the mutiny
within' and did not transform 'to potable gold the poisonous waters
which flow from death through life'.[8] For all his greatness,
Rousseau was not able to achieve the desired internal equilibrium,
as his *Confessions* had demonstrated: they were, said Shelley,

'either a disgrace to the confessor or a string of falsehoods'. To make such inadequacies public was a dangerous proceeding: in spite of his humanitarian intentions, 'Rousseau gave license by his writings to passions that only incapacitate and contract the human heart'. In one sense, then, he was as much a tyrant as the French monarchs whom he despised or as Napoleon for whom he paved the way: his words were 'seeds of misery' and 'he prepared the necks of his fellow-beings for that galling and dishonourable servitude which at this moment it bears'.[9] As *Prometheus Unbound* so forcefully asserts, man cannot be free until he dethrones the tyrants of his own soul, a process which involves self-knowledge, self-control, and self-reliance. To concentrate, as Rousseau does, on one's own weakness, gloatingly as it seems, is to subject oneself to a despotic control as ruthless and as destructive as any which is exercised from the customary seats of power.

The sense of moral responsibility which informs this passage is characteristic of Shelley, whose conception of poetry had little to do with what was merely fashionable or charming. Though he valued increasingly the aesthetic virtues of poetry, he habitually approached it in terms of its relations to society. A passage in the draft of *Prometheus Unbound* reveals how conscientiously Shelley responded to these claims. Mercury is cataloguing a variety of monsters who can deputize for the Furies in their efforts to overcome the heroic resolve of Prometheus. One of these is the Sphinx, 'subtlest of fiends, / Who ministered to Thebes Heaven's poisoned wine — / Unnatural love, and more unnatural hate' (I. 347-9), a reference to the story of how Oedipus solved the riddle of the Sphinx, thus making possible his incestuous marriage and the fatal curse which he invoked on his sons. Shelley was exercised by the formulation of the last line and reflected in a note: 'The contrast would have been [more complete] if the sentiment had been transposed: but wherefore sacrifice the philosophical truth, that love however monstrous in its expression is still less worthy of horror than hatred.'[10] Here Shelley prefers moral truth to a rhetorical contrast which is more satisfying in terms of aesthetics.

As a rule Shelley manages to satisfy both his conscience and his artistic sensibility; nonetheless, it is ironical that a man of such moral tenacity should have been misrepresented for so long as primarily a lyrical poet with little or nothing to say. Critics who questioned his ultimate stature have always been ready to acknowledge that he had a rare lyrical faculty (or facility, as they might prefer to put it). Indeed, this lyrical ease has often been related to their own critical attitudes, since it was Shelley's fluency, his apparantly uncontrolled emotionalism, his habit of going on 'till I am stopped', which produced those results which they found so irritating. 'The effect of Shelley's eloquence is to hand poetry over to a sensibility that has no more dealings with intelligence than it can help', wrote Dr Leavis, notoriously. For Shelley's admirers the poems often provided a similar experience but their conclusions were exactly the opposite — for them the lack of 'meaning' was a positive virtue, a sign of the highest poetic achievement. For critics such as these, Shelley (like Blake) moved in a world of pure poetry, uncontaminated by realities, insulated from the harsh necessities of meaning. The main result of this unholy alliance between those who despised Shelley and those who adored him was that, between the two extremes, the real Shelley was persistently neglected. To concentrate on Shelley's lyrical poetry was to ignore the poetry by which he would have wished to be judged and remembered, the long and complex poems which grapple with the problems of politics, society, philosophy, love, art and religion. To assess Shelley's achievement on the basis of 'The Indian Serenade' or 'When the lamp is shattered' was to exhibit a seriously distorted perspective, as if one were to base a final judgment of Shakespeare on the songs from the plays. It is true that recent critical trends have enabled us to recognize new virtues in these poems.[11] We can now see that many of Shelley's lyrics belong to identifiable poetic traditions rather than to the pathology of Romantic narcissism or to the poetry of the higher nonsense. It is now evident that many of Shelley's shorter poems address themselves to moral or meta-physical problems of some complexity with great intellectual rigour and precision of inquiry. 'When passion's trance is overpast' explores the decline of love from its first intensity with unsenti-mental directness; 'Mutability' is also a tightly controlled sequence of logic; more extensive lyrics like 'Lines Written in the Bay of Lerici' and 'To Jane: The Recollection' combine a delicate sense of atmosphere with painful but incisive psychological probings. Be-neath these graceful surfaces there is a bony framework, a careful formal patterning which binds all together. Yet, in spite of their excellence, Shelley regarded these poems as the marginalia to far greater enterprises. Critics have persisted in thinking otherwise; perhaps Mrs Shelley was not alone in confusing the heart and the liver.

II

Politics were probably the dominating concern of Shelley's intellectual life. His earliest poetry, most of which is bad by any standards, is an unhappy mixture of Gothic melodramatics and political invective. Throughout his brief life, Shelley was never entirely free from the temptation to blend the two worlds, to turn Lord Castlereagh and Lord Sidmouth, king, priest and politician, into ghouls and vampires, evil monsters from the novels of Monk Lewis and Mrs Radcliffe (Shelley himself had successfully published a Gothic novel while still at school). Yet this fierce indignation, this painful awareness of man's inhumanity to man, was the directing force behind much of his greatest poetry. Shelley was one of those (in Keats' phrase) 'to whom the miseries of the world / Are misery, and will not let them rest'.[12]

He had been born (in 1792) into a family with political connections. His father, Sir Timothy, was a Sussex landowner, a Whig M.P. attached to the liberal faction of the Duke of Norfolk; his liberalism did not extend to the behaviour of his own son with whom he was permanently at odds after Shelley was sent down from Oxford in 1811 for refusing to acknowledge his authorship of an inquiring pamphlet called *The Necessity of Atheism*. Shelley had been intended to succeed his father in the House when he came of age; from his early years he was politically conscious and his whole career was marked by an unswerving adherence to the principles of political reform and a firm belief in the rightness of his own convictions. Thus, though Shelley was always in opposition and generally derided or ignored, he characteristically expresses himself with an impressive air of authority.

He grew up in that grim period sometimes known as the Bleak Age, the period of profound moral unrest and increasing political agitation which marked the years between the failure of the French Revolution and the passing of the Reform Bill in 1832. The first and perhaps the greatest influence on his political thinking was William Godwin, who later became his father-in-law. In 1812 Shelley described to its author how *An Enquiry Concerning Political Justice* (1793) had 'materially influenced my character':

> I was no longer the votary of Romance; till then I had existed in an ideal world; now I found that in this universe of ours was enough to excite the interest of the heart, enough to employ the discussions of Reason. I beheld in short that I had duties to perform. (*Letters*, i. 227-8).

Godwin had imagined a Utopian society in which there would be no
need for government; much of Shelley's poetry, early and late,
delights in presenting visions of a free and regenerated society, yet a
growing sense of what was politically possible and a deeper under-
standing of human nature soon modified his belief in perfecti-
bility.[13] Equality was 'unattainable except by a parcel of peas or
beans' and so was perfection yet 'my principles incite me to take all
the good I can get in politics, for ever aspiring to something more'.[14]
Shelley's main aim was to abolish the inequalities in society, to
undermine the system of power and privilege on which they were
based. In particular, this involved a reform of the electoral system
which currently excluded the vast majority of the population from
the right to vote. The unfinished *A Philosophical View of Reform*
(1819) intended to be 'an instructive and readable book, appealing
from the passions to the reason of men'[15] attracted no publisher but
it is a shrewd and comprehensive account which places its subject in
the context of European history. Shelley also attacked the unequal
distribution of property; paper currency, the 'Ghost of Gold, whose
consequences 'have been the establishment of a new aristocracy,
which has its basis in fraud as the old one has its basis in force'; the
operation of the National Debt; the use of the standing army; the
legal system including the barbaric Game Laws; and the rigid
marriage laws which underestimated both the rights of women and
the holiness of the heart's affections.[16] Binding together all these
abuses were the Church and the monarchy ('the only string which
ties the robber's bundle'),[17] who had combined themselves for their
own benefit and to 'the destruction of the real interest of all'.
Shelley crusaded with great energy: this infuses *Queen Mab* (1813)
and its supporting array of essays on social and political problems.
It also took Shelley to Dublin where he addressed public meetings,
distributed pamphlets and wrote his *Address to the Irish People*.
Yet, most of his activity was closer to home and aligned him with
those moderate radicals who were working for reform by peaceful
means. Among these was Leigh Hunt, editor of *The Examiner* and
later a close friend, for whose paper he produced a number of
poems on political subjects (including 'England in 1819', *The Mask
of Anarchy* and *Peter Bell the Third*) which were not published for
discretionary reasons. (Hunt had already spent two years in prison
for criticizing the Prince Regent.)[18]

   Shelley became increasingly disillusioned both with direct
political activity and with poetry which was bluntly didactic. Yet,
when the situation demanded it, he could still produce popular

verse such as *The Mask of Anarchy* which was specifically intended for a wide reading public. Poems like these were classed as *exoteric*; in his later years, Shelley preferred to concentrate on poetry of the *esoteric* species, aimed at the 'more select classes of poetical readers'. The aim was no longer simply didactic, but the predominating concerns were still moral and political. In *A Defence of Poetry* (1821) Shelley argues eloquently that poetry has an important social function; history shows that it is closely related to moral and social progress. In his own age the failure of the Industrial Revolution to increase the sum of human happiness could be attributed, along with the other excesses and imbalances of a capitalist economy, to a failure to 'imagine that which we know'. If man 'having enslaved the elements, remains himself a slave', it is because of 'an excess of the selfish and calculating principle' at the expense of imagination and its vehicle, poetry. The battle-lines are clearly drawn: 'Poetry and the principle of Self, of which money is the visible incarnation, are the God and Mammon of the world.'[19]

Poetry is an act of hope; 'it is ever still the light of life; the source of whatever of beautiful or generous or true can have place in an evil time'.[20] Shelley argues for the necessity of hope in the preface to *Laon and Cythna; or, The Revolution of the Golden City: A Vision of the Nineteenth Century* (1817) (published for reasons of discretion under the title *The Revolt of Islam*). There he claims that 'gloom and misanthropy have become the characteristics of the age in which we live, the solace of a disappointment that unconsciously finds relief only in the wilful exaggeration of its own despair'. Yet the signs are that England has survived and that 'a slow, gradual, silent change' is beginning to take place. Shelley dedicated his talents to the service of that change. *Laon and Cythna* describes the efforts of two revolutionary leaders, brother and sister, who briefly achieve the overthrow of the Ottoman empire but are finally defeated and subsumed into a mysterious Valhalla of fame after their death. This immensely ambitious epic poem is not totally successful in fusing its narrative structure with its philosophical concerns: yet it is a serious and original achievement which attempts to explore the moral and political implications of a revolutionary situation. Some of Shelley's critics pretended that they saw nothing of interest in the Ottoman empire but most of his readers must have recognized that he was attempting to analyse the reasons for the ultimate failure of the French Revolution and that his conclusions were not unconnected with politics in England. Though he allowed his heroes to be executed, Shelley intended his

poem both as a primer in moral and political education and a
contribution to hope: it was written 'in the view of kindling within
the bosoms of my readers a virtuous enthusiasm for those doctrines
of liberty and justice, that faith and hope in something good, which
neither violence nor misrepresentation nor prejudice can ever
totally extinguish among mankind'.

Laon and Cythna was soon followed by *Prometheus Unbound*
(1818-19), a mythological drama which is certainly Shelley's
greatest achievement. The *Prometheus Bound* of Aeschylus had
shown the archetypal revolutionary hero at odds with a tyrannical
father-god; here Shelley provides a highly personal revisionary
version and brings it to a conclusion which elicits its full potential
for hope. In rewriting Aeschylus Shelley seems to have discovered
new uses for Greek, Christian, and Oriental mythology;[21] the
psychological profundity of his conception and the brilliantly
daring imagery give to this play a satisfying complexity which raises
it far above the level of *Laon and Cythna*. Shelley's gift was not for
narrative but for psychological and moral explanation and for
evoking states of mind; *Prometheus Unbound* is successful because,
as Northrop Frye put it, 'it has attained the plotless or actionless
narrative which seems to be characteristic of the mythopoeic
genre'.[22] Shelley himself declared his intention of familiarizing his
readers with 'beautiful idealisms of moral excellence': *Prometheus
Unbound* is not didactic nor does it give in to despair. It is an
attempt to show what man might achieve if he devoted himself to
the principles of reform, abolished those false constraints which he
has permitted to exert their tyranny over him, and reclaimed the
human condition from the moral ice and snow which binds us in
shivering isolation, each on our barren mountain peak. Shelley
emphasizes both the necessity for resisting force from without and
the insinuating pressure of our own weakness from within. The
play's vocabulary insists on potential; many of the negatives
(*unpastured, unreclaiming*) imply that if the present situation is not
satisfactory it is because man himself has failed to take the
necessary action. Yet, although *Prometheus Unbound* is quite
deliberately an idealism, much of it deals with the unreclaimed
human condition and the insidious and recurrent temptations to
despair and apathy. Shelley insists on the necessity of a continuous
effort; unlike Godwin, he also recognizes that should man achieve
his Utopian society on earth he will still be merely man, still subject
to many limitations and always in danger of sliding back into an
unregenerated state.

Thus, even in his most optimistic works, Shelley's idealism does not preclude some salutary examples of psychological realism; his hope was never naive or simple-minded. In other works, he argued against his own best inclinations; *Julian and Maddalo* presents a disillusioning reply to Julian's question 'if we were not weak / Should we be less in deed than in desire?' while *The Cenci* portrays in Beatrice a character of Promethean potential who does not possess his moral self-restraint, gives in to revenge and murders her father: 'all best things are thus confused to ill.' *Hellas*, which anticipates the success of the Greek War of Independence, begins its final chorus on a note of joyful celebration. Yet, before the chorus has ended, the joy has modulated into doubt: 'O cease! must hate and death return? / Cease! must men kill and die? / Cease! drain not to its dregs the urn / Of bitter prophecy.' Shelley delineated with grim precision the *danse macabre* of *The Triumph of Life* yet he also wrote that 'Poetry is the record of the best and happiest moments of the happiest and best minds' and believed that 'Hope . . . is a solemn duty which we owe alike to ourselves & to the world'.[23] A number of Shelley's shorter poems obviously follow a dialectical pattern (e.g. 'Ode to Heaven', 'The Two Spirits' and the songs of Apollo and Pan, which contrast with and balance each other). It is part of Shelley's particular subtlety that he argues against himself within the confines of individual poems and that he also sets up poem against poem. The result is a continuous and fruitful dialectic, an energizing tension which gives force to most of his poetry. Perhaps not a little of Shelley's famous 'ungraspability' might be traced to this constant shifting of the terms of reference. What has often been interpreted as mere incoherence or self-contradiction should be acknowledged as a never-ending process of intellectual adjustment, a perpetual balancing of hypothesis against hypothesis, a guarded series of approaches to the ultimately unknowable truth. Sometimes the poem will finish nearer to hope (*Adonais*, 'The Sensitive Plant') sometimes nearer despair (*The Cenci*); mostly the endings are ambivalent, the final assertions tentative and qualified. Sometimes the aspiring flight towards hope and vision is wrecked in a carefully calculated collapse of poetic inspiration (*Epipsychidion*). Shelley's supposedly contradictory endings can thus be seen not as literary failures but as paradoxes justified and even predestined by the very nature of the poems out of which they emerge.[24]

Behind this shifting dialectic we can detect the influence of Shelley's own temperament, given to violent oscillations of mood.

But the changes of mood were conditioned not only by Shelley's own variations of health and of happiness but by a much more profound inquisition into the facts of existence. From an early age Shelley was fascinated both by science and philosophy. Although his scientific sophistication has sometimes been exaggerated (according to A. N. Whitehead he would have been 'a Newton among chemists' if he had been born a hundred years later)[25] Shelley once possessed a microscope and conducted scientific experiments; he also took the trouble to read and take notes from recent books such as Humphry Davy's *Elements of Agricultural Chemistry* and he was well informed on theories of light, electricity, the nature of matter and the behaviour of volcanoes. His letters from Italy also show that he was a meticulous observer of cloud formations (an obvious influence both on 'Ode to the West Wind' and 'The Cloud').[26] Many passages in his poetry which were once dismissed as charming but meaningless are now known to be closely related to his philosophical investigations; both were directed towards the discovery of the secret principle of life. Shelley's nature had a strong leavening of scepticism which checks even his most enthusiastic assertions: the sky-lark is located in 'Heaven, or near it' while his passionate affirmation of the immortality of Keats/ Adonais is fastidiously explicated — 'He wakes or sleeps with the enduring dead' (336). This tendency was strengthened by his reading of the eighteenth-century sceptics and perhaps also of Plato, two of whose dialogues he translated and whose view of the world as 'but a spume that plays / Upon a ghostly paradigm of things' (Yeats) was undoubtedly an influence on his own more melancholy musings.[27] Yet he also possessed a capacity for a very personal kind of religious faith, not related to any institutionalized church, placing a considerable emphasis on man's own potential divinity but acknowledging the existence of a Power in the universe; this Power he defined as the 'over-ruling Spirit of the collective energy of the moral and material world',[28] the plastic (shaping) stress which he celebrates in *Adonais*. This feeling influences even heterodox poems like 'Hymn to Intellectual Beauty' and apparently secular poems such as 'Ode to the West Wind'. It appears that Shelley also experienced direct and vivid intimations of immortality, through the almost mystical process of poetic inspiration so magnificently analysed in *A Defence of Poetry*.

III

Shelley provided a shrewd analysis of his own abilities in a letter of 1817 to William Godwin:

> I am formed, — if for any thing not in common with the herd of mankind — to apprehend minute & remote distinctions of feeling whether relative to external nature, or the living beings which surround us, & to communicate the conceptions which result from considering either the moral or the material universe as a whole. (*Letters*, i. 577)

The ability to concentrate on the whole rather than on the details is certainly a feature of his work. The attention to minute and remote distinctions of feeling is also characteristic both of his best lyrics and of more detailed explorations such as 'Mont Blanc', *Prometheus Unbound, Epipsychidion*, and *The Triumph of Life*. Shelley had a highly attuned moral sense; he was also gifted with a delicate insight into the operations of mind, which is the distinguishing feature of many of his greatest poems. Learning from the Greek tragedians and Dante and profiting from the recent example of Wordsworth, Shelley developed a subtle poetry of mind which demands vigilant attention from the reader. Take for example these lines from *Prometheus Unbound*:

> . . . terror, madness, crime, remorse,
> Which from the links of the great chain of things
> To every thought within the mind of man
> Sway and drag heavily, and each one reels
> Under the load towards the pit of death . . . (II. iv. 19-23)

This pessimistic image of the human condition is derived from the sight of fettered convicts hoeing the weeds in St Peter's Square in Rome. There are suggestions here of the great chain of being and of the iron chain of necessity which links cause to effect with inexorable consequence; as a whole the passage illustrates Shelley's ability to give concrete form to the most abstract activities of mind and to invest them with a directing emotional intensity. The strength of *Prometheus Unbound* is largely derived from the skill with which Shelley relates the outer world of politics to the inner world of mind; it is implied that the repressive systems of politics and religion represented by Jupiter are intimately related to the psychological and moral weaknesses of those who tolerate them. Shelley does not deny the political realities of Regency England — indeed, he details them with brutal immediacy in 'England in 1819' and *The Mask of Anarchy* — but he insists on exploring the interior complexities of evil. *The Triumph of Life* investigates the ways in which even those with the best intentions and the most humane aspirations may be defeated by the process of life. In these explorations Shelley discovers important connections between politics and religion; 'Mont Blanc' and *Prometheus Unbound* both trace a link between the false divinities which man has imposed on himself and his acquiescence in the prevailing political system.

Yet if Shelley's most distinctive literary achievement is his development of the richly symbolic poetry of mind, he was highly accomplished in many other areas. No poet of his period, and few in the history of English literature, can rival the scope and range of his poetic activities. Contrary to popular opinion, he was not a poet of one style (the impassioned and lyrical) but of many. He could produce with equal skill and technical dexterity the learned formal ode in the high style (*Ode to Liberty*), the familiar verse epistle (*Letter to Maria Gisborne*), the satire (fiercely animated as in *The Mask of Anarchy* or more jocular as in *Peter Bell the Third*), the relaxed conversation poem (*Julian and Maddalo*), the Dantean history of love (*Epipsychidion*), the carefully wrought classical elegy (*Adonais*), the extended exploratory lyric ('Lines Written in the Bay of Lerici', 'To Edward Williams'), the flyting ('To the Lord Chancellor'), the delighted celebration of natural energies ('The Cloud'). Even within his slighter lyrics there is a rich variety ranging from the simple cry of 'O World, O Life, O Time' to the elegant self-translation of 'Goodnight'. His descriptions of nature can range from the metaphysical analogies of 'Mont Blanc' to the precise but densely symbolic imagery of 'Ode to the West Wind' to the simple clarities with which *Julian and Maddalo* begins. His voice can encompass the charming domestic detail ('We sate there, rolling billiard balls about'), the compressed and paradoxical ('It is the unpastured Sea hungering for calm'), the profoundly philosophical ('The One remains, the many change and pass; / Heaven's light forever shines, Earth's shadows fly; / Life, like a dome of many-coloured glass, / Stains the white radiance of Eternity'), the bluntly comic ('He touched the hem of Nature's shift, / Felt faint — and never dared uplift / The closest, all-concealing tunic'), the grotesque ('His big tears, for he wept well, / Turned to millstones as they fell'), the drily witty ('Now he obliquely through the keyhole passed, / Like a thin mist or an autumnal blast'), the morally incisive ('The good want power, but to weep barren tears. / The powerful goodness want: worse need for them. / The wise want love; and those who love want wisdom; / And all best things are thus confused to ill.').[29] There is the ruthlessly unsentimental portrayal of sexual attraction in *The Triumph of Life*, the urbane conclusion to 'The Sensitive Plant', the joyful dance of the universe in Act IV of *Prometheus Unbound*, the Byronic poise of Mephistopheles in the Goethe translation, the gently chiding satire of 'An Exhortation', the pungently unsparing social and political analysis of 'England in 1819'. Shelley was also a fertile and intuitive translator who achieved particular success with the untranslatable *Prologue in Heaven* from Goethe's *Faust* and the light-hearted Homeric *Hymn to Mercury* (both represented here) and in scenes from Calderón's *El mágico prodigioso*. Such versatility makes Shelley not only the most European of English poets between Dryden and Eliot but goes a long way towards justifying Wordsworth's statement that 'Shelley is one of the best *artists* of us all: I mean in workmanship of style'.[30]

Though he could assume so many voices, there are three qualities which link all his best poems together. First, there is a general fluency, a controlling impetus which derives both from Shelley's habit of reading aloud and from the urgency of his conviction. Shelley's voice is always assured even when he is expressing his doubts. Secondly, many of his poems, particularly those which deal with the world of nature, exhibit what Shelley once called 'the animation of delight'.[31] The operations of the West Wind, the dance of matter in *Prometheus Unbound*, the onset of spring in *Adonais*, the fresh morning setting of *The Triumph of Life* are all given life by an informing source of energy, a vitality which cannot be ignored. Thirdly, the best of Shelley's poetry is born from a fusing of passion and precision which is achieved at a very high level of intensity. Admittedly, the pressure is sometimes too great (Shelley himself once lamented the absence of 'that tranquillity which is the attribute & the accompaniment of power'):[32] both *Prometheus Unbound* and *Epipsychidion* are overheated in places. Much more frequently, however, Shelley achieves a highly impressive blend of imaginative intensity with precise philosophical definition. This is very similar to the balance which Shelley had detected in the 'intense but regulated passion' of a painting by Correggio, and in that 'calm & sustained energy without which true greatness cannot be' which he identified in Dante and in the masterpieces of Greek sculpture.[33] Shelley's own miraculous equilibrium received its most perceptive tribute from Walter Bagehot:

The peculiarity of his style is its intellectuality; and this strikes us the more from its contrast with his impulsiveness. . . . So in his writings; over the most intense excitement, the grandest objects, the keenest agony, the most buoyant joy, he throws an air of subtle mind. His language is minutely and acutely searching; at the dizziest height of meaning the keenness of the word is greatest. . . . In the wildest of ecstasies his self-anatomising intellect is equal to itself.[34]

No critic has come closer to defining the secret of Shelley's particular excellence.

NOTES TO INTRODUCTION

Names in capitals signify that full details can be found in the Select Bibliography. Prose is cited from the edition by D. L. Clark (Albuquerque, New Mexico, 1966), corrected where necessary and possible.

1   *Prose*, p. 281; *Letters*, ii. 310.
2   'Tradition and the Individual Talent', *Selected Essays* (3rd edn, 1951), p. 22.
3   Discussed in detail by MATTHEWS ('Shelley's Lyrics') LEVIN and CHERNAIK.
4   *Modern Poetry and the Tradition* (Chapel Hill, North Carolina, 1939; new edn, 1965), p. 237.
5   See POTTLE ('The Case of Shelley') and BLOOM (*Shelley's Mythmaking*).
6   See HUGHES ('Kindling and Dwindling: The Poetic Process in Shelley' and 'Coherence and Collapse in Shelley'); WEBB (*Shelley: A Voice Not Understood*).
7   Based on Bod. MS. Shelley adds.e.9, p. 24, which reads *Aeschylus* rather than *Greek tragedians* and does not include Chaucer; these additions are based on Shelley's statements elsewhere.
8   *Prose*, p. 295.
9   On Rousseau: *Letters*, i. 84; *Prose*, pp. 67, 209.
10 Cited in ZILLMAN. Cf. 'I have confidence in my moral sense alone; but that is a kind of originality' (*Letters*, ii. 153).
11 For an excellent critical account, see CHERNAIK; for a collection of essays, see SWINDEN.

12 *The Fall of Hyperion*, i. 148-9.
13 See CAMERON (*passim*) and MCNIECE.
14 *Letters*, i. 127; ii. 153.
15 *Letters*, ii. 164.
16 Most of these topics are extensively discussed in the Notes to *Queen Mab* or in *A Philosophical View of Reform* (*Prose*, pp. 229-61; quotation from p. 244).
17 *Prose*, p. 243.
18 Hunt's letters to and critical appraisals of Shelley can be found in BRIMLEY JOHNSON; see also Hunt's *Autobiography*.
19 All quotations from *Prose*, p. 293.
20 *Prose*, p. 286.
21 For Greek and Christian, see BLOOM (*Shelley's Mythmaking*), WASSERMAN (*Shelley: A Critical Reading*), WEBB (*Shelley: A Voice Not Understood*); for Oriental, see CURRAN (*Shelley's Annus Mirabilis*).
22 *A Study of English Romanticism* (New York, 1968), p. 110.
23 *Prose*, p. 294; *Letters*, ii. 125.
24 Analysed brilliantly by WASSERMAN (*Shelley: A Critical Reading*).
25 *Science and the Modern World* (Harmondsworth, 1938), p. 103.
26 For Davy, see WEBB (*Shelley: A Voice Not Understood*); for light, electricity and matter, see GRABO and BUTTER; for volcanoes, see MATTHEWS ('A Volcano's Voice in Shelley'); for clouds, see KING-HELE and LUDLAM.
27 Yeats, 'Among School Children': for scepticism, see PULOS and WASSERMAN (*Shelley: A Critical Reading*); for Platonism, see NOTOPOULOS and ROGERS (*Shelley at Work*).
28 *Prose*, p. 202.
29 *Julian and Maddalo*, 157; *Prometheus Unbound*, III. ii. 49; *Adonais*, 460-3; *Peter Bell the Third*, 313-7, here 167-71; *The Mask of Anarchy*, 16-17; *Hymn to Mercury*, 188-9; *Prometheus Unbound*, I. 625-8.
30 An oral judgment recorded by Christopher Wordsworth in 1827; see M. L. Peacock, Jnr, ed., *The Critical Opinions of William Wordsworth* (Baltimore, 1950).
31 *Prometheus Unbound*, IV. 322.
32 *Letters*, i. 578.
33 *Letters*, ii. 50, 20.
34 'Percy Bysshe Shelley' (1856), *Literary Studies* (Everyman edn, 1911; reprint 1951), i. 110-11.

SELECT BIBLIOGRAPHY

Texts

At present the standard complete edition of Shelley's poetry is still the Oxford edition by Thomas Hutchinson (1904) but this is textually inadequate. The five-volume edition by Neville Rogers which was intended to replace it has resulted in only two volumes, both of which have proved controversial, especially in matters of punctuation. Geoffrey Matthews is working on a two-volume annotated edition for Longman. The most authoritative text currently available is *Shelley's Poetry and Prose*, ed. Donald H. Reiman and Sharon B. Powers (New York, 1977). This contains most of Shelley's best poetry, some prose, a selection of criticism and excellent and copious annotation. Other useful editions of separate works or groups of poems are as follows: *Alastor . . . Prometheus Unbound . . . Adonais*, ed. Peter Butter (1970; richly annotated edition of Shelley's collections of 1816, 1820 and of *Adonais*); *The Esdaile Poems*, ed. K. N. Cameron (1964; Shelley's youthful poems, annotated); *The Lyrics of Shelley*, ed. Judith Chernaik (Cleveland and London, 1972; text of shorter poems as appendix to critical discussions); *Shelley's 'Prometheus Unbound': The Text and the Drafts*, ed. Lawrence J. Zillman (New Haven and London, 1968; over adventurous but contains invaluable manuscript evidence); *Shelley: Selected Poems and Prose*, ed. G. M. Matthews (1964; succinct and helpful notes; good text); *Shelley's 'The Triumph of Life'*, ed. D. H. Reiman (Urbana, Illinois, 1965; all the manuscript evidence and a critical study). *Shelley: Selected Poetry*, ed. Neville Rogers (1969) advances little on Hutchinson in textual matters; its notes are largely devoted to interpreting Shelley in Platonic terms.

At present there is no reliable edition of the prose, though E. B. Murray and Timothy Webb are currently working on a new and comprehensive edition for the Clarendon Press. The 1880 edition in four volumes by H. B. Forman is still perhaps the best, though convenience often dictates a consultation of *The Complete Works of Percy Bysshe Shelley*, ed. R. Ingpen and W. E. Peck (1926–30; the Julian edition) or of *Shelley's Prose: The Trumpet of a Prophecy*, ed. David Lee Clark (Albuquerque, New Mexico, 1966). Shelley's translations from Plato have been edited by James A. Notopoulos, *The Platonism of Shelley* (Durham, North Carolina, 1949). The standard edition of the correspondence is *The Letters of Percy Bysshe Shelley*, ed. F. L. Jones (2 vols, Oxford, 1964). A usefully annotated edition of *A Defence of Poetry* is that by H. F. B. Brett-Smith (reprinted edn, Oxford, 1953).

Biographies
Edmund Blunden, *Shelley: A Life Story* (1946); K. N. Cameron, *The Young Shelley: Genesis of a Radical* (New York, 1950; London, 1951; up to end of 1814); K. N. Cameron, *Shelley: The Golden Years* (Cambridge, Mass., 1974; covers 1814–22; very good on specific biographical problems but highly selective as biography. Most of the book is devoted to an analysis of Shelley's ideas and a study of his major works with particular reference to contemporary thought and politics); Richard Holmes, *Shelley: The Pursuit* (1974); Sylva Norman, *Flight of the Skylark* (Norman, Oklahoma, 1954; on biographical legend and the development of Shelley's reputation); Newman Ivey White, *Shelley* (2 vols, New York, 1940; still the standard life).

Valuable, if sometimes distorted, contemporary records are provided by: *The Letters of Mary W. Shelley*, ed. Betty Bennett (vol 1, Baltimore and London, 1980); *Mary Shelley's Journal*, ed. F. L. Jones (Norman, Oklahoma, 1947; new ed. forthcoming); *The Journals of Claire Clairmont*, ed. Marion Kingston Stocking (Cambridge, Mass., 1968); *Maria Gisborne and Edward E. Williams, Their Journals and Letters*, ed. F. L. Jones (Norman, Oklahoma, 1951); Thomas Jefferson Hogg, *The Life of Shelley* (1858); Thomas Love Peacock, *Memoirs of Shelley* (1858–62); Edward John Trelawny, *Recollections of Shelley and Byron* (1858), collected in a two-volume edition by Humbert Wolfe (1933); Edward J. Trelawny, *Records of Shelley, Byron and the Author* (1878), ed. David Wright (Harmondsworth, 1973); Thomas Medwin, *The Life of Percy Bysshe Shelley* (1847), revised edn by H. B. Forman (1913); *The Autobiography of Leigh Hunt*, ed. J. E. Morpurgo (1949). Byron's conversations may also be consulted usefully. *Shelley and his Circle* is an invaluable aid. This ten-volume project sponsored by the Pforzheimer Foundation in New York is based on original materials and provides an exhaustive study both of the texts in question and of many matters relating to Shelley, his friends and the details of contemporary life. So far 6 volumes have appeared, 1-4 edited by K. N. Cameron, 5-6 edited by D. H. Reiman.

Critical or General Books on Shelley
Miriam Allott, ed., *Essays on Shelley* (Liverpool, 1982); Carlos Baker, *Shelley's Major Poetry: The Fabric of a Vision* (Princeton, 1948); Ellsworth

Barnard, *Shelley's Religion* (Minneapolis, 1937); Harold Bloom, *Shelley's Mythmaking* (New Haven, Conn., 1959); Nathaniel Brown, *Sexuality and Feminism in Shelley* (Cambridge, Mass., and London, 1979); Peter Butter, *Shelley's Idols of the Cave* (Edinburgh, 1954); K. N. Cameron, *Shelley: The Golden Years* (Cambridge, Mass., 1974; see *Biographies*); Judith Chernaik, *The Lyrics of Shelley* (Cleveland, Ohio and London, 1972); Richard Cronin, *Shelley's Poetic Thoughts* (1981); Stuart Curran, *Shelley's 'Cenci': Scorpions Ringed with Fire* (Princeton, 1970); Stuart Curran, *Shelley's Annus Mirabilis* (San Marino, California, 1975); P. M. S. Dawson, *The Unacknowledged Legislator: Shelley and Politics* (Oxford, 1980); Edward Duffy, *Rousseau in England: The Context for Shelley's Critique of the Enlightenment* (Berkeley, Los Angeles, London, 1979); Kelvin Everest, ed., *Shelley Revalued: Essays from the Gregynog Conference* (Leicester, 1983); Carl Grabo, *A Newton among Poets* (Chapel Hill, North Carolina, 1930); Jean Hall, *The Transforming Image: A Study of Shelley's Major Poetry* (Illinois, 1980); A. M. D. Hughes, *The Nascent Mind of Shelley* (Oxford, 1971); Desmond King-Hele, *Shelley: His Thought and Work* (2nd edn, 1971; excellent on science but weak on criticism); Hélène Lemaitre, *Shelley: poète des éléments* (Paris, 1962); Gerald McNiece, *Shelley and the Revolutionary Idea* (Cambridge, Mass., 1969); Glen O'Malley, *Shelley and Synaesthesia* (Chicago, 1964); Jean Perrin, *Les structures de l'imaginaire shelleyen* (Grenoble, 1973); C. E. Pulos, *The Deep Truth: A Study of Shelley's Scepticism* (Lincoln, Nebraska, 1954); Donald H. Reiman, *Percy Bysshe Shelley* (New York, 1969); Neville Rogers, *Shelley at Work* (2nd edn, Oxford, 1967); Michael H. Scrivener, *Radical Shelley: The Philosophical Anarchism and Utopian Thought of Percy Bysshe Shelley* (Princeton, 1982); Earl Wasserman, *Shelley: A Critical Reading* (Baltimore, Maryland and London, 1971); Timothy Webb, *Shelley: A Voice Not Understood* (Manchester, 1977); Timothy Webb, *The Violet in the Crucible: Shelley and Translation* (Oxford, 1976); Milton Wilson, *Shelley's Later Poetry: A Study of his Prophetic Imagination* (New York, 1959); Ross G. Woodman, *The Apocalyptic Vision in the Poetry of Shelley* (Toronto, 1964).

Books including chapters or sections on Shelley
M. H. Abrams, *The Mirror and the Lamp* (New York, 1953); M. H. Abrams, *Natural Supernaturalism* (1971); Walter Bagehot, *Literary Studies* (Shelley essay, 1856); Francis Berry, *Poetry and the Physical Voice* (1963); Francis Berry, *Poets' Grammar* (1958); Harold Bloom, *The Ringers in the Tower: Studies in Romantic Tradition* (Chicago and London, 1971); Harold Bloom, *The Visionary Company* (revised edn, Ithaca and London, 1971); A. C. Bradley, *Oxford Lectures on Poetry* (2nd edn, 1909);

Marilyn Butler, *Romantics, Rebels, and Reactionaries: English Literature and Its Background 1760–1830* (1981); Donald Davie, *Purity of Diction in English Verse* (Oxford, 1967); R. A. Foakes, *The Romantic Assertion: A Study in the Language of Nineteenth-Century Poetry* (1958); R. H. Fogle, *The Imagery of Keats and Shelley: A Comparative Study* (Chapel Hill, North Carolina, 1949); J. R. de J. Jackson, *Poetry of the Romantic Period* (London, Boston and Henley, 1980); G. Wilson Knight, *The Starlit Dome: Studies in the Poetry of Vision* (1971); F. R. Leavis, *Revaluation* (1936); Howard Mills, *Peacock, his Circle and his Age* (Cambridge, 1969); I. A. Richards, *Beyond* (New York, 1974); Charles E. Robinson, *Shelley and Byron: The Snake and Eagle Wreathed in Fight* (Baltimore, Maryland and London, 1976); Roger Sales, *English Literature in History: 1780–1830 Pastoral and Politics* (1983); Leone Vivante, *English Poetry and its Contribution to the Knowledge of a Creative Principle* (1950); Earl R. Wasserman, *The Subtler Language* (Baltimore, 1959; includes discussions of 'Mont Blanc', 'The Sensitive Plant', *Adonais*); Brian Wilkie, *Romantic Poets and Epic Tradition* (Milwaukee, Wisconsin, 1965); Carl R. Woodring, *Politics and English Romantic Poetry* (Cambridge, Mass., 1970); W. B. Yeats, *Essays and Introductions* (1961).

Critical Anthologies

M. H. Abrams, ed., *English Romantic Poets* (2nd edn, Oxford, 1975) = ERP; George M. Ridenour, ed., *Shelley* (*Twentieth Century Views*; Englewood Cliffs, New Jersey, 1965) = TCV; Patrick Swinden, ed., *Shelley: Shorter Poems and Lyrics* (*Casebook*; 1976) = CB; R. B. Woodings, ed., *Shelley* (*Modern Judgements*; 1968) = MJ. Earlier criticism is collected in Newman I. White, ed., *The Unextinguished Hearth* (Durham, North Carolina, 1938; London, 1966). James E. Barcus, ed., *Shelley: The Critical Heritage* (London and Boston, 1975) covers much the same ground as White with less detail on the circumstances of publication and a rather arbitrary additional selection of American criticism. Theodore Redpath, ed., *The Young Romantics and Critical Opinion, 1807–1824* (1973) offers a well chosen, but briefer collection. Another valuable book is R. Brimley Johnson, *Shelley – Leigh Hunt: How Friendship Made History* (1928) which provides an illuminating record of Hunt's letters to and criticism of Shelley.

Articles

John Ross Baker, 'Poetry and Language in Shelley's *Defence of Poetry*', *The Journal of Aesthetics and Art Criticism*, 39 (1981), 437–49; Ronald E.

Becht, 'Shelley's *Adonais*: Formal Design and the Lyric Speaker's Crisis of Imagination', *Studies in Philology*, 78 (1981), 194–210; Stephen C. Behrendt, 'The Exoteric Species: The Popular Idiom in Shelley's Poetry', *Genre* (1981), 473–92; M. K. Bequette, 'Shelley and Smith: Two Sonnets on Ozymandias', *Keats-Shelley Journal*, xxvi (1977), 29–31; Leslie Brisman, 'Mysterious Tongue: Shelley and the Language of Christianity', *Texas Studies in Language and Literature*, 23 (1981), 389–417; Susan Hawk Brisman, ' "Unsaying His High Language": The Problem of Voice in *Prometheus Unbound*', *Studies in Romanticism*, 16 (1977), 51–86; Frederick Burwick, 'The Language of Causality in *Prometheus Unbound*', *Keats-Shelley Journal*, xxxi (1982), 136–58; Peter Butter, 'Sun and Shape in Shelley's *The Triumph of Life*', *Review of English Studies*, xiii (1962), 40–51; John Buxton, 'On Reading Shelley' in *Essays and Poems Presented to Lord David Cecil*, ed. W. W. Robson (1970), 109–25; Richard S. Caldwell, ' "The Sensitive Plant" as Original Fantasy', *Studies in Romanticism*, 15 (1976), 221–52; K. N. Cameron, 'Shelley and Marx', *Wordsworth Circle*, 10 (1979), 234–9; Yvonne M. Carothers, '*Alastor*: Shelley Corrects Wordsworth', *Modern Language Quarterly*, 42 (1981), 21–47; Frederick S. Colwell, 'Shelley and Italian Painting', *Keats-Shelley Journal*, xxix (1980), 43–66; Frederick S. Colwell, 'Shelley on Sculpture: The Uffizi Notes', *Keats-Shelley Journal*, xxviii (1979), 59–77; Richard Cronin, 'Shelley's Language of Dissent', *Essays in Criticism*, 27 (1977), 203–15; Martyn Crucefix, 'Wordsworth, Superstition, and Shelley's *Alastor*', *Essays in Criticism*, xxxiii (1983), 126–47; P. M. S. Dawson, ' "King Over Himself": Shelley's Philosophical Anarchism', *Keats-Shelley Memorial Bulletin*, xxx (1979), 16–35; P. M. S. Dawson, 'Shelley and the *Improvvisatore* Sgricci: An Unpublished Review', *Keats-Shelley Memorial Bulletin*, xxxii (1981), 19–29; V. A. de Luca, 'The Style of Millennial Announcement in *Prometheus Unbound*', *Keats-Shelley Journal*, xxviii (1979), 78–101; Paul de Man, 'Shelley Transfigured' in Harold Bloom *et al.*, *Deconstruction and Criticism* (New York, 1979), 39–73; Joseph W. Donohue, 'Shelley's Beatrice and the Romantic Concept of Tragic Character', *Keats-Shelley Journal*, xvii (1968), 53–73; James C. Evans, 'Masks of the Poet: A Study of Self-Confrontation in Shelley's Poetry', *Keats-Shelley Journal*, xxiv (1975), 70–88; R. H. Fogle, 'Dante and Shelley's *Adonais*', *Bucknell Review*, xv (1967), 11–12; R. H. Fogle, 'Image and Imagelessness: A Limited Reading of *Prometheus Unbound*', *Keats-Shelley Journal*, i (1952), 23–36; Newell F. Ford, 'Paradox and Irony in Shelley's Poetry', *Studies in Philology*, lvii (1960), 648–62; Newell F. Ford, 'The Wit in Shelley's Poetry', *Studies in English Literature*, i (1961), 1–22; Jack Benoit Gohn, 'Did Shelley Know Wordsworth's *Peter Bell*?', *Keats-Shelley Journal*, xxviii (1979), 20–4; D. Harrington-Lueker, 'Imagination versus Intro-spection: *The Cenci* and *Macbeth*', *Keats-Shelley Journal*, xxxii (1983), 172–89; R. A. Hartley, 'The Uroboros in Shelley's Poetry', *Journal of English and Germanic Philology*, lxxiii (1974), 524–42; Richard H. Has-well, 'Shelley's *The Revolt of Islam*: "The Connection of Its Parts"', *Keats-Shelley Journal*, xxv (1976), 81–102; Helen E. Haworth, '*Ode to the West Wind* and the Sonnet Form', *Keats-Shelley Journal*, xx (1971), 71–7; Richard Hendrix, 'The Necessity of Response: How Shelley's Radical Poetry Works', *Keats-Shelley Journal*, xxvii (1978), 45–69; W. H. Hilde-brand, 'A Look at the Third and Fourth Spirit Songs: *Prometheus Unbound*, I', *Keats-Shelley Journal*, xx (1971), 87–99; William H. Hilde-brand, 'Naming-Day in Asia's Vale', *Keats-Shelley Journal*, xxxii (1983), 190–203; J. A. Hodgson, 'The World's Mysterious Doom: Shelley's *The Triumph of Life*', *English Literary History*, xlii (1975), 595–622; Jerrold E. Hogle, 'Metaphor and Metamorphosis in Shelley's "The Witch of Atlas"', *Studies in Romanticism*, 19 (1980), 327–53; Jerrold E. Hogle, 'Shelley's Fiction: The "Stream of Fate"', *Keats-Shelley Journal*, xxx (1981), 78–99; Jerrold E. Hogle, 'Shelley's Poetics: The Power as Metaphor', *Keats-Shelley Journal*, xxxi (1982), 159–97; John Holloway, Introduction to *Selected Poems of Percy Bysshe Shelley* (1960) (CB); Ralph Houston, 'Shelley and the Principle of Association' (1953) (CB); Daniel J. Hughes, 'Coherence and Collapse in Shelley', *English Literary History*, xxviii (1961), 260–83; Daniel J. Hughes, 'Kindling and Dwindling: The Poetic Process in Shelley', *Keats-Shelley Journal*, xiii (1964), 13–28; Daniel J. Hughes, 'Potentiality in *Prometheus Unbound*' (1965) (MJ); Daniel J. Hughes, 'Shelley, Leonardo and the Monsters of Thought', *Criticism*, 12 (1970), 195–212; I. J. Kapstein, 'The Mean-ing of *Mont Blanc*' (1947) (CB); William Keach, 'Obstinate Question-ings: The Immortality Ode and *Alastor*', *Wordsworth Circle*, 12 (1981), 36–44; William Keach, 'Reflexive Imagery in Shelley', *Keats-Shelley Journal*, xxiv (1975), 49–69; E. H. King, 'Beattie and Shelley: The Making of the Poet', *English Studies*, 61 (1980), 338–53; Karl Kroeber, 'Experience as History: Shelley's Venice, Turner's Carthage', *English Literary History*, 41 (1974), 321–39; John J. Lavelle, 'Shelley's Pythagorean Daemons' in *The Evidence of the Imagination*, ed. Donald H. Reiman, Michael C. Jaye and Betty T. Bennett (New York, 1978), 264–84; Angela Leighton, '*Adonais*: The Voice and the Text', *Keats-Shelley Memorial Bulletin*, xxxi (1980), 39–51; John Robert Leo, 'Critic-ism of Consciousness in Shelley's "A Defence of Poetry"', *Philosophy and Literature*, 2 (1978), 46–59; Richard Levin, 'Shelley's "Indian Serenade": A Re-Revaluation', *College English*, 24 (1963), 305–7; F. H. Ludlam, 'The Meteorology of the *Ode to the West Wind*' (1972) (CB);

Jerome J. McGann, 'The Secrets of an Elder Day: Shelley after *Hellas*' (1966) (MJ); Gerald McNiece, 'The Poet as Ironist in "Mont Blanc" and "Hymn to Intellectual Beauty" ', *Studies in Romanticism*, 14 (1975), 311–36; R. R. Male and J. A. Notopoulos, 'Shelley's Copy of Diogenes Laertius', *Modern Language Review*, liv (1959), 10–21; Geoffrey Matthews, 'A Volcano's Voice in Shelley' (1957) (TCV; MJ); Geoffrey Matthews, ' "Julian and Maddalo": The Draft and the Meaning', *Studia Neophilologica*, xxxv (1963), 57–84; Geoffrey Matthews, 'On Shelley's *Triumph of Life*', *Studia Neophilologica*, xxxiv (1962), 104–34; Geoffrey Matthews, 'Shelley's Lyrics' (1969) (CB); J. Hillis Miller, 'The Critic as Host' in Harold Bloom *et al.*, *Deconstruction and Criticism* (New York, 1979), 217–53; Fred L. Milne, 'The Eclipsed Imagination in Shelley's "The Triumph of Life" ', *Studies in English Literature*, 21 (1981), 681–702; Peter Mortenson, 'Image and Structure in Shelley's Longer Lyrics', *Studies in Romanticism*, iv (1965), 104–10; E. B. Murray, 'Annotated Manuscript Corrections of Shelley's Prose Essays', *Keats-Shelley Journal*, xxvi (1977), 10–21; E. B. Murray, '*Mont Blanc*'s Unfurled Veil', *Keats-Shelley Journal*, xviii (1969), 39–48; E. B. Murray, 'Shelley's Contribution to Mary's *Frankenstein*', *Keats-Shelley Memorial Bulletin*, xxix (1978), 50–68; E. B. Murray, 'Shelley's *Notes on Sculptures*: The Provenance and Authority of the Text', *Keats-Shelley Journal*, xxxii (1983), 150–71; Leonard N. Neufeldt, 'Poetry as Subversion: The Unbinding of Shelley's Prometheus', *Anglia*, 95 (1977), 60–86; Michael O'Neill, 'Shelley's *The Triumph of Life*: Questioning and Imagining' in *An Infinite Complexity: Essays in Romanticism*, ed. J. R. Watson (Edinburgh, 1983), 161–80; Ants Oras, 'The Multitudinous Orb: Some Miltonic Elements in Shelley', *Modern Language Quarterly*, xvi (1955), 247–57; Jean de Palacio, 'Shelley traducteur de soi-même', *Revue des sciences humaines*, 158 (1975), 223–44; Coleman Parsons, 'Shelley's Prayer to the West Wind', *Keats-Shelley Journal*, xi (1962), 31–7; Jean Perrin, 'The Actaeon Myth in Shelley's Poetry', *Essays and Studies*, 28 (1975), 29–46; Frederick A. Pottle, 'The Case of Shelley' (1952; 1960) (MJ; ERP); Frederick A. Pottle, 'The Role of Asia in the Dramatic Action of *Prometheus Unbound*' (1965) (TCV); A. A. Prins, 'The Religious Background of Shelley's *Prometheus Unbound*', *English Studies Presented to R. W. Zandvoort . . . A Supplement to English Studies*, xlv (1964), 223–34; Joseph Raben, 'Shelley's *Prometheus Unbound*: Why the Indian Caucasus?', *Keats-Shelley Journal*, xii (1963), 95–106; Melvin M. Rader, 'Shelley's Theory of Evil' (1930) (TCV); Joanna E. Rapf, 'A Spirit in Search of Itself: Non-Narrative Structure in Act IV of Shelley's *Prometheus Unbound*', *Keats-Shelley Memorial Bulletin*, xxx (1979), 36–47; D. H. Reiman, 'Roman Scenes in *Prometheus Unbound* III. iv', *Philological*

Quarterly, xlvi (1967), 69–78; D. H. Reiman, 'Shelley as Agrarian Reactionary', *Keats-Shelley Memorial Bulletin*, xxx (1979), 5–15; D. H. Reiman, 'Structure, Symbol and Theme in "Lines Written Among the Euganean Hills" ', *Publications of the Modern Language Association*, lxxvii (1962), 404–13; H. M. Richmond, 'Ozymandias and the Travellers', *Keats-Shelley Journal*, xi (1962) 65–71; John Rieder, 'Shelley's "Mont Blanc": Landscape and the Ideology of the Sacred Text', *English Literary History*, 48 (1981), 778–98; James Rieger, 'Shelley's Paterin Beatrice', *Studies in Romanticism* (1965); reprinted in *The Mutiny Within* (New York, 1967); Charles E. Robinson, 'The Shelleys to Leigh Hunt: A New Letter of 5 April 1821', *Keats-Shelley Memorial Bulletin*, xxxi (1980), 52–6; Neville Rogers, 'Shelley and the Visual Arts', *Keats-Shelley Memorial Bulletin*, xii (1961), 9–17; Merle E. Rubin, 'Shelley's Skepticism: A Detachment Beyond Despair', *Philological Quarterly*, 59 (1980), 353–73; John F. Slater, 'Self-Concealment and Self-Revelation in Shelley's *Epipsychidion*', *Papers on Language and Literature*, 11 (1975), 279–92; Stuart M. Sperry, 'Necessity and the Role of the Hero in Shelley's *Prometheus Unbound*', *Publications of the Modern Language Association*, 96 (1981), 242–54; David M. Stocking and Marion Kingston Stocking, 'New Shelley Letters in a John Gisborne Notebook', *Keats-Shelley Memorial Bulletin*, xxxi (1980), 1–9; Patrick Story, 'Pope, Pageantry, and Shelley's *Triumph of Life*', *Keats-Shelley Journal*, xxi–xxii (1972–3), 145–59; Ronald Tetreault, 'Quest and Caution: Psychomachy in Shelley's *Alastor*', *English Studies in Canada*, 3 (1977), 289–306; Ronald Tetreault, 'Shelley at the Opera', *English Literary History*, 48 (1981), 144–71; Ann Thompson, 'Shelley and Satire's Scourge' in *Literature of the Romantic Period, 1750–1850*, ed. R. T. Davies and B. G. Beatty (Liverpool, 1976), 135–50; Norman Thurston, 'Author, Narrator, and Hero in Shelley's *Alastor*', *Studies in Romanticism*, xiv (1975), 119–31; Norman Thurston, 'The Second Language of *Prometheus Unbound*', *Philological Quarterly*, 55 (1976), 126–33; Norman Thurston, 'Shelley and the Duty of Hope', *Keats-Shelley Journal*, xxvi (1977), 22–8; Paul Turner, 'Shelley and Lucretius', *Review of English Studies*, x (1959), 269–82; James B. Twitchell, 'Shelley's Metapsychological System in Act IV of *Prometheus Unbound*', *Keats-Shelley Journal*, xxiv (1975), 29–48; James B. Twitchell, 'Shelley's Use of Vampirism in *The Cenci*', *Tennessee Studies in Literature*, 24 (1979), 120–33; L. Waldoff, 'The Father-Son Conflict in *Prometheus Unbound*', *Psychoanalytic Review*, 62 (1975), 75–96; Constance Walker, 'The Urn of Bitter Prophecy: Antithetical Patterns in *Hellas*', *Keats-Shelley Memorial Bulletin*, xxxiii (1982), 36–48; Earl Wasserman, 'Shelley's Last Poetics' in *From Sensibility to Romanticism*, ed. F. W. Hilles and H. Bloom (1965);

Timothy Webb, 'Shelley and the Religion of Joy', *Studies in Romanticism*, 15 (1976), 357–82; Harry White, 'Shelley's Defence of Science', *Studies in Romanticism*, 16 (1977), 319–30; S. C. Wilcox, 'Sources, Symbolism, and Unity of Shelley's *Skylark*', *Studies in Philology*, xlvi (1949), 560–76; Andelys Wood, 'Shelley's Ironic Vision: *The Witch of Atlas*', *Keats-Shelley Journal*, xxix (1980), 67–82; R. B. Woodings, ' "A Devil of a Nut to Crack": Shelley's *Charles the First*', *Studia Neophilologica*, xl (1968), 216–37; Ross Woodman, 'The Androgyne in *Prometheus Unbound*', *Studies in Romanticism*, 20 (1981), 225–47; Curt R. Zimansky, 'Cause and Effect: A Symbolism for Shelley's Poetry', *Journal of English and Germanic Philology*, 78 (1979), 209–26.

Reference Works

F. S. Ellis, *A Lexical Concordance to the Poetical Works of Percy Bysshe Shelley* (1892) is very useful but will need to be heavily revised when the definitive text of Shelley has been established. Useful bibliographies can be found in the *New Cambridge Bibliography of English Literature* and in Clement Dunbar, *A Bibliography of Shelley Studies: 1823–1950* (New York and London, 1976); a critical account can be found in *The English Romantic Poets: A Review of Research and Criticism*, ed. Frank Jordan, Jnr (Modern Language Association of America, New York; 3rd edn, 1972). The student may also consult the bibliography in Ian Jack, *English Literature, 1815–1832* (1963; Vol. X of the *Oxford History of English Literature*). Comprehensive annual bibliographies are provided by the *Keats-Shelley Journal*.

HYMN TO INTELLECTUAL BEAUTY

1. The awful shadow of some unseen Power
        Floats though unseen amongst us,—visiting
        This various world with as inconstant wing
    As summer winds that creep from flower to flower.—
    Like moonbeams that behind some piny mountain shower,
            It visits with inconstant glance
            Each human heart and countenance;
    Like hues and harmonies of evening,—
            Like clouds in starlight widely spread,—
            Like memory of music fled,—   10
            Like aught that for its grace may be
    Dear, and yet dearer for its mystery.

2. Spirit of BEAUTY, that doth consecrate
        With thine own hues all thou dost shine upon
        Of human thought or form,—where art thou gone?
    Why dost thou pass away and leave our state,
    This dim vast vale of tears, vacant and desolate?
            Ask why the sunlight not forever
            Weaves rainbows o'er yon mountain river,
    Why aught should fail and fade that once is shown,   20
            Why fear and dream and death and birth
            Cast on the daylight of this earth
            Such gloom,—why man has such a scope
    For love and hate, despondency and hope?

3. No voice from some sublimer world hath ever
        To sage or poet these responses given—
        Therefore the name of God and ghosts and Heaven,
    Remain the records of their vain endeavour,
    Frail spells—whose uttered charm might not avail to sever
            From all we hear and all we see,   30
            Doubt, chance, and mutability.
    Thy light alone—like mist o'er mountains driven,
            Or music by the night wind sent
            Through strings of some still instrument,
            Or moonlight on a midnight stream,
    Gives grace and truth to life's unquiet dream.

4. Love, Hope, and Self-esteem, like clouds depart
        And come, for some uncertain moments lent.
        Man were immortal, and omnipotent,
    Didst thou, unknown and awful as thou art,   40
    Keep with thy glorious train firm state within his heart.
            Thou messenger of sympathies,
            That wax and wane in lovers' eyes—
    Thou—that to human thought art nourishment,
            Like darkness to a dying flame!
            Depart not as thy shadow came,
            Depart not—lest the grave should be,
    Like life and fear, a dark reality.

5. While yet a boy I sought for ghosts, and sped
        Through many a listening chamber, cave and ruin,   50
        And starlight wood, with fearful steps pursuing
    Hopes of high talk with the departed dead.
    I called on poisonous names with which our youth is fed,
            I was not heard—I saw them not—
            When musing deeply on the lot
    Of life, at that sweet time when winds are wooing
            All vital things that wake to bring
            News of buds and blossoming,—
            Sudden, thy shadow fell on me;
    I shrieked, and clasped my hands in ecstasy!   60

6. I vowed that I would dedicate my powers
        To thee and thine—have I not kept the vow?
        With beating heart and streaming eyes, even now
    I call the phantoms of a thousand hours
    Each from his voiceless grave: they have in visioned bowers
            Of studious zeal or love's delight
            Outwatched with me the envious night—
    They know that never joy illumed my brow
            Unlinked with hope that thou wouldst free
            This world from its dark slavery,   70
            That thou—O awful LOVELINESS,
    Wouldst give whate'er these words cannot express.

7. The day becomes more solemn and serene
        When noon is past—there is a harmony
        In autumn, and a lustre in its sky,

Which through the summer is not heard or seen,
As if it could not be, as if it had not been!
    Thus let thy power, which like the truth
    Of nature on my passive youth
Descended, to my onward life supply   80
    Its calm—to one who worships thee,
    And every form containing thee,
    Whom, SPIRIT fair, thy spells did bind
To fear himself, and love all human kind.

MONT BLANC
Lines Written in the Vale of Chamouni

1.   The everlasting universe of things
    Flows through the mind, and rolls its rapid waves,
    Now dark—now glittering—now reflecting gloom—
    Now lending splendour, where from secret springs
    The source of human thought its tribute brings
    Of waters,—with a sound but half its own,
    Such as a feeble brook will oft assume
    In the wild woods, among the mountains lone,
    Where waterfalls around it leap forever,
    Where woods and winds contend, and a vast river   10
    Over its rocks ceaselessly bursts and raves.

2.   Thus thou, Ravine of Arve—dark, deep Ravine—
    Thou many-coloured, many-voicèd vale,
    Over whose pines, and crags, and caverns sail
    Fast cloud-shadows and sunbeams: awful scene,
    Where Power in likeness of the Arve comes down
    From the ice gulfs that gird his secret throne,
    Bursting through these dark mountains like the flame
    Of lightning through the tempest;—thou dost lie,
    Thy giant brood of pines around thee clinging,   20
    Children of elder time, in whose devotion
    The chainless winds still come and ever came
    To drink their odours, and their mighty swinging
    To hear—an old and solemn harmony;
    Thine earthly rainbows stretched across the sweep
    Of the aethereal waterfall, whose veil

Robes some unsculptured image; the strange sleep
Which when the voices of the desert fail
Wraps all in its own deep eternity;—
Thy caverns echoing to the Arve's commotion,   30
A loud, lone sound no other sound can tame;
Thou art pervaded with that ceaseless motion,
Thou art the path of that unresting sound—
Dizzy Ravine!—and when I gaze on thee
I seem as in a trance sublime and strange
To muse on my own separate phantasy,
My own, my human mind, which passively
Now renders and receives fast influencings,
Holding an unremitting interchange
With the clear universe of things around;   40
One legion of wild thoughts, whose wandering wings
Now float above thy darkness, and now rest
Where that or thou art no unbidden guest,
In the still cave of the witch Poesy,
Seeking among the shadows that pass by,
Ghosts of all things that are, some shade of thee,
Some phantom, some faint image; till the breast
From which they fled recalls them, thou art there!

3.   Some say that gleams of a remoter world
Visit the soul in sleep,—that death is slumber,   50
And that its shapes the busy thoughts outnumber
Of those who wake and live.—I look on high;—
Has some unknown omnipotence unfurled
The veil of life and death? or do I lie
In dream, and does the mightier world of sleep
Spread far around and inaccessibly
Its circles? For the very spirit fails,
Driven like a homeless cloud from steep to steep
That vanishes among the viewless gales!
Far, far above, piercing the infinite sky,   60
Mont Blanc appears,—still, snowy, and serene;
Its subject mountains their unearthly forms
Pile round it, ice and rock; broad vales between
Of frozen floods, unfathomable deeps,
Blue as the overhanging heaven, that spread
And wind among the accumulated steeps:—
A desert peopled by the storms alone,

Save when the eagle brings some hunter's bone,
And the wolf tracks her there—how hideously
Its shapes are heaped around! rude, bare, and high,   70
Ghastly, and scarred, and riven.—Is this the scene
Where the old Earthquake-dæmon taught her young
Ruin? Were these their toys? or did a sea
Of fire envelop once this silent snow?
None can reply—all seems eternal now.
The wilderness has a mysterious tongue
Which teaches awful doubt, or faith so mild,
So solemn, so serene, that man may be
But for such faith with nature reconciled;
Thou has a voice, great Mountain, to repeal   80
Large codes of fraud and woe; not understood
By all, but which the wise, and great, and good
Interpret, or make felt, or deeply feel.

4.   The fields, the lakes, the forests, and the streams,
Ocean, and all the living things that dwell
Within the dædal earth; lightning, and rain,
Earthquake, and fiery flood, and hurricane,
The torpor of the year when feeble dreams
Visit the hidden buds, or dreamless sleep
Holds every future leaf and flower;—the bound   90
With which from that detested trance they leap;
The works and ways of man, their death and birth,
And that of him and all that his may be;
All things that move and breathe with toil and sound
Are born and die; revolve, subside and swell.
Power dwells apart in its tranquillity
Remote, serene, and inaccessible:
And *this*, the naked countenance of earth,
On which I gaze, even these primæval mountains
Teach the adverting mind. The glaciers creep   100
Like snakes that watch their prey, from their far fountains,
Slow rolling on; there, many a precipice,
Frost and the Sun in scorn of mortal power
Have piled: dome, pyramid, and pinnacle,
A city of death, distinct with many a tower
And wall impregnable of beaming ice.
Yet not a city, but a flood of ruin
Is there, that from the boundaries of the sky

Rolls its perpetual stream; vast pines are strewing
Its destined path, or in the mangled soil   110
Branchless and shattered stand; the rocks, drawn down
From yon remotest waste, have overthrown
The limits of the dead and living world,
Never to be reclaimed. The dwelling-place
Of insects, beasts, and birds becomes its spoil;
Their food and their retreat forever gone,
So much of life and joy is lost. The race
Of man flies far in dread; his work and dwelling
Vanish, like smoke before the tempest's stream,
And their place is not known. Below, vast caves   120
Shine in the rushing torrents' restless gleam,
Which from those secret chasms in tumult welling
Meet in the vale, and one majestic River,
The breath and blood of distant lands, forever
Rolls its loud waters to the ocean waves,
Breathes its swift vapours to the circling air.

5. Mont Blanc yet gleams on high:—the power is there,
    The still and solemn power of many sights,
    And many sounds, and much of life and death.
    In the calm darkness of the moonless nights,   130
    In the lone glare of day, the snows descend
    Upon that Mountain; none beholds them there,
    Nor when the flakes burn in the sinking sun,
    Or the star-beams dart through them.—Winds contend
    Silently there, and heap the snow with breath
    Rapid and strong, but silently! Its home
    The voiceless lightning in these solitudes
    Keeps innocently, and like vapour broods
    Over the snow. The secret strength of things
    Which governs thought, and to the infinite dome   140
    Of heaven is as a law, inhabits thee!
    And what were thou, and earth, and stars, and sea,
    If to the human mind's imaginings
    Silence and solitude were vacancy?

VERSES WRITTEN ON RECEIVING A CELANDINE
IN A LETTER FROM ENGLAND

I thought of thee, fair Celandine,
    As of a flower aery blue
Yet small—thy leaves methought were wet
    With the light of morning dew.
In the same glen thy star did shine
As the primrose and the violet,
And the wild briar bent over thee
And the woodland brook danced under thee.

Lovely thou wert in thine own glen
    Ere thou didst dwell in song or story;   10
Ere the moonlight of a Poet's mind
    Had arrayed thee with the glory
Whose fountains are the hearts of men—
Many a thing of vital kind
Had fed and sheltered under thee,
Had nourished their thoughts near to thee.

Yes, gentle flower in thy recess,
    None might a sweeter aspect wear,
Thy young bud drooped so gracefully,
    Thou wert so very fair,—   20
Among the fairest, ere the stress
Of exile, death and injury,
Thus withering and deforming thee,
Had made a mournful type of thee,

A type of that when I and thou
    Are thus familiar, Celandine—
A deathless Poet whose young prime
    Was as serene as thine!
But he is changed and withered now,
Fallen on a cold and evil time;   30
His heart is gone—his fame is dim,
And Infamy sits mocking him.

Celandine! Thou art pale and dead,
    Changed from thy fresh and woodland state;
Oh! that thy bard were cold, but he

Has lived too long and late.
Would he were in an honoured grave!
But that, men say, now must not be,
Since he for impious gold could sell
The love of those who loved him well.   40

That he, with all hope else of good
   Should be thus transitory,
I marvel not; but that his lays
   Have spared not their own glory—
That blood, even the foul god of blood
With most inexpiable praise,
Freedom and truth left desolate,
He has been bought to celebrate!

They were his hopes which he doth scorn;
   They were his foes the fight that won;   50
That sanction and that condemnation
   Are now forever gone.
They need them not! Truth may not mourn
That with a liar's inspiration
Her majesty he did disown
Ere he could overlive his own.

They need them not, for Liberty,
   Justice and philosophic truth
From his divine and simple song
   Shall draw immortal youth,   60
When he and thou shall cease to be
Or be some other thing,—so long
As men may breathe or flowers may blossom
O'er the wide earth's maternal bosom.

The stem whence thou wert disunited
   Since thy poor self was banished hither,
Now, by that priest of Nature's care
   Who sent thee forth to wither,
His window with its blooms has lighted,
And I shall see thy brethren there.   70
And each, like thee, will aye betoken
Love sold, hope dead, and honour broken.

TO THE LORD CHANCELLOR

1.   Thy country's curse is on thee, darkest crest
       Of that foul, knotted, many-headed worm
    Which rends our Mother's bosom—Priestly Pest!
       Masked Resurrection of a buried Form!

2.   Thy country's curse is on thee! Justice sold,
       Truth trampled, Nature's landmarks overthrown,
    And heaps of fraud-accumulated gold
       Plead, loud as thunder, at Destruction's throne.

3.   And, whilst that sure slow Angel which aye stands
       Watching the beck of Mutability   10
    Delays to execute her high commands,
       And, though a nation weeps, spares thine and thee,

4.   O, let a father's curse be on thy soul,
       And let a daughter's hope be on thy tomb;
    Be both, on thy grey head, a leaden cowl
       To weigh thee down to thy approaching doom!

5.   I curse thee—by a parent's outraged love,
       By hopes long cherished and too lately lost,
    By gentle feelings thou couldst never prove,
       By griefs which thy stern nature never crossed;   20

6.   By those infantine smiles of happy light,
       Which were a fire within a stranger's hearth,
    Quenched even when kindled, in untimely night
       Hiding the promise of a lovely birth;

7.   By those unpractised accents of young speech,
       Which he who is a father thought to frame
    To gentlest lore, such as the wisest teach—
       Thou strike the lyre of mind!—oh, grief and shame!

8.   By all the happy see in children's growth—
       That undeveloped flower of budding years—   30
    Sweetness and sadness interwoven both,
       Source of the sweetest hopes and saddest fears;

9. By all the days, under a hireling's care,
        Of dull constraint and bitter heaviness,—
    O wretched ye if ever any were,—
        Sadder than orphans, yet not fatherless;

10. By the false cant which on their innocent lips
        Must hang like poison on an opening bloom;
    By the dark creeds which cover with eclipse
        Their pathway from the cradle to the tomb;   40

11. By thy most impious Hell, and all its terror;
        By all the grief, the madness, and the guilt
    Of thine impostures, which must be their error—
        That sand on which thy crumbling Power is built;

12. By thy complicity with lust and hate—
        Thy thirst for tears—thy hunger after gold—
    The ready frauds which ever on thee wait—
        The servile arts in which thou hast grown old;

13. By thy most killing sneer, and by thy smile,
        By all the snares and nets of thy black den;   50
    And—for thou canst outweep the crocodile—
        By thy false tears—those millstones braining men—

14. By all the hate which checks a father's love—
        By all the scorn which kills a father's care—
    By those most impious hands which dared remove
        Nature's high bounds—by thee—and by despair—

15. Yes, the despair which bids a father groan,
        And cry, 'My children are no longer mine—
    The blood within those veins may be mine own,
        But, Tyrant, their polluted souls are thine!'—   60

16. I curse thee, though I hate thee not.—O slave!
        If thou couldst quench the earth-consuming Hell
    Of which thou art a daemon, on thy grave
        This curse should be a blessing. Fare thee well!

OZYMANDIAS

I met a traveller from an antique land
Who said: 'Two vast and trunkless legs of stone
Stand in the desert. Near them, on the sand,
Half sunk, a shattered visage lies, whose frown,
And wrinkled lip, and sneer of cold command,
Tell that its sculptor well those passions read
Which yet survive, stamped on these lifeless things,
The hand that mocked them and the heart that fed;
And on the pedestal these words appear:
"My name is Ozymandias, king of kings: 10
Look on my works, ye Mighty, and despair!"
Nothing beside remains. Round the decay
Of that colossal wreck, boundless and bare
The lone and level sands stretch far away.'

STANZAS WRITTEN IN DEJECTION —
December 1818, near Naples

The Sun is warm, the sky is clear,
The waves are dancing fast and bright,
Blue isles and snowy mountains wear
The purple noon's transparent might,
The breath of the moist earth is light
Around its unexpanded buds;
Like many a voice of one delight
The winds, the birds, the Ocean-floods;
The City's voice itself is soft, like Solitude's.

I see the Deep's untrampled floor   10
With green and purple seaweeds strown,
I see the waves upon the shore
Like light dissolved in star-showers, thrown;
I sit upon the sands alone;
The lightning of the noontide Ocean
Is flashing round me, and a tone
Arises from its measured motion,
How sweet! did any heart now share in my emotion.

Alas, I have nor hope nor health,
Nor peace within nor calm around,   20
Nor that content surpassing wealth
The sage in meditation found,
And walked with inward glory crowned;
Nor fame nor power nor love nor leisure—
Others I see whom these surround,
Smiling they live and call life pleasure:
To me that cup has been dealt in another measure.

Yet now despair itself is mild,
Even as the winds and waters are;
I could lie down like a tired child   30
And weep away the life of care
Which I have borne and yet must bear,
Till Death like Sleep might steal on me,
And I might feel in the warm air
My cheek grow cold, and hear the Sea
Breathe o'er my dying brain its last monotony.

Some might lament that I were cold,
As I, when this sweet day is gone,
Which my lost heart, too soon grown old,
Insults with this untimely moan—   40
They might lament,—for I am one
Whom men love not, and yet regret;
Unlike this day, which, when the Sun
Shall on its stainless glory set,
Will linger, though enjoyed, like joy in memory yet.

JULIAN AND MADDALO
A Conversation

PREFACE

The meadows with fresh streams, the bees with thyme,
The goats with the green leaves of budding Spring,
Are saturated not—nor Love with tears.—*Virgil*, Ecl. X.

Count Maddalo is a Venetian nobleman of ancient family and of
great fortune, who, without mixing much in the society of his

countrymen, resides chiefly at his magnificent palace in that city. He is a person of the most consummate genius, and capable, if he would direct his energies to such an end, of becoming the redeemer of his degraded country. But it is his weakness to be proud: he derives, from a comparison of his own extraordinary mind with the dwarfish intellects that surround him, an intense apprehension of the nothingness of human life. His passions and his powers are incomparably greater then those of other men; and, instead of the latter having been employed in curbing the former, they have mutually lent each other strength. His ambition preys upon itself, for want of objects which it can consider worthy of exertion. I say that Maddalo is proud, because I can find no other word to express the concentered and impatient feelings which consume him; but it is on his own hopes and affections only that he seems to trample, for in social life no human being can be more gentle, patient, and unassuming than Maddalo. He is cheerful, frank, and witty. His more serious conversation is a sort of intoxication; men are held by it as by a spell. He has travelled much; and there is an inexpressible charm in his relation of his adventures in different countries.

Julian is an Englishman of good family, passionately attached to those philosophical notions which assert the power of man over his own mind, and the immense improvements of which, by the extinction of certain moral superstitions, human society may be yet susceptible. Without concealing the evil in the world, he is for ever speculating how good may be made superior. He is a complete infidel, and a scoffer at all things reputed holy; and Maddalo takes a wicked pleasure in drawing out his taunts against religion. What Maddalo thinks on these matters is not exactly known. Julian, in spite of his heterodox opinions, is conjectured by his friends to possess some good qualities. How far this is possible the pious reader will determine. Julian is rather serious.

Of the Maniac I can give no information. He seems, by his own account, to have been disappointed in love. He was evidently a very cultivated and amiable person when in his right senses. His story, told at length, might be like many other stories of the same kind: the unconnected exclamations of his agony will perhaps be found a sufficient comment for the text of every heart.

I rode one evening with Count Maddalo
Upon the bank of land which breaks the flow
Of Adria towards Venice:—a bare strand

Of hillocks, heaped from ever-shifting sand,
Matted with thistles and amphibious weeds,
Such as from earth's embrace the salt ooze breeds,
Is this;—an uninhabitable sea-side,
Which the lone fisher, when his nets are dried,
Abandons; and no other object breaks
The waste, but one dwarf tree and some few stakes   10
Broken and unrepaired, and the tide makes
A narrow space of level sand thereon,
Where 'twas our wont to ride while day went down.
This ride was my delight.—I love all waste
And solitary places; where we taste
The pleasure of believing what we see
Is boundless, as we wish our souls to be:
And such was this wide ocean, and this shore
More barren than its billows;—and yet more
Than all, with a remembered friend I love   20
To ride as then I rode;—for the winds drove
The living spray along the sunny air
Into our faces; the blue heavens were bare,
Stripped to their depths by the awakening North
And from the waves, sound like delight broke forth
Harmonizing with solitude, and sent
Into our hearts aërial merriment. . .
So, as we rode, we talked; and the swift thought,
Winging itself with laughter, lingered not
But flew from brain to brain,—such glee was ours—   30
Charged with light memories of remembered hours,
None slow enough for sadness; till we came
Homeward, which always makes the spirit tame.
This day had been cheerful but cold, and now
The sun was sinking, and the wind also.
Our talk grew somewhat serious, as may be
Talk interrupted with such raillery
As mocks itself, because it cannot scorn
The thoughts it would extinguish:—'twas forlorn
Yet pleasing, such as once, so poets tell,   40
The devils held within the dales of Hell
Concerning God, freewill and destiny:
Of all that earth has been or yet may be,
All that vain men imagine or believe,
Or hope can paint or suffering may achieve,

We descanted, and I (for ever still
Is it not wise to make the best of ill?)
Argued against despondency, but pride
Made my companion take the darker side.
The sense that he was greater than his kind   50
Had struck, methinks, his eagle spirit blind
By gazing on its own exceeding light.
—Meanwhile the sun paused ere it should alight,
Over the horizon of the mountains;—Oh,
How beautiful is sunset, when the glow
Of Heaven descends upon a land like thee,
Thou Paradise of exiles, Italy!
Thy mountains, seas and vineyards and the towers
Of cities they encircle!—it was ours
To stand on thee, beholding it; and then   60
Just where we had dismounted the Count's men
Were waiting for us with the gondola.—
As those who pause on some delightful way
Though bent on pleasant pilgrimage, we stood
Looking upon the evening and the flood
Which lay between the city and the shore
Paved with the image of the sky . . . the hoar
And aëry Alps towards the North appeared
Through mist, an heaven-sustaining bulwark reared
Between the East and West; and half the sky   70
Was roofed with clouds of rich emblazonry
Dark purple at the zenith, which still grew
Down the steep West into a wondrous hue
Brighter than burning gold, even to the rent
Where the swift sun yet paused in his descent
Among the many-folded hills: they were
Those famous Euganean hills, which bear
As seen from Lido through the harbour piles
The likeness of a clump of peakèd isles—
And then—as if the Earth and Sea had been   80
Dissolved into one lake of fire, were seen
Those mountains towering as from waves of flame
Around the vaporous sun, from which there came
The inmost purple spirit of light, and made
Their very peaks transparent. 'Ere it fade,'
Said my companion, 'I will show you soon
A better station'—so, o'er the lagune

We glided, and from that funereal bark
I leaned, and saw the city, and could mark
How from their many isles in evening's gleam   90
Its temples and its palaces did seem
Like fabrics of enchantment piled to Heaven.
I was about to speak, when—'We are even
Now at the point I meant,' said Maddalo,
And bade the gondolieri cease to row.
'Look, Julian, on the west, and listen well
If you hear not a deep and heavy bell.'
I looked, and saw between us and the sun
A building on an island; such a one
As age to age might add, for uses vile,   100
A windowless, deformed and dreary pile,
And on the top an open tower, where hung
A bell, which in the radiance swayed and swung—
We could just hear its hoarse and iron tongue:
The broad sun sunk behind it, and it tolled
In strong and black relief.—'What we behold
Shall be the madhouse and its belfry tower,'
Said Maddalo, 'and ever at this hour
Those who may cross the water, hear that bell
Which calls the maniacs each one from his cell   110
To vespers.'—'As much skill as need to pray
In thanks or hope for their dark lot have they
To their stern maker,' I replied. 'O ho!
You talk as in years past,' said Maddalo.
''Tis strange men change not. You were ever still
Among Christ's flock a perilous infidel,
A wolf for the meek lambs—if you can't swim
Beware of Providence.' I looked on him,
But the gay smile had faded in his eye:
'And such,'—he cried, 'is our mortality   120
And this must be the emblem and the sign
Of what should be eternal and divine!—
And like that black and dreary bell, the soul,
Hung in a heaven-illumined tower, must toll
Our thoughts and our desires to meet below
Round the rent heart and pray—as madmen do
For what? they know not,—till the night of death
As sunset that strange vision, severeth
Our memory from itself, and us from all

We sought and yet were baffled!' I recall   130
The sense of what he said, although I mar
The force of his expressions. The broad star
Of day meanwhile had sunk behind the hill
And the black bell became invisible
And the red tower looked grey, and all between
The churches, ships and palaces were seen
Huddled in gloom;—into the purple sea
The orange hues of heaven sunk silently.
We hardly spoke, and soon the gondola
Conveyed me to my lodging by the way.   140

 The following morn was rainy, cold and dim:
Ere Maddalo arose, I called on him,
And whilst I waited with his child I played;
A lovelier toy sweet Nature never made,
A serious, subtle, wild, yet gentle being,
Graceful without design and unforeseeing,
With eyes—oh speak not of her eyes!—which seem
Twin mirrors of Italian Heaven, yet gleam
With such deep meaning, as we never see
But in the human countenance: with me   150
She was a special favourite: I had nursed
Her fine and feeble limbs when she came first
To this bleak world; and she yet seemed to know
On second sight her ancient playfellow,
Less changed than she was by six months or so;
For after her first shyness was worn out
We sate there, rolling billiard balls about.
When the Count entered—salutations past—
'The words you spoke last night might well have cast
A darkness on my spirit—if man be   160
The passive thing you say, I should not see
Much harm in the religions and old saws
(Though I may never own such leaden laws)
Which break a teachless nature to the yoke:
Mine is another faith'—thus much I spoke,
And noting he replied not, added: 'See
This lovely child, blithe, innocent and free;
She spends a happy time with little care
While we to such sick thoughts subjected are
As came on you last night—it is our will   170

That thus enchains us to permitted ill—
We might be otherwise—we might be all
We dream of happy, high, majestical.
Where is the love, beauty and truth we seek
But in our mind? and if we were not weak
Should we be less in deed than in desire?'
'Aye, if we were not weak—and we aspire
How vainly to be strong!' said Maddalo:
'You talk Utopia.' 'It remains to know,'
I then rejoined, 'and those who try may find   180
How strong the chains are which our spirit bind;
Brittle perchance as straw . . . We are assured
Much may be conquered, much may be endured
Of what degrades and crushes us. We know
That we have power over ourselves to do
And suffer—what, we know not till we try;
But something nobler than to live and die—
So taught those kings of old philosophy
Who reigned, before Religion made men blind;
And those who suffer with their suffering kind   190
Yet feel their faith, religion.' 'My dear friend,'
Said Maddalo, 'my judgement will not bend
To your opinion, though I think you might
Make such a system refutation-tight
As far as words go. I knew one like you
Who to this city came some months ago
With whom I argued in this sort, and he
Is now gone mad,—and so he answered me,—
Poor fellow! but if you would like to go
We'll visit him, and his wild talk will show   200
How vain are such aspiring theories.'
'I hope to prove the induction otherwise,
And that a want of that true theory, still
Which seeks a "soul of goodness" in things ill
Or in himself or others has thus bowed
His being—there are some by nature proud,
Who patient in all else demand but this:
To love and be beloved with gentleness;
And being scorned, what wonder if they die
Some living death? this is not destiny   210
But man's own wilfull ill.' As thus I spoke,

Servants announced the gondola, and we
Through the fast-falling rain and high-wrought sea
Sailed to the island where the madhouse stands.
We disembarked. The clap of tortured hands,
Fierce yells and howlings and lamentings keen,
And laughter where complaint had merrier been,
Moans, shrieks and curses and blaspheming prayers
Accosted us. We climbed the oozy stairs
Into an old courtyard. I heard on high,   220
Then, fragments of most touching melody
But looking up saw not the singer there—
Through the black bars in the tempestuous air
I saw, like weeds on a wrecked palace growing,
Long tangled locks flung wildly forth, and flowing,
Of those who on a sudden were beguiled
Into strange silence, and looked forth and smiled
Hearing sweet sounds.—Then I: 'Methinks there were
A cure of these with patience and kind care,
If music can thus move . . . but what is he   230
Whom we seek here?' 'Of his sad history
I know but this,' said Maddalo: 'he came
To Venice a dejected man, and fame
Said he was wealthy, or he had been so;
Some thought the loss of fortune wrought him woe;
But he was ever talking in such sort
As you do—far more sadly—he seemed hurt,
Even as a man with his peculiar wrong,
To hear but of the oppression of the strong,
Or those absurd deceits (I think with you   240
In some respects, you know) which carry through
The excellent impostors of this earth
When they outface detection—he had worth,
Poor fellow! but a humourist in his way'—
'Alas, what drove him mad?' 'I cannot say:
A lady came with him from France, and when
She left him and returned, he wandered then
About yon lonely isles of desert sand
Till he grew wild—he had no cash or land
Remaining,—the police had brought him here—   250
Some fancy took him and he would not bear
Removal; so I fitted up for him
Those rooms beside the sea, to please his whim,

And sent him busts and books and urns for flowers
Which had adorned his life in happier hours,
And instruments of music—you may guess
A stranger could do little more or less
For one so gentle and unfortunate,
And those are his sweet strains which charm the weight
From madmen's chains, and make this Hell appear   260
A heaven of sacred silence, hushed to hear.'—
'Nay, this was kind of you—he had no claim,
As the world says'—'None—but the very same
Which I on all mankind were I as he
Fallen to such deep reverse;—his melody
Is interrupted now—we hear the din
Of madmen, shriek on shriek again begin;
Let us now visit him; after this strain
He ever communes with himself again,
And sees nor hears not any.' Having said   270
These words we called the keeper, and he led
To an apartment opening on the sea—
There the poor wretch was sitting mournfully
Near a piano, his pale fingers twined
One with the other, and the ooze and wind
Rushed through an open casement, and did sway
His hair, and starred it with the brackish spray;
His head was leaning on a music book,
And he was muttering, and his lean limbs shook;
His lips were pressed against a folded leaf   280
In hue too beautiful for health, and grief
Smiled in their motions as they lay apart—
As one who wrought from his own fervid heart
The eloquence of passion, soon he raised
His sad meek face and eyes lustrous and glazed
And spoke—sometimes as one who wrote and thought
His words might move some heart that heeded not
If sent to distant lands: and then as one
Reproaching deeds never to be undone
With wondering self-compassion; then his speech   290
Was lost in grief, and then his words came each
Unmodulated, cold, expressionless;
But that from one jarred accent you might guess
It was despair made them so uniform:
And all the while the loud and gusty storm

Hissed through the window, and we stood behind
Stealing his accents from the envious wind
Unseen. I yet remember what he said
Distinctly: such impression his words made.

'Month after month,' he cried, 'to bear this load   300
And as a jade urged by the whip and goad
To drag life on, which like a heavy chain
Lengthens behind with many a link of pain!—
And not to speak my grief—o not to dare
To give a human voice to my despair
But live and move, and wretched thing! smile on
As if I never went aside to groan
And wear this mask of falsehood even to those
Who are most dear—not for my own repose—
Alas, no scorn or pain or hate could be   310
So heavy as that falsehood is to me—
But that I cannot bear more altered faces
Than needs must be, more changed and cold embraces,
More misery, disappointment and mistrust
To own me for their father . . . Would the dust
Were covered in upon my body now!
That the life ceased to toil within my brow!
And then these thoughts would at the least be fled;
Let us not fear such pain can vex the dead.

'What Power delights to torture us? I know   320
That to myself I do not wholly owe
What now I suffer, though in part I may.
Alas, none strewed sweet flowers upon the way
Where wandering heedlessly, I met pale Pain,
My shadow, which will leave me not again—
If I have erred, there was no joy in error,
But pain and insult and unrest and terror;
I have not as some do, bought penitence
With pleasure, and a dark yet sweet offence,
For then,—if love and tenderness and truth   330
Had overlived hope's momentary youth,
My creed should have redeemed me from repenting;
But loathèd scorn and outrage unrelenting
Met love excited by far other seeming

Until the end was gained . . . as one from dreaming
Of sweetest peace, I woke, and found my state
Such as it is.——

　　　　　　　'O thou, my spirit's mate
Who, for thou art compassionate and wise,
Wouldst pity me from thy most gentle eyes
If this sad writing thou shouldst ever see—   340
My secret groans must be unheard by thee,
Thou wouldst weep tears bitter as blood to know
Thy lost friend's incommunicable woe.

　　'Ye few by whom my nature has been weighed
In friendship, let me not that name degrade
By placing on your hearts the secret load
Which crushes mine to dust. There is one road
To peace and that is truth, which follow ye!
Love sometimes leads astray to misery.
Yet think not though subdued—and I may well   350
Say that I am subdued—that the full Hell
Within me would infect the untainted breast
Of sacred nature with its own unrest;
As some perverted beings think to find
In scorn or hate a medicine for the mind
Which scorn or hate have wounded—o how vain!
The dagger heals not but may rend again . . .
Believe that I am ever still the same
In creed as in resolve, and what may tame
My heart, must leave the understanding free   360
Or all would sink in this keen agony—
Nor dream that I will join the vulgar cry,
Or with my silence sanction tyranny,
Or seek a moment's shelter from my pain
In any madness which the world calls gain,
Ambition or revenge or thoughts as stern
As those which make me what I am, or turn
To avarice or misanthropy or lust . . .
Heap on me soon, o grave, thy welcome dust!
Till then the dungeon may demand its prey,   370
And Poverty and Shame may meet and say—
Halting beside me on the public way—
"That love-devoted youth is ours—let's sit

Beside him—he may live some six months yet."
Or the red scaffold, as our country bends,
May ask some willing victim, or ye friends
May fall under some sorrow which this heart
Or hand may share or vanquish or avert;
I am prepared: in truth with no proud joy   380
To do or suffer aught, as when a boy
I did devote to justice and to love
My nature, worthless now! . . .

     'I must remove
A veil from my pent mind. 'Tis torn aside!
O, pallid as Death's dedicated bride,
Thou mockery which art sitting by my side,
Am I not wan like thee? at the grave's call
I haste, invited to thy wedding-ball
To greet the ghastly paramour, for whom
Thou hast deserted me . . . and made the tomb
Thy bridal bed . . . But I beside your feet   390
Will lie and watch ye from my winding sheet—
Thus. . .wide awake, though dead. . .yet stay, o stay!
Go not so soon—I know not what I say—
Hear but my reasons . . . I am mad, I fear,
My fancy is o'erwrought . . . thou art not here . . .
Pale art thou, 'tis most true . . . but thou art gone,
Thy work is finished . . . I am left alone!—

.   .   .   .

 'Nay, was it I who wooed thee to this breast
Which, like a serpent, thou envenomest
As in repayment of the warmth it lent?   400
Didst thou not seek me for thine own content?
Did not thy love awaken mine? I thought
That thou wert she who said, "You kiss me not
Ever, I fear you do not love me now"—
In truth I loved even to my overthrow
Her, who would fain forget these words: but they
Cling to her mind, and cannot pass away.

.   .   .   .

 'You say that I am proud—that when I speak
My lip is tortured with the wrongs which break
The spirit it expresses . . . Never one   410

Humbled himself before, as I have done!
Even the instinctive worm on which we tread
Turns, though it wound not—then with prostrate head
Sinks in the dust and writhes like me—and dies?
No: wears a living death of agonies!
As the slow shadows of the pointed grass
Mark the eternal periods, his pangs pass
Slow, ever-moving,—making moments be
As mine seem—each an immortality!

. . . .

'That you had never seen me—never heard   420
My voice, and more than all had ne'er endured
The deep pollution of my loathed embrace—
That your eyes ne'er had lied love in my face—
That, like some maniac monk, I had torn out
The nerves of manhood by their bleeding root
With mine own quivering fingers, so that ne'er
Our hearts had for a moment mingled there
To disunite in horror—these were not
With thee, like some suppressed and hideous thought
Which flits athwart our musings, but can find   430
No rest within a pure and gentle mind . . .
Thou sealedst them with many a bare broad word,
And cearedst my memory o'er them,—for I heard
And can forget not . . . they were ministered
One after one, those curses. Mix them up
Like self-destroying poisons in one cup,
And they will make one blessing which thou ne'er
Didst imprecate for, on me,—death.

. . . .

                                        'It were
A cruel punishment for one most cruel,
If such can love, to make that love the fuel   440
Of the mind's hell; hate, scorn, remorse, despair:
But *me*—whose heart a stranger's tear might wear
As water-drops the sandy fountain-stone,
Who loved and pitied all things, and could moan
For woes which others hear not, and could see
The absent with the glance of phantasy,
And with the poor and trampled sit and weep,
Following the captive to his dungeon deep;

Me—who am as a nerve o'er which do creep
The else unfelt oppressions of this earth   450
And was to thee the flame upon thy hearth
When all beside was cold—that thou on me
Shouldst rain these plagues of blistering agony—
Such curses are from lips once eloquent
With love's too partial praise—let none relent
Who intend deeds too dreadful for a name
Henceforth, if an example for the same
They seek . . . for thou on me lookedst so, and so—
And didst speak thus. . .and thus. . .I live to show
How much men bear and die not!   460
·   ·   ·   ·   ·   ·   ·   ·   ·   ·   ·   ·   ·   ·

                              'Thou wilt tell
With the grimace of hate how horrible
It was to meet my love when thine grew less;
Thou wilt admire how I could e'er address
Such features to love's work . . . this taunt, though true,
(For indeed nature nor in form nor hue
Bestowed on me her choicest workmanship)
Shall not be thy defence . . . for since thy lip
Met mine first, years long past, since thine eye kindled
With soft fire under mine, I have not dwindled
Nor changed in mind or body, or in aught   470
But as love changes what it loveth not
After long years and many trials.

                              'How vain
Are words! I thought never to speak again,
Not even in secret,—not to my own heart—
But from my lips the unwilling accents start
And from my pen the words flow as I write,
Dazzling my eyes with scalding tears . . . my sight
Is dim to see that charactered in vain
On this unfeeling leaf which burns the brain
And eats into it . . . blotting all things fair   480
And wise and good which time had written there.

'Those who inflict must suffer, for they see
The work of their own hearts and this must be
Our chastisement or recompense—O child!

I would that thine were like to be more mild
For both our wretched sakes . . . for thine the most
Who feelest already all that thou hast lost
Without the power to wish it thine again;
And as slow years pass, a funereal train
Each with the ghost of some lost hope or friend   490
Following it like its shadow, wilt thou bend
No thought on my dead memory?

.   .   .   .

                                        'Alas, love,
Fear me not . . . against thee I would not move
A finger in despite. Do I not live
That thou mayst have less bitter cause to grieve?
I give thee tears for scorn and love for hate;
And that thy lot may be less desolate
Than his on whom thou tramplest, I refrain
From that sweet sleep which medicines all pain.
Then, when thou speakest of me, never say   500
"He could forgive not." Here I cast away
All human passions, all revenge, all pride;
I think, speak, act no ill; I do but hide
Under these words like embers, every spark
Of that which has consumed me—quick and dark
The grave is yawning . . . as its roof shall cover
My limbs with dust and worms under and over
So let Oblivion hide this grief . . . the air
Closes upon my accents, as despair
Upon my heart—let death upon despair!'   510

    He ceased, and overcome leant back awhile,
Then rising, with a melancholy smile
Went to a sofa, and lay down, and slept
A heavy sleep, and in his dreams he wept
And muttered some familiar name, and we
Wept without shame in his society.
I think I never was impressed so much;
The man who were not, must have lacked a touch
Of human nature . . . then we lingered not,
Although our argument was quite forgot,   520
But calling the attendants, went to dine
At Maddalo's; yet neither cheer nor wine

Could give us spirits, for we talked of him
And nothing else, till daylight made stars dim;
And we agreed his was some dreadful ill
Wrought on him boldly, yet unspeakable,
By a dear friend; some deadly change in love
Of one vowed deeply which he dreamed not of;
For whose sake he, it seemed, had fixed a blot
Of falsehood on his mind which flourished not   530
But in the light of all-beholding truth;
And having stamped this canker on his youth
She had abandoned him—and how much more
Might be his woe, we guessed not—he had store
Of friends and fortune once, as we could guess
From his nice habits and his gentleness;
These were now lost . . . it were a grief indeed
If he had changed one unsustaining reed
For all that such a man might else adorn.
The colours of his mind seemed yet unworn;   540
For the wild language of his grief was high,
Such as in measure were called poetry;
And I remember one remark which then
Maddalo made. He said: 'Most wretched men
Are cradled into poetry by wrong,
They learn in suffering what they teach in song.'

      If I had been an unconnected man
I, from this moment, should have formed some plan
Never to leave sweet Venice,—for to me
It was delight to ride by the lone sea;   550
And then, the town is silent—one may write
Or read in gondolas by day or night,
Having the little brazen lamp alight,
Unseen, uninterrupted; books are there,
Pictures, and casts from all those statues fair
Which were twin-born with poetry, and all
We seek in towns, with little to recall
Regrets for the green country. I might sit
In Maddalo's great palace, and his wit
And subtle talk would cheer the winter night   560
And make me know myself, and the firelight
Would flash upon our faces, till the day
Might dawn and make me wonder at my stay:

But I had friends in London too: the chief
Attraction here, was that I sought relief
From the deep tenderness that maniac wrought
Within me—'twas perhaps an idle thought,
But I imagined that if day by day
I watched him, and but seldom went away,
And studied all the beatings of his heart   570
With zeal, as men study some stubborn art
For their own good, and could by patience find
An entrance to the caverns of his mind,
I might reclaim him from his dark estate:
In friendships I had been most fortunate—
Yet never saw I one whom I would call
More willingly my friend; and this was all
Accomplished not; such dreams of baseless good
Oft come and go in crowds or solitude
And leave no trace—but what I now designed   580
Made for long years impression on my mind.
The following morning urged by my affairs
I left bright Venice.

                    After many years
And many changes I returned; the name
Of Venice, and its aspect, was the same;
But Maddalo was travelling far away
Among the mountains of Armenia.
His dog was dead. His child had now become
A woman; such as it has been my doom
To meet with few,—a wonder of this earth   590
Where there is little of transcendent worth,—
Like one of Shakespeare's women: kindly she
And with a manner beyond courtesy
Received her father's friend; and when I asked
Of the lorn maniac, she her memory tasked
And told as she had heard the mournful tale:
'That the poor sufferer's health began to fail
Two years from my departure, but that then
The lady who had left him, came again.
Her mien had been imperious, but she now   600
Looked meek—perhaps remorse had brought her low.
Her coming made him better, and they stayed
Together at my father's—for I played

As I remember with the lady's shawl—
I might be six years old—but after all
She left him' . . . 'Why, her heart must have been tough:
How did it end?' 'And was not this enough?
They met—they parted'—'Child, is there no more?'
'Something within that interval which bore
The stamp of *why* they parted, *how* they met;—   610
Yet if thine agèd eyes disdain to wet
Those wrinkled cheeks with youth's remembered tears,
Ask me no more, but let the silent years
Be closed and ceared over their memory
As yon mute marble where their corpses lie.'
I urged and questioned still, she told me how
All happened—but the cold world shall not know.

FROM PROMETHEUS UNBOUND

A Lyrical Drama
in Four Acts

AUDISNE HAEC, AMPHIARAE, SUB TERRAM ABDITE?

PREFACE

The Greek tragic writers, in selecting as their subject any portion of
their national history or mythology, employed in their treatment of
it a certain arbitrary discretion. They by no means conceived
themselves bound to adhere to the common interpretation or to
imitate in story as in title their rivals and predecessors. Such a
system would have amounted to a resignation of those claims to
preference over their competitors which incited the composition.
The Agamemnonian story was exhibited on the Athenian theatre
with as many variations as dramas.

I have presumed to employ a similar licence. The *Prometheus
Unbound* of Aeschylus supposed the reconciliation of Jupiter with
his victim as the price of the disclosure of the danger threatened to
his empire by the consummation of his marriage with Thetis.
Thetis, according to this view of the subject, was given in marriage
to Peleus, and Prometheus, by the permission of Jupiter, delivered
from his captivity by Hercules. Had I framed my story on this

model, I should have done no more than have attempted to restore
the lost drama of Aeschylus; an ambition which, if my preference to
this mode of treating the subject had incited me to cherish, the
recollection of the high comparison such an attempt would
challenge might well abate. But, in truth, I was averse from a
catastrophe so feeble as that of reconciling the Champion with the
Oppressor of mankind. The moral interest of the fable, which is so
powerfully sustained by the sufferings and endurance of Prome-
theus, would be annihilated if we could conceive of him as unsaying
his high language and quailing before his successful and perfidious
adversary. The only imaginary being resembling in any degree
Prometheus, is Satan; and Prometheus is, in my judgement, a more
poetical character than Satan, because, in addition to courage, and
majesty, and firm and patient opposition to omnipotent force, he is
susceptible of being described as exempt from the taints of
ambition, envy, revenge, and a desire for personal aggrandisement,
which, in the Hero of *Paradise Lost*, interfere with the interest. The
character of Satan engenders in the mind a pernicious casuistry
which leads us to weigh his faults with his wrongs, and to excuse the
former because the latter exceed all measure. In the minds of those
who consider that magnificent fiction with a religious feeling it
engenders something worse. But Prometheus is, as it were, the type
of the highest perfection of moral and intellectual nature, impelled
by the purest and the truest motives to the best and noblest ends.

This Poem was chiefly written upon the mountainous ruins of
the Baths of Caracalla, among the flowery glades, and thickets of
odoriferous blossoming trees, which are extended in ever winding
labyrinths upon its immense platforms and dizzy arches suspended
in the air. The bright blue sky of Rome, and the effect of the
vigorous awakening spring in that divinest climate, and the new life
with which it drenches the spirits even to intoxication, were the
inspiration of this drama.

The imagery which I have employed will be found, in many
instances, to have been drawn from the operations of the human
mind, or from those external actions by which they are expressed.
This is unusual in modern poetry, although Dante and Shakespeare
are full of instances of the same kind: Dante indeed more than any
other poet, and with greater success. But the Greek poets, as writers
to whom no resource of awakening the sympathy of their
contemporaries was unknown, were in the habitual use of this
power; and it is the study of their works (since a higher merit would
probably be denied me) to which I am willing that my readers

should impute this singularity.

One word is due in candour to the degree in which the study of contemporary writings may have tinged my composition, for such has been a topic of censure with regard to poems far more popular, and indeed more deservedly popular, than mine. It is impossible that any one who inhabits the same age with such writers as those who stand in the foremost ranks of our own, can conscientiously assure himself that his language and tone of thought may not have been modified by the study of the productions of those extraordinary intellects. It is true that, not the spirit of their genius, but the forms in which it has manifested itself, are due less to the peculiarities of their own minds than to the peculiarity of the moral and intellectual condition of the minds among which they have been produced. Thus a number of writers possess the form, whilst they want the spirit of those whom, it is alleged, they imitate; because the former is the endowment of the age in which they live, and the latter must be the uncommunicated lightning of their own mind.

The peculiar style of intense and comprehensive imagery which distinguishes the modern literature of England, has not been, as a general power, the product of the imitation of any particular writer. The mass of capabilities remains at every period materially the same; the circumstances which awaken it to action perpetually change. If England were divided into forty republics, each equal in population and extent to Athens, there is no reason to suppose but that, under institutions not more perfect than those of Athens, each would produce philosophers and poets equal to those who (if we except Shakespeare) have never been surpassed. We owe the great writers of the golden age of our literature to that fervid awakening of the public mind which shook to dust the oldest and most oppressive form of the Christian religion. We owe Milton to the progress and development of the same spirit: the sacred Milton was, let it ever be remembered, a republican, and a bold inquirer into morals and religion. The great writers of our own age are, we have reason to suppose, the companions and forerunners of some unimagined change in our social condition or the opinions which cement it. The cloud of mind is discharging its collected lightning, and the equilibrium between institutions and opinions is now restoring, or is about to be restored.

As to imitation, poetry is a mimetic art. It creates, but it creates by combination and representation. Poetical abstractions are beautiful and new, not because the portions of which they are

composed had no previous existence in the mind of man or in
nature, but because the whole produced by their combination has
some intelligible and beautiful analogy with those sources of
emotion and thought, and with the contemporary condition of
them: one great poet is a masterpiece of nature which another not
only ought to study but must study. He might as wisely and as easily
determine that his mind should no longer be the mirror of all that is
lovely in the visible universe, as exclude from his contemplation the
beautiful which exists in the writings of a great contemporary. The
pretence of doing it would be a presumption in any but the greatest;
the effect, even in him, would be strained, unnatural, and
ineffectual. A poet is the combined product of such internal powers
as modify the nature of others; and of such external influences as
excite and sustain these powers; he is not one, but both. Every
man's mind is, in this respect, modified by all the objects of nature
and art; by every word and every suggestion which he ever admitted
to act upon his consciousness; it is the mirror upon which all forms
are reflected, and in which they compose one form. Poets, not
otherwise than philosophers, painters, sculptors, and musicians,
are, in one sense, the creators, and, in another, the creations, of
their age. From this subjection the loftiest do not escape. There is a
similarity between Homer and Hesiod, between Aeschylus and
Euripides, between Virgil and Horace, between Dante and Petrarch,
between Shakespeare and Fletcher, between Dryden and Pope;
each has a generic resemblance under which their specific
distinctions are arranged. If this similarity be the result of imitation,
I am willing to confess that I have imitated.

Let this opportunity be conceded to me of acknowledging that I
have, what a Scotch philosopher characteristically terms, 'a passion
for reforming the world': what passion incited him to write and
publish his book, he omits to explain. For my part I had rather be
damned with Plato and Lord Bacon, than go to Heaven with Paley
and Malthus. But it is a mistake to suppose that I dedicate my
poetical compositions solely to the direct enforcement of reform,
or that I consider them in any degree as containing a reasoned
system on the theory of human life. Didactic poetry is my
abhorrence; nothing can be equally well expressed in prose that is
not tedious and supererogatory in verse. My purpose has hitherto
been simply to familiarize the highly refined imagination of the
more select classes of poetical readers with beautiful idealisms of
moral excellence; aware that until the mind can love, and admire,
and trust, and hope, and endure, reasoned principles of moral

conduct are seeds cast upon the highway of life which the unconscious passenger tramples into dust, although they would bear the harvest of his happiness. Should I live to accomplish what I purpose, that is, produce a systematical history of what appear to me to be the genuine elements of human society, let not the advocates of injustice and superstition flatter themselves that I should take Aeschylus rather than Plato as my model.

The having spoken of myself with unaffected freedom will need little apology with the candid; and let the uncandid consider that they injure me less than their own hearts and minds by misrepresentation. Whatever talents a person may possess to amuse and instruct others, be they ever so inconsiderable, he is yet bound to exert them: if his attempt be ineffectual, let the punishment of an unaccomplished purpose have been sufficient; let none trouble themselves to heap the dust of oblivion upon his efforts; the pile they raise will betray his grave which might otherwise have been unknown.

ACT I Scene i

> SCENE: *a ravine of icy rocks in the Indian Caucasus.*
> PROMETHEUS *is discovered bound to the precipice.*
> PANTHEA *and* IONE *are seated at his feet. Time, night.*
> *During the scene, morning slowly breaks.*

Prometheus.   Monarch of Gods and Dæmons, and all Spirits
But One, who throng those bright and rolling worlds
Which Thou and I alone of living things
Behold with sleepless eyes! regard this Earth
Made multitudinous with thy slaves, whom thou
Requitest for knee-worship, prayer and praise,
And toil, and hecatombs of broken hearts,
With fear and self-contempt and barren hope;
Whilst me, who am thy foe, eyeless in hate,
Hast thou made reign and triumph, to thy scorn,   10
O'er mine own misery and thy vain revenge.
Three thousand years of sleep-unsheltered hours,
And moments aye divided by keen pangs
Till they seemed years, torture and solitude,
Scorn and despair,—these are mine empire:
More glorious far than that which thou surveyest

From thine unenvied throne, O Mighty God!
Almighty, had I deigned to share the shame
Of thine ill tyranny, and hung not here
Nailed to this wall of eagle-baffling mountain,   20
Black, wintry, dead, unmeasured; without herb,
Insect, or beast, or shape or sound of life.
Ah me! alas, pain, pain ever, forever!

No change, no pause, no hope! Yet I endure.
I ask the Earth, have not the mountains felt?
I ask yon Heaven—the all-beholding Sun,
Has it not seen? the Sea, in storm or calm
Heaven's ever-changing Shadow, spread below,
Have its deaf waves not heard my agony?
Ah me! alas, pain, pain ever, forever!   30

The crawling glaciers pierce me with the spears
Of their moon-freezing crystals; the bright chains
Eat with their burning cold into my bones.
Heaven's wingèd hound, polluting from thy lips
His beak in poison not his own, tears up
My heart; and shapeless sights come wandering by,
The ghastly people of the realm of dream,
Mocking me: and the Earthquake-fiends are charged
To wrench the rivets from my quivering wounds
When the rocks split and close again behind;   40
While from their loud abysses howling throng
The genii of the storm, urging the rage
Of whirlwind, and afflict me with keen hail.
And yet to me welcome is day and night,
Whether one breaks the hoar frost of the morn,
Or starry, dim, and slow, the other climbs
The leaden-coloured east; for then they lead
Their wingless, crawling Hours, one among whom
—As some dark Priest hales the reluctant victim—
Shall drag thee, cruel King, to kiss the blood   50
From these pale feet, which then might trample thee
If they disdained not such a prostrate slave.
Disdain? Ah no! I pity thee. What ruin
Will hunt thee undefended through wide Heaven!
How will thy soul, cloven to its depth with terror,
Gape like a Hell within! I speak in grief,

Not exultation, for I hate no more,
As then ere misery made me wise. The Curse
Once breathed on thee I would recall. Ye Mountains,
Whose many-voicèd Echoes, through the mist   60
Of cataracts, flung the thunder of that spell;
Ye icy Springs, stagnant with wrinkling frost,
Which vibrated to hear me and then crept
Shuddering through India; thou serenest Air,
Through which the Sun walks burning without beams;
And ye swift Whirlwinds, who on poisèd wings
Hung mute and moveless o'er yon hushed abyss,
As thunder louder than your own made rock
The orbèd world—if then my words had power,
Though I am changed so that aught evil wish   70
Is dead within; although no memory be
Of what is hate—let them not lose it now!
What was that curse? for ye all heard me speak.

First Voice   (from the Mountains)
Thrice three hundred thousand years
    O'er the Earthquake's couch we stood:
Oft, as men convulsed with fears,
    We trembled in our multitude.

Second Voice   (from the Springs)
Thunderbolts had parched our water,
    We had been stained with bitter blood,
And had run mute, mid shrieks of slaughter,   80
    Through a city and a solitude.

Third Voice   (from the Air)
I had clothed, since Earth uprose,
    Its wastes in colours not their own;
And oft had my serene repose
    Been cloven by many a rending groan.

Fourth Voice   (from the Whirlwinds)
We had soared beneath these mountains
    Unresting ages; nor had thunder,
Nor yon volcano's flaming fountains,
    Nor any power above or under
    Ever made us mute with wonder.   90

First Voice.
>   But never bowed our snowy crest
>   As at the voice of thine unrest.

Second Voice.
>   Never such a sound before
>   To the Indian waves we bore.
>   A pilot asleep on the howling sea
>   Leaped up from the deck in agony
>   And heard, and cried, 'Ah, woe is me!'
>   And died as mad as the wild waves be.

Third Voice.
>   By such dread words from Earth to Heaven
>   My still realm was never riven: 100
>   When its wound was closed, there stood
>   Darkness o'er the day like blood.

Fourth Voice.
>   And we shrank back: for dreams of ruin
>   To frozen caves our flight pursuing
>   Made us keep silence—thus—and thus—
>   Though silence is as hell to us.

The Earth.   The tongueless Caverns of the craggy hills
>   Cried, 'Misery!' then the hollow Heaven replied,
>   'Misery!' and the Ocean's purple waves,
>   Climbing the land, howled to the lashing winds,   110
>   And the pale nations heard it,—'Misery!'
Prometheus.   I hear a sound of voices—not the voice
>   Which I gave forth. Mother, thy sons and thou
>   Scorn him, without whose all-enduring will
>   Beneath the fierce omnipotence of Jove,
>   Both they and thou had vanished like thin mist
>   Unrolled on the morning wind. Know ye not me,
>   The Titan? he who made his agony
>   The barrier to your else all-conquering foe?
>   O rock-embosomed lawns, and snow-fed streams,   120
>   Now seen athwart frore vapours, deep below,
>   Through whose o'ershadowing woods I wandered once
>   With Asia, drinking life from her loved eyes,
>   Why scorns the spirit which informs ye, now

To commune with me? me alone, who checked—
As one who checks a fiend-drawn charioteer—
The falsehood and the force of Him who reigns
Supreme, and with the groans of pining slaves
Fills your dim glens and liquid wildernesses?
Why answer ye not, still? Brethren!
The Earth.   They dare not.   130
Prometheus.   Who dares? for I would hear that curse again . . .
Ha, what an awful whisper rises up!
'Tis scarce like sound: it tingles through the frame
As lightning tingles, hovering ere it strike.
Speak, Spirit! from thine inorganic voice
I only know that thou art moving near
And love. How cursed I him?
The Earth.   How canst thou hear,
Who knowest not the language of the dead?
Prometheus.   Thou art a living spirit; speak as they.
The Earth.   I dare not speak like life, lest Heaven's fell King 140
Should hear, and link me to some wheel of pain
More torturing than the one whereon I roll.
Subtle thou art and good; and though the Gods
Hear not this voice, yet thou art more than God
Being wise and kind: earnestly hearken now.
Prometheus.   Obscurely through my brain, like shadows dim,
Sweep awful thoughts, rapid and thick. I feel
Faint, like one mingled in entwining love;
Yet 'tis not pleasure.
The Earth.   No, thou canst not hear:
Thou art immortal, and this tongue is known   150
Only to those who die . . .
Prometheus.   And what art thou,
O melancholy Voice?
The Earth.   I am the Earth,
Thy mother; she within whose stony veins,
To the last fibre of the loftiest tree
Whose thin leaves trembled in the frozen air,
Joy ran, as blood within a living frame,
When thou didst from her bosom, like a cloud
Of glory, arise—a spirit of keen joy!
And at thy voice her pining sons uplifted
Their prostrate brows from the polluting dust,   160
And our almighty Tyrant with fierce dread

Grew pale—until his thunder chained thee here.
Then—see those million worlds which burn and roll
Around us: their inhabitants beheld
My spherèd light wane in wide Heaven; the sea
Was lifted by strange tempest, and new fire
From earthquake-rifted mountains of bright snow
Shook its portentous hair beneath Heaven's frown;
Lightning and Inundation vexed the plains;
Blue thistles bloomed in cities; foodless toads   170
Within voluptuous chambers panting crawled;
When Plague had fallen on man and beast and worm,
And Famine,—and black blight on herb and tree;
And in the corn, and vines, and meadow-grass
Teemed ineradicable poisonous weeds
Draining their growth, for my wan breast was dry
With grief; and the thin air, my breath, was stained
With the contagion of a mother's hate
Breathed on her child's destroyer—aye, I heard
Thy curse, the which, if thou rememberest not,   180
Yet my innumerable seas and streams,
Mountains, and caves, and winds, and yon wide air,
And the inarticulate people of the dead,
Preserve, a treasured spell. We meditate
In secret joy and hope those dreadful words,
But dare not speak them.
Prometheus.   Venerable Mother!
All else who live and suffer take from thee
Some comfort; flowers, and fruits, and happy sounds,
And love, though fleeting; these may not be mine.
But mine own words, I pray, deny me not.   190
The Earth.   They shall be told. Ere Babylon was dust,
The Magus Zoroaster, my dead child,
Met his own image walking in the garden.
That apparition, sole of men, he saw.
For know, there are two worlds of life and death:
One that which thou beholdest; but the other
Is underneath the grave, where do inhabit
The shadows of all forms that think and live
Till death unite them and they part no more;
Dreams and the light imaginings of men,   200
And all that faith creates or love desires,
Terrible, strange, sublime and beauteous shapes.

> There thou art, and dost hang, a writhing shade
> Mid whirlwind-peopled mountains; all the Gods
> Are there, and all the Powers of nameless worlds,
> Vast, sceptred Phantoms; heroes, men, and beasts;
> And Demogorgon, a tremendous Gloom;
> And he, the Supreme Tyrant, on his throne
> Of burning gold. Son, one of these shall utter
> The curse which all remember. Call at will   210
> Thine own ghost, or the ghost of Jupiter,
> Hades, or Typhon, or what mightier Gods
> From all-prolific Evil since thy ruin
> Have sprung, and trampled on my prostrate sons.
> Ask, and they must reply: so the revenge
> Of the Supreme may sweep through vacant shades,
> As rainy wind through the abandoned gate
> Of a fallen palace.

Prometheus.   Mother, let not aught
> Of that which may be evil, pass again
> My lips, or those of aught resembling me.   220
> Phantasm of Jupiter, arise, appear!

Ione.
> My wings are folded o'er mine ears:
>   My wings are crossed over mine eyes:
> Yet through their silver shade appears,
>   And through their lulling plumes arise,
> A Shape, a throng of sounds;
>   May it be no ill to thee,
> O thou of many wounds!
> Near whom, for our sweet sister's sake,
> Ever thus we watch and wake.   230

Panthea.
> The sound is of whirlwind underground,
>   Earthquake, and fire, and mountains cloven;
> The Shape is awful like the sound,
>   Clothed in dark purple, star-inwoven.
> A sceptre of pale gold
>   To stay steps proud, o'er the slow cloud
> His veinèd hand doth hold.
> Cruel he looks, but calm and strong,
> Like one who does, not suffers wrong.

Phantasm of Jupiter.   Why have the secret
                powers of this strange world   240
    Driven me, a frail and empty phantom, hither
    On direst storms? What unaccustomed sounds
    Are hovering on my lips, unlike the voice
    With which our pallid race hold ghastly talk
    In darkness? And, proud Sufferer, who art thou?
Prometheus.   Tremendous Image, as thou art must be
    He whom thou shadowest forth. I am his foe,
    The Titan. Speak the words which I would hear,
    Although no thought inform thine empty voice.
The Earth.   Listen! And though your echoes must be mute, 250
    Grey mountains, and old woods, and haunted springs,
    Prophetic caves, and isle-surrounding streams,
    Rejoice to hear what yet ye cannot speak.
Phantasm.   A spirit seizes me and speaks within:
    It tears me as fire tears a thunder-cloud.
Panthea.   See, how he lifts his mighty looks, the Heaven
    Darkens above.
Ione.   He speaks! O shelter me!
Prometheus.   I see the curse on gestures proud and cold,
    And looks of firm defiance, and calm hate,
    And such despair as mocks itself with smiles,   260
    Written as on a scroll . . . yet speak—O speak!

Phantasm.
    Fiend, I defy thee! with a calm, fixed mind,
        All that thou canst inflict I bid thee do;
    Foul Tyrant both of Gods and Humankind,
        One only being shalt thou not subdue.
    Rain then thy plagues upon me here,
    Ghastly disease, and frenzying fear;
    And let alternate frost and fire
    Eat into me, and be thine ire
Lightning, and cutting hail, and legioned forms   270
Of furies, driving by upon the wounding storms.

    Aye, do thy worst. Thou art omnipotent.
        O'er all things but thyself I gave thee power,
    And my own will. Be thy swift mischiefs sent
        To blast mankind, from yon aetherial tower.

Let thy malignant spirit move
Its darkness over those I love:
On me and mine I imprecate
The utmost torture of thy hate;
And thus devote to sleepless agony   280
This undeclining head while thou must reign on high.

But thou who art the God and Lord—O thou
    Who fillest with thy soul this world of woe,
To whom all things of Earth and Heaven do bow
    In fear and worship—all-prevailing foe!
I curse thee! let a sufferer's curse
Clasp thee, his torturer, like remorse,
'Till thine Infinity shall be
A robe of envenomed agony,
And thine Omnipotence a crown of pain   290
To cling like burning gold round thy dissolving brain.

Heap on thy soul, by virtue of this Curse,
    Ill deeds, then be thou damned, beholding good—
Both infinite as is the Universe,
    And thou, and thy self-torturing solitude.
An awful image of calm power
Though now thou sittest, let the hour
Come, when thou must appear to be
That which thou art internally,
And after many a false and fruitless crime   300
Scorn track thy lagging fall through boundless space and time.

Prometheus.   Were these my words, O Parent?
The Earth.   They were thine.
Prometheus.   It doth repent me: words are quick and vain;
    Grief for awhile is blind, and so was mine.
    I wish no living thing to suffer pain.

The Earth.
    Misery, O misery to me,
    That Jove at length should vanquish thee.
    Wail, howl aloud, Land and Sea;
    The Earth's rent heart shall answer ye.
    Howl, Spirits of the living and the dead;   310
    Your refuge, your defence lies fallen and vanquishèd.

First Echo.
    Lies fallen and vanquishèd!

Second Echo.
    Fallen and vanquishèd!

Ione.
    Fear not: 'tis but some passing spasm;
        The Titan is unvanquished still.
    But see, where through the azure chasm
        Of yon forked and snowy hill
    Trampling the slant winds on high
        With golden-sandalled feet, that glow
    Under plumes of purple dye,   320
    Like rose-ensanguined ivory,
        A Shape comes now,
    Stretching on high from his right hand
    A serpent-cinctured wand.

Panthea.
    'Tis Jove's world-wandering herald, Mercury.

Ione.
    And who are those with hydra tresses
        And iron wings that climb the wind,
    Whom the frowning God represses
        Like vapours steaming up behind,
    Clanging loud, an endless crowd—   330

Panthea.
    These are Jove's tempest-walking hounds,
    Whom he gluts with groans and blood,
    When charioted on sulphurous cloud
        He bursts Heaven's bounds.

Ione.
    Are they now led from the thin dead,
    On new pangs to be fed?

Panthea.   The Titan looks as ever, firm, not proud.
First Fury.   Ha! I scent life!
Second Fury.   Let me but look into his eyes!

Third Fury.   The hope of torturing him smells like a heap
   Of corpses to a death-bird after battle   340
First Fury.   Darest thou delay, O Herald! take cheer, Hounds
   Of Hell—what if the Son of Maia soon
   Should make us food and sport? who can please long
   The Omnipotent?

Mercury.   Back to your towers of iron,
   And gnash beside the streams of fire and wail
   Your foodless teeth! . . . Geryon, arise! and Gorgon,
   Chimæra, and thou Sphinx, subtlest of fiends,
   Who ministered to Thebes Heaven's poisoned wine—
   Unnatural love, and more unnatural hate:
   These shall perform your task.
First Fury.   O mercy! mercy!   350
   We die with our desire—drive us not back!
Mercury.   Crouch then in silence.
                  Awful Sufferer,
   To thee unwilling, most unwillingly
   I come, by the great Father's will driven down
   To execute a doom of new revenge.
   Alas! I pity thee, and hate myself
   That I can do no more: aye from thy sight
   Returning, for a season, Heaven seems Hell,
   So thy worn form pursues me night and day,
   Smiling reproach. Wise art thou, firm and good,   360
   But vainly wouldst stand forth alone in strife
   Against the Omnipotent; as yon clear lamps
   That measure and divide the weary years
   From which there is no refuge, long have taught
   And long must teach. Even now thy Torturer arms
   With the strange might of unimagined pains
   The powers who scheme slow agonies in Hell,
   And my commission is to lead them here,
   Or what more subtle, foul, or savage fiends
   People the abyss, and leave them to their task.   370
   Be it not so! . . . there is a secret known
   To thee and to none else of living things,
   Which may transfer the sceptre of wide Heaven,
   The fear of which perplexes the Supreme:
   Clothe it in words, and bid it clasp his throne
   In intercession; bend thy soul in prayer,

And like a suppliant in some gorgeous fane
Let the will kneel within thy haughty heart:
For benefits and meek submission tame
The fiercest and the mightiest.
Prometheus.   Evil minds   380
Change good to their own nature. I gave all
He has; and in return he chains me here
Years, ages, night and day: whether the Sun
Split my parched skin, or in the moony night
The crystal-wingèd snow cling round my hair—
Whilst my belovèd race is trampled down
By his thought-executing ministers.
Such is the tyrant's recompense—'tis just:
He who is evil can receive no good;
And for a world bestowed, or a friend lost,   390
He can feel hate, fear, shame—not gratitude:
He but requites me for his own misdeed.
Kindness to such is keen reproach, which breaks
With bitter stings the light sleep of Revenge.
Submission, thou dost know, I cannot try:
For what submission but that fatal word,
The death-seal of mankind's captivity,
Like the Sicilian's hair-suspended sword
Which trembles o'er his crown, would he accept,
Or could I yield?—Which yet I will not yield.   400
Let others flatter Crime, where it sits throned
In brief Omnipotence; secure are they:
For Justice, when triumphant, will weep down
Pity, not punishment, on her own wrongs,
Too much avenged by those who err. I wait,
Enduring thus, the retributive hour
Which since we spake is even nearer now—
But hark, the hell-hounds clamour: fear delay:
Behold! Heaven lowers under thy Father's frown.
Mercury.   O that we might be spared: I to inflict   410
And thou to suffer! Once more answer me:
Thou knowest not the period of Jove's power?
Prometheus.   I know but this, that it must come.
Mercury.   Alas,
Thou canst not count thy years to come of pain?
Prometheus.   They last while Jove must reign: nor more, nor less
Do I desire or fear.

Mercury.   Yet pause, and plunge
   Into Eternity, where recorded time,
   Even all that we imagine, age on age,
   Seems but a point, and the reluctant mind
   Flags wearily in its unending flight,   420
   Till it sink, dizzy, blind, lost, shelterless;
   Perchance it has not numbered the slow years
   Which thou must spend in torture, unreprieved.
Prometheus.   Perchance no thought can count them—yet
      they pass.
Mercury.   If thou might'st dwell among the Gods the while,
   Lapped in voluptuous joy?
Prometheus.   I would not quit
   This bleak ravine, these unrepentant pains.
Mercury.   Alas! I wonder at, yet pity thee.
Prometheus.   Pity the self-despising slaves of Heaven,
   Not me, within whose mind sits peace serene,   430
   As light in the sun, throned . . . How vain is talk!
   Call up the fiends.
Ione.   O sister, look! White fire
   Has cloven to the roots yon huge snow-loaded cedar;
   How fearfully God's thunder howls behind!
Mercury.   I must obey his words and thine—alas!
   Most heavily remorse hangs at my heart!
Panthea.   See where the child of Heaven with wingèd feet
   Runs down the slanted sunlight of the dawn.
Ione.   Dear sister, close thy plumes over thine eyes
   Lest thou behold and die—they come, they come   440
   Blackening the birth of day with countless wings,
   And hollow underneath, like death.
First Fury.   Prometheus!
Second Fury.   Immortal Titan!
Third Fury.   Champion of Heaven's slaves!
Prometheus.   He whom some dreadful voice invokes is here,
   Prometheus, the chained Titan. Horrible forms,
   What and who are ye? Never yet there came
   Phantasms so foul through monster-teeming Hell
   From the all-miscreative brain of Jove;
   Whilst I behold such execrable shapes
   Methinks I grow like what I contemplate,   450
   And laugh and stare in loathsome sympathy.
First Fury.   We are the ministers of pain and fear,

And disappointment, and mistrust, and hate,
And clinging crime; and as lean dogs pursue
Through wood and lake some struck and sobbing fawn,
We track all things that weep, and bleed, and live,
When the great King betrays them to our will.
Prometheus.   O many fearful natures in one name,
I know ye; and these lakes and echoes know
The darkness and the clangour of your wings.   460
But why more hideous than your loathèd selves
Gather ye up in legions from the deep?
Second Fury.   We knew not that: Sisters, rejoice, rejoice!
Prometheus.   Can aught exult in its deformity?
Second Fury.   The beauty of delight makes lovers glad,
Gazing on one another: so are we.
As from the rose which the pale priestess kneels
To gather for her festal crown of flowers
The aërial crimson falls, flushing her cheek,
So from our victim's destined agony   470
The shade which is our form invests us round,
Else are we shapeless as our mother Night.
Prometheus.   I laugh your power, and his who sent you here,
To lowest scorn. Pour forth the cup of pain.
First Fury.   Thou thinkest we will rend thee bone from bone,
And nerve from nerve, working like fire within?
Prometheus.   Pain is my element, as hate is thine;
Ye rend me now: I care not.
Second Fury.   Dost imagine
We will but laugh into thy lidless eyes?
Prometheus.   I weigh not what ye do, but what ye suffer,   480
Being evil. Cruel was the Power which called
You, or aught else so wretched, into light.
Third Fury.   Thou think'st we will live through thee,
one by one,
Like animal life, and though we can obscure not
The soul which burns within, that we will dwell
Beside it, like a vain loud multitude
Vexing the self-content of wisest men;
That we will be dread thought beneath thy brain,
And foul desire round thine astonished heart,
And blood within thy labyrinthine veins   490
Crawling like agony?
Prometheus.   Why, ye are thus now;

Yet am I king over myself, and rule
The torturing and conflicting throngs within,
As Jove rules you when Hell grows mutinous.

Chorus of Furies.
From the ends of the Earth, from the ends of the Earth,
Where the night has its grave and the morning its birth,
     Come, come, come!
O ye who shake hills with the scream of your mirth
When cities sink howling in ruin; and ye
Who with wingless footsteps trample the Sea,   500
And close upon Shipwreck and Famine's track
Sit chattering with joy on the foodless wreck:
     Come, come, come!
  Leave the bed, low, cold, and red,
  Strewed beneath a nation dead;
  Leave the hatred, as in ashes
    Fire is left for future burning—
  It will burst in bloodier flashes
    When ye stir it, soon returning;
  Leave the self-contempt implanted   510
  In young spirits, sense-enchanted,
    Misery's yet unkindled fuel;
  Leave Hell's secrets half-unchanted
    To the maniac dreamer: cruel
  More than ye can be with hate
    Is he with fear.
     Come, come, come!
  We are steaming up from Hell's wide gate,
    And we burthen the blasts of the atmosphere,
    But vainly we toil till ye come here.   520
Ione.   Sister, I hear the thunder of new wings.
Panthea.   These solid mountains quiver with the sound
  Even as the tremulous air: their shadows make
  The space within my plumes more black than night.

First Fury.
  Your call was as a wingèd car
  Driven on whirlwinds fast and far;
  It rapt us from red gulfs of war.

Second Fury.
  From wide cities, famine-wasted;

Third Fury.
  Groans half heard, and blood untasted;

Fourth Fury.
  Kingly conclaves stern and cold,   530
  Where blood with gold is bought and sold;

Fifth Fury.
  From the furnace, white and hot,
  In which—

A Fury.
      Speak not—whisper not:
  I know all that ye would tell,
  But to speak might break the spell
  Which must bend the Invincible,
    The stern of thought;
  He yet defies the deepest power of Hell.

Fury.
  Tear the veil!

Another Fury.
  It is torn!

Chorus.
      The pale stars of the morn
  Shine on a misery dire to be borne.   540
  Dost thou faint, mighty Titan? We laugh thee to scorn.
  Dost thou boast the clear knowledge thou waken'dst for man?
  Then was kindled within him a thirst which outran
  Those perishing waters: a thirst of fierce fever,
  Hope, love, doubt, desire—which consume him for ever.
    One came forth of gentle worth
    Smiling on the sanguine earth;
  His words outlived him, like swift poison
    Withering up truth, peace, and pity.
  Look! where round the wide horizon   550
    Many a million-peopled city

    Vomits smoke in the bright air.
    Hark that outcry of despair!
    'Tis his mild and gentle ghost
        Wailing for the faith he kindled:
    Look again, the flames almost
        To a glow-worm's lamp have dwindled:
    The survivors round the embers
        Gather in dread.
           Joy, joy, joy!   560
Past ages crowd on thee, but each one remembers;
And the future is dark, and the present is spread
Like a pillow of thorns for thy slumberless head.

Semichorus I.
    Drops of bloody agony flow
    From his white and quivering brow.
    Grant a little respite now—
    See, a disenchanted nation
    Springs like day from desolation;
    To Truth its state is dedicate,
    And Freedom leads it forth, her mate;   570
    A legioned band of linkèd brothers
    Whom Love calls children—

Semichorus II.
        'Tis another's—
    See how kindred murder kin!
    'Tis the vintage-time for Death and Sin:
    Blood, like new wine, bubbles within,
        Till Despair smothers
The struggling World—which slaves and tyrants win.
                [*All the* Furies *vanish, except one.*

Ione.   Hark, sister! what a low yet dreadful groan
    Quite unsuppressed is tearing up the heart
    Of the good Titan, as storms tear the deep,   580
    And beasts hear the sea moan in inland caves.
    Darest thou observe how the fiends torture him?
Panthea.   Alas! I looked forth twice, but will no more.
Ione.   What didst thou see?
Panthea.   A woeful sight: a youth
    With patient looks nailed to a crucifix.

Ione.   What next?
Panthea.   The Heaven around, the Earth below
   Was peopled with thick shapes of human death,
   All horrible, and wrought by human hands,
   Though some appeared the work of human hearts,
   For men were slowly killed by frowns and smiles: 590
   And other sights too foul to speak and live
   Were wandering by. Let us not tempt worse fear
   By looking forth: those groans are grief enough.
Fury.   Behold an emblem: those who do endure
   Deep wrongs for man, and scorn, and chains, but heap
   Thousandfold torment on themselves and him.
Prometheus.   Remit the anguish of that lighted stare;
   Close those wan lips; let that thorn-wounded brow
   Stream not with blood—it mingles with thy tears!
   Fix, fix those tortured orbs in peace and death,   600
   So thy sick throes shake not that crucifix,
   So those pale fingers play not with thy gore.
   O, horrible! Thy name I will not speak;
   It hath become a curse. I see, I see
   The wise, the mild, the lofty, and the just,
   Whom thy slaves hate for being like to thee,
   Some hunted by foul lies from their heart's home,
   An early-chosen, late-lamented home,
   As hooded ounces cling to the driven hind;
   Some linked to corpses in unwholesome cells;   610
   Some—hear I not the multitude laugh loud?—
   Impaled in lingering fire: and mighty realms
   Float by my feet like sea-uprooted isles,
   Whose sons are kneaded down in common blood
   By the red light of their own burning homes.
Fury.   Blood thou canst see, and fire; and canst hear groans;
   Worse things, unheard, unseen, remain behind.
Prometheus.   Worse?
Fury.   In each human heart terror survives
   The ravin it has gorged: the loftiest fear
   All that they would disdain to think were true: 620
   Hypocrisy and custom make their minds
   The fanes of many a worship, now outworn.
   They dare not devise good for man's estate,
   And yet they know not that they do not dare.
   The good want power, but to weep barren tears.

The powerful goodness want: worse need for them.
The wise want love; and those who love want wisdom;
And all best things are thus confused to ill.
Many are strong and rich,—and would be just—
But live among their suffering fellow men   630
As if none felt: they know not what they do.
Prometheus.   Thy words are like a cloud of wingèd snakes;
And yet I pity those they torture not.
Fury.   Thou pitiest them? I speak no more!

                                                    [*Vanishes.*

Prometheus.   Ah woe!
Ah woe! Alas! pain, pain ever, for ever!
I close my tearless eyes, but see more clear
Thy works within my woe-illumèd mind,
Thou subtle tyrant! . . . Peace is in the grave.
The grave hides all things beautiful and good:
I am a God and cannot find it there,   640
Nor would I seek it: for, though dread revenge,
This is defeat, fierce King, not victory!
The sights with which thou torturest gird my soul
With new endurance, till the hour arrives
When they shall be no types of things which are.
Panthea.   Alas! what sawest thou?
Prometheus.   There are two woes:
To speak, and to behold; thou spare me one.
Names are there, Nature's sacred watchwords—they
Were borne aloft in bright emblazonry;
The nations thronged around, and cried aloud,   650
As with one voice, 'Truth, Liberty, and Love!'
Suddenly fierce confusion fell from Heaven
Among them: there was strife, deceit, and fear;
Tyrants rushed in, and did divide the spoil.
This was the shadow of the truth I saw.
The Earth.   I felt thy torture, Son, with such mixed joy
As pain and virtue give. To cheer thy state
I bid ascend those subtle and fair spirits
Whose homes are the dim caves of human thought,
And who inhabit, as birds wing the wind,   660
Its world-surrounding æther; they behold
Beyond that twilight realm, as in a glass,
The future: may they speak comfort to thee!

Panthea.   Look, sister, where a troop of spirits gather,
     Like flocks of clouds in spring's delightful weather,
     Thronging in the blue air!
Ione.   And see! more come,
     Like fountain-vapours when the winds are dumb,
     That climb up the ravine in scattered lines.
     And, hark! is it the music of the pines?
     Is it the lake? is it the waterfall?   670
Panthea.   'Tis something sadder, sweeter far than all.

Chorus of Spirits.
     From unremembered ages we
     Gentle guides and guardians be
     Of Heaven-oppressed mortality;
     And we breathe, and sicken not,
     The atmosphere of human thought:
     Be it dim, and dank, and grey,
     Like a storm-extinguished day,
     Travelled o'er by dying gleams;
          Be it bright as all between   680
     Cloudless skies and windless streams,
          Silent, liquid, and serene—
     As the birds within the wind,
          As the fish within the wave,
     As the thoughts of man's own mind
          Float through all above the grave,
     We make there our liquid lair,
     Voyaging cloudlike and unpent
     Through the boundless element—
     Thence we bear the prophecy   690
     Which begins and ends in thee!

Ione.   More yet come, one by one: the air around them
     Looks radiant as the air around a star.

First Spirit.
     On a battle-trumpet's blast
     I fled hither, fast, fast, fast,
     Mid the darkness upward cast—
     From the dust of creeds outworn,
     From the tyrant's banner torn,
     Gathering round me, onward borne,

There was mingled many a cry— 700
'Freedom! Hope! Death! Victory!'
Till they faded through the sky;
And one sound, above, around,
One sound beneath, around, above,
Was moving; 'twas the soul of love;
'Twas the hope, the prophecy,
Which begins and ends in thee.

Second Spirit.
A rainbow's arch stood on the sea,
Which rocked beneath, immoveably;
And the triumphant Storm did flee, 710
Like a conqueror, swift and proud,
Between, with many a captive cloud,
A shapeless, dark and rapid crowd,
Each by lightning riven in half—
I heard the thunder hoarsely laugh—
Mighty fleets were strewn like chaff
And spread beneath a hell of death
O'er the white waters. I alit
On a great ship lightning-split,
And speeded hither on the sigh 720
Of one who gave an enemy
His plank—then plunged aside to die.

Third Spirit.
I sate beside a Sage's bed,
And the lamp was burning red
Near the book where he had fed,
When a Dream with plumes of flame
To his pillow hovering came,
And I knew it was the same
Which had kindled long ago
Pity, eloquence, and woe; 730
And the world awhile below
Wore the shade its lustre made.
It has borne me here as fleet
As Desire's lightning feet:
I must ride it back ere morrow,
Or the sage will wake in sorrow.

Fourth Spirit.
    On a Poet's lips I slept
    Dreaming like a love-adept
    In the sound his breathing kept;
    Nor seeks nor finds he mortal blisses,   740
    But feeds on the aërial kisses
    Of shapes that haunt thought's wildernesses.
    He will watch from dawn to gloom
    The lake-reflected sun illume
    The yellow bees i' the ivy-bloom,
    Nor heed nor see, what things they be;
    But from these create he can
    Forms more real than living man,
    Nurslings of immortality!
    One of these awakened me,   750
    And I sped to succour thee.

Ione.
    Behold'st thou not two shapes from the east and west
    Come, as two doves to one belovèd nest,
    Twin nurslings of the all-sustaining air,
    On swift still wings glide down the atmosphere?
    And hark! their sweet, sad voices; 'tis despair
    Mingled with love and then dissolved in sound.

Panthea.
    Canst thou speak, sister? all my words are drowned.

Ione.   Their beauty gives me voice. See how they float
    On their sustaining wings of skiey grain,   760
    Orange and azure deepening into gold:
    Their soft smiles light the air like a star's fire.

Chorus of Spirits.
    Hast thou beheld the form of Love?

Fifth Spirit.
          As over wide dominions
    I sped, like some swift cloud that wings the wide air's
        wildernesses,
    That planet-crested Shape swept by on lightning-braided
        pinions,

Scattering the liquid joy of life from his ambrosial tresses:
His footsteps paved the world with light—but as I passed
    'twas fading,
And hollow Ruin yawned behind: great sages bound in
    madness,
And headless patriots, and pale youths who perished,
    unupbraiding,
Gleamed in the night I wandered o'er—till thou, O
    King of sadness,   770
Turned by thy smile the worst I saw to recollected gladness.

Sixth Spirit.
    Ah, sister! Desolation is a delicate thing:
    It walks not on the earth, it floats not on the air,
    But treads with lulling footstep, and fans with silent wing
    The tender hopes which in their hearts the best and gentlest bear;
    Who, soothed to false repose by the fanning plumes above,
    And the music-stirring motion of its soft and busy feet,
    Dream visions of aërial joy, and call the monster Love,
    And wake, and find the shadow Pain—as he whom now
        we greet.

Chorus.
    Though Ruin now Love's shadow be,   780
    Following him destroyingly
        On Death's white and wingèd steed,
    Which the fleetest cannot flee—
        Trampling down both flower and weed,
    Man and beast, and foul and fair,
    Like a tempest through the air;
    Thou shalt quell this Horseman grim,
    Woundless though in heart or limb.

Prometheus.   Spirits! how know ye this shall be?

Chorus.
    In the atmosphere we breathe—   790
  As buds grow red when snow-storms flee
    From spring gathering up beneath,
    Whose mild winds shake the elder brake,
    And the wandering herdsmen know
    That the white-thorn soon will blow—

Wisdom, Justice, Love, and Peace,
When they struggle to increase,
        Are to us as soft winds be
        To shepherd boys—the prophecy
        Which begins and ends in thee.   800

Ione.   Where are the Spirits fled?

Panthea.

                    Only a sense
Remains of them, like the omnipotence
Of music, when the inspired voice and lute
Languish, ere yet the responses are mute
Which through the deep and labyrinthine soul,
Like echoes through long caverns, wind and roll.

Prometheus.   How fair these air-born shapes! and yet I feel
Most vain all hope but love; and thou art far,
Asia! who, when my being overflowed,
Wert like a golden chalice to bright wine   810
Which else had sunk into the thirsty dust.
All things are still: alas! how heavily
This quiet morning weighs upon my heart;
Though I should dream, I could even sleep with grief
If slumber were denied not. I would fain
Be what it is my destiny to be,
The saviour and the strength of suffering man,
Or sink into the original gulf of things . . .
There is no agony, and no solace left;
Earth can console, Heaven can torment no more.   820
Panthea.   Hast thou forgotten one who watches thee
The cold dark night, and never sleeps but when
The shadow of thy spirit falls on her?
Prometheus.   I said all hope was vain but love: thou lovest.
Panthea.   Deeply in truth; but the eastern star looks white,
And Asia waits in that far Indian vale,
The scene of her sad exile—rugged once
And desolate and frozen, like this ravine;
But now invested with fair flowers and herbs,
And haunted by sweet airs and sounds, which flow   830
Among the woods and waters, from the æther
Of her transforming presence—which would fade
If it were mingled not with thine. Farewell!

ACT II   Scene iv

The Cave of Demogorgon. ASIA and PANTHEA.

Panthea.   What veilèd form sits on that ebon throne?
Asia.   The veil has fallen. . . .
Panthea.   I see a mighty Darkness
    Filling the seat of power; and rays of gloom
    Dart round, as light from the meridian sun,
    Ungazed upon and shapeless—neither limb,
    Nor form, nor outline; yet we feel it is
    A living Spirit.
Demogorgon.   Ask what thou wouldst know.
Asia.   What canst thou tell?
Demogorgon.   All things thou dar'st demand.
Asia.   Who made the living world?
Demogorgon.   God.
Asia.   Who made all
    That it contains—thought, passion, reason, will,   10
    Imagination?
Demogorgon.   God: Almighty God.
Asia.   Who made that sense which, when the winds of spring
    In rarest visitation, or the voice
    Of one belovèd heard in youth alone,
    Fills the faint eyes with falling tears which dim
    The radiant looks of unbewailing flowers,
    And leaves this peopled earth a solitude
    When it returns no more?
Demogorgon.   Merciful God.
Asia.   And who made terror, madness, crime, remorse,
    Which from the links of the great chain of things   20
    To every thought within the mind of man
    Sway and drag heavily, and each one reels
    Under the load towards the pit of death;
    Abandoned hope, and love that turns to hate;
    And self-contempt, bitterer to drink than blood;
    Pain, whose unheeded and familiar speech
    Is howling, and keen shrieks, day after day;
    And Hell, or the sharp fear of Hell?
Demogorgon.   He reigns.
Asia.   Utter his name: a world pining in pain
    Asks but his name: curses shall drag him down.   30

Demogorgon.   He reigns.
Asia.   I feel, I know it: who?
Demogorgon.   He reigns.
Asia.   Who reigns? There was the Heaven and Earth at first,
And Light and Love; then Saturn, from whose throne
Time fell, an envious shadow; such the state
Of the earth's primal spirits beneath his sway
As the calm joy of flowers and living leaves
Before the wind or sun has withered them
And semivital worms; but he refused
The birthrights of their being, knowledge, power,
The skill which wields the elements, the thought   40
Which pierces this dim universe like light,
Self-empire, and the majesty of love;
For thirst of which they fainted. Then Prometheus
Gave wisdom, which is strength, to Jupiter,
And with this law alone, 'Let man be free,'
Clothed him with the dominion of wide Heaven.
To know nor faith, nor love, nor law; to be
Omnipotent but friendless is to reign;
And Jove now reigned; for on the race of man
First famine, and then toil, and then disease,   50
Strife, wounds, and ghastly death unseen before,
Fell; and the unseasonable seasons drove
With alternating shafts of frost and fire,
Their shelterless, pale tribes to mountain caves;
And in their desert hearts fierce wants he sent,
And mad disquietudes, and shadows idle
Of unreal good, which levied mutual war,
So ruining the lair wherein they raged.
Prometheus saw, and waked the legioned hopes
Which sleep within folded Elysian flowers,   60
Nepenthe, Moly, Amaranth, fadeless blooms,
That they might hide with thin and rainbow wings
The shape of Death; and Love he sent to bind
The disunited tendrils of that vine
Which bears the wine of life, the human heart;
And he tamed fire which, like some beast of chase,
Most terrible, but lovely, played beneath
The frown of man; and tortured to his will
Iron and gold, the slaves and signs of power,
And gems and poisons, and all subtlest forms   70

Hidden beneath the mountains and the waves.
He gave man speech, and speech created thought,
Which is the measure of the universe;
And Science struck the thrones of Earth and Heaven,
Which shook, but fell not; and the harmonious mind
Poured itself forth in all-prophetic song;
And music lifted up the listening spirit
Until it walked, exempt from mortal care,
Godlike, o'er the clear billows of sweet sound;
And human hands first mimicked and then mocked,   80
With moulded limbs more lovely than its own,
The human form, till marble grew divine;
And mothers, gazing, drank the love men see
Reflected in their race—behold, and perish.
He told the hidden power of herbs and springs,
And Disease drank and slept. Death grew like sleep.
He taught the implicated orbits woven
Of the wide-wandering stars; and how the Sun
Changes his lair, and by what secret spell
The pale Moon is transformed, when her broad eye   90
Gazes not on the interlunar sea.
He taught to rule, as life directs the limbs,
The tempest-wingèd chariots of the Ocean,
And the Celt knew the Indian. Cities then
Were built, and through their snow-like columns flowed
The warm winds, and the azure æther shone,
And the blue sea and shadowy hills were seen. . .
Such the alleviations of his state
Prometheus gave to man—for which he hangs
Withering in destined pain: but who rains down   100
Evil, the immedicable plague, which, while
Man looks on his creation like a God
And sees that it is glorious, drives him on,
The wreck of his own will, the scorn of Earth,
The outcast, the abandoned, the alone?
Not Jove: while yet his frown shook heaven, aye when
His adversary from adamantine chains
Cursed him, he trembled like a slave. Declare
Who is his master? Is he too a slave?
Demogorgon.   All spirits are enslaved which serve things
        evil: 110
    Thou knowest if Jupiter be such or no.

Asia.   Whom called'st thou God?
Demogorgon.   I spoke but as ye speak,
  For Jove is the supreme of living things.
Asia.   Who is the master of the slave?
Demogorgon.   If the abysm
  Could vomit forth its secrets:—but a voice
  Is wanting, the deep truth is imageless;
  For what would it avail to bid thee gaze
  On the revolving world? what to bid speak
  Fate, Time, Occasion, Chance and Change? To these
  All things are subject but eternal Love.   120
Asia.   So much I asked before, and my heart gave
  The response thou hast given; and of such truths
  Each to itself must be the oracle.—
  One more demand; and do thou answer me
  As my own soul would answer, did it know
  That which I ask. Prometheus shall arise
  Henceforth the Sun of this rejoicing world:
  When will the destined hour arrive?
Demogorgon.   Behold!
Asia.   The rocks are cloven, and through the purple night
  I see cars drawn by rainbow-wingèd steeds   130
  Which trample the dim winds: in each there stands
  A wild-eyed charioteer, urging their flight.
  Some look behind, as fiends pursued them there,
  And yet I see no shapes but the keen stars;
  Others, with burning eyes, lean forth, and drink
  With eager lips the wind of their own speed,
  As if the thing they loved fled on before,
  And now, even now, they clasped it. Their bright locks
  Stream like a comet's flashing hair: they all
  Sweep onward.
Demogorgon.   These are the immortal Hours,   140
  Of whom thou didst demand. One waits for thee.
Asia.   A spirit with a dreadful countenance
  Checks its dark chariot by the craggy gulf.
  Unlike thy brethren, ghastly charioteer,
  What art thou? Whither wouldst thou bear me? Speak!
Spirit.   I am the shadow of a destiny
  More dread than is my aspect: ere yon planet
  Has set, the Darkness which ascends with me
  Shall wrap in lasting night Heaven's kingless throne.

Asia.   What meanest thou?
Panthea.   That terrible shadow floats   150
   Up from its throne, as may the lurid smoke
   Of earthquake-ruined cities o'er the sea.
   Lo! it ascends the car . . . the coursers fly
   Terrified: watch its path among the stars
   Blackening the night!
Asia.   Thus I am answered: strange!
Panthea.   See, near the verge, another chariot stays;
   An ivory shell inlaid with crimson fire,
   Which comes and goes within its sculptured rim
   Of delicate strange tracery; the young spirit
   That guides it has the dove-like eyes of hope;   160
   How its soft smiles attract the soul! as light
   Lures wingèd insects through the lampless air.

Spirit.
   My coursers are fed with the lightning,
     They drink of the whirlwind's stream,
   And when the red morning is bright'ning
     They bathe in the fresh sunbeam;
     They have strength for their swiftness I deem,
   Then ascend with me, daughter of Ocean.
   I desire: and their speed makes night kindle;
     I fear: they outstrip the Typhoon;   170
   Ere the cloud piled on Atlas can dwindle
     We encircle the earth and the moon:
     We shall rest from long labours at noon:
   Then ascend with me, daughter of Ocean.

FROM ACT III Scene iv

Spirit of the Earth.   Mother, I am grown wiser, though a child
   Cannot be wise like thee, within this day;
   And happier too; happier and wiser both.
   Thou knowest that toads, and snakes, and loathly worms,
   And venomous and malicious beasts, and boughs
   That bore ill berries in the woods, were ever
   An hindrance to my walks o'er the green world;
   And that, among the haunts of humankind,

Hard-featured men, or with proud, angry looks,
Or cold, staid gait, or false and hollow smiles,   10
Or the dull sneer of self-loved ignorance,
Or other such foul masks, with which ill thoughts
Hide that fair being whom we spirits call man;
And women too, ugliest of all things evil,
(Though fair, even in a world where thou art fair,
When good and kind, free and sincere like thee)
When false or frowning made me sick at heart
To pass them, though they slept, and I unseen.
Well, my path lately lay through a great city
Into the woody hills surrounding it.   20
A sentinel was sleeping at the gate—
When there was heard a sound, so loud, it shook
The towers amid the moonlight, yet more sweet
Than any voice but thine, sweetest of all;
A long, long sound, as it would never end:
And all the inhabitants leapt suddenly
Out of their rest, and gathered in the streets,
Looking in wonder up to Heaven, while yet
The music pealed along. I hid myself
Within a fountain in the public square,   30
Where I lay like the reflex of the moon
Seen in a wave under green leaves—and soon
Those ugly human shapes and visages
Of which I spoke as having wrought me pain,
Passed floating through the air, and fading still
Into the winds that scattered them, and those
From whom they passed seemed mild and lovely forms
After some foul disguise had fallen—and all
Were somewhat changed—and after brief surprise
And greetings of delighted wonder, all   40
Went to their sleep again; and when the dawn
Came—would'st thou think that toads, and snakes, and efts
Could e'er be beautiful? yet so they were,
And that with little change of shape or hue:
All things had put their evil nature off.
I cannot tell my joy, when o'er a lake,
Upon a drooping bough with night-shade twined,
I saw two azure halcyons clinging downward
And thinning one bright bunch of amber berries
With quick long beaks, and in the deep there lay   50

Those lovely forms imaged as in a sky—
So with my thoughts full of these happy changes,
We meet again, the happiest change of all.

*   *   *   *   *   *

Spirit of the Hour.   Thrones, altars, judgement-seats, and
    prisons—wherein,
And beside which, by wretched men were borne
Sceptres, tiaras, swords, and chains, and tomes
Of reasoned wrong, glozed on by ignorance,
Were like those monstrous and barbaric shapes,
The ghosts of a no-more-remembered fame,
Which, from their unworn obelisks, look forth   60
In triumph o'er the palaces and tombs
Of those who were their conquerors, mouldering round.
These imaged to the pride of kings and priests
A dark yet mighty faith, a power as wide
As is the world it wasted, and are now
But an astonishment; even so the tools
And emblems of its last captivity,
Amid the dwellings of the peopled earth,
Stand, not o'erthrown, but unregarded now.
And those foul shapes, abhorred by God and man,   70
Which, under many a name and many a form,
Strange, savage, ghastly, dark, and execrable,
Were Jupiter, the tyrant of the world;
And which the nations, panic-stricken, served
With blood, and hearts broken by long hope, and love
Dragged to his altars soiled and garlandless,
And slain among men's unreclaiming tears,
Flattering the thing they feared, which fear was hate—
Frown, mouldering fast, o'er their abandoned shrines.
The painted veil, by those who were, called life,   80
Which mimicked, as with colours idly spread,
All men believed and hoped, is torn aside;
The loathsome mask has fallen, the man remains
Sceptreless, free, uncircumscribed—but man:
Equal, unclassed, tribeless, and nationless;
Exempt from awe, worship, degree,—the king
Over himself; just, gentle, wise—but man:
Passionless? no—yet free from guilt or pain,

Which were, for his will made, or suffered them;
Nor yet exempt, though ruling them like slaves,   90
From chance, and death, and mutability,
The clogs of that which else might oversoar
The loftiest star of unascended Heaven,
Pinnacled dim in the intense inane.

FROM ACT IV

Demogorgon.
This is the Day, which down the void abysm
At the Earth-born's spell yawns for Heaven's despotism,
    And Conquest is dragged captive through the deep;
Love, from its awful throne of patient power
In the wise heart, from the last giddy hour
    Of dread endurance, from the slippery, steep,
And narrow verge of crag-like agony, springs
And folds over the world its healing wings.

Gentleness, Virtue, Wisdom, and Endurance,—
These are the seals of that most firm assurance   10
    Which bars the pit over Destruction's strength;
And if, with infirm hand, Eternity,
Mother of many acts and hours, should free
    The serpent that would clasp her with his length,—
These are the spells by which to re-assume
An empire o'er the disentangled Doom.

To suffer woes which Hope thinks infinite;
To forgive wrongs darker than Death or Night;
    To defy Power, which seems omnipotent;
To love, and bear; to hope, till Hope creates   20
From its own wreck the thing it contemplates;
    Neither to change, nor falter, nor repent:
This, like thy glory, Titan, is to be
Good, great and joyous, beautiful and free;
This is alone Life, Joy, Empire, and Victory.

THE MASK OF ANARCHY
written on the Occasion of the Massacre at Manchester

As I lay asleep in Italy
There came a voice from over the Sea,
And with great power it forth led me
To walk in the Visions of Poesy.

I met Murder on the way—
He had a mask like Castlereagh,
Very smooth he looked, yet grim;
Seven bloodhounds followed him:

All were fat; and well they might
Be in admirable plight,   10
For one by one, and two by two,
He tossed them human hearts to chew
Which from his wide cloak he drew.

Next came Fraud, and he had on,
Like Eldon, an ermined gown;
His big tears, for he wept well,
Turned to mill-stones as they fell,

And the little children who
Round his feet played to and fro,
Thinking every tear a gem,   20
Had their brains knocked out by them.

Clothed with the Bible, as with light,
And the shadows of the night,
Like Sidmouth next, Hypocrisy
On a crocodile rode by.

And many more Destructions played
In this ghastly masquerade,
All disguised, even to the eyes,
Like Bishops, lawyers, peers or spies.

Last came Anarchy: he rode   30
On a white horse, splashed with blood;

He was pale even to the lips,
Like Death in the Apocalypse.

And he wore a kingly crown;
And in his grasp a sceptre shone;
On his brow this mark I saw—
'I AM GOD AND KING AND LAW.'

With a pace stately and fast,
Over English land he passed,
Trampling to a mire of blood   40
The adoring multitude.

And a mighty troop around,
With their trampling shook the ground,
Waving each a bloody sword,
For the service of their Lord;

And with glorious triumph, they
Rode through England proud and gay,
Drunk as with intoxication
Of the wine of desolation.

O'er fields and towns, from sea to sea,   50
Passed that Pageant swift and free,
Tearing up and trampling down
Till they came to London town;

And each dweller, panic-stricken,
Felt his heart with terror sicken
Hearing the tempestuous cry
Of the triumph of Anarchy.

For with pomp to meet him came
Clothed in arms like blood and flame
The hired Murderers, who did sing   60
'Thou art God and Law and King.

'We have waited weak and lone
For thy coming, Mighty One!
Our purses are empty, our swords are cold,
Give us glory and blood and gold.'

Lawyers and priests, a motley crowd,
To the Earth their pale brows bowed,
Like a bad prayer not overloud
Whispering—'Thou art Law and God.'

Then all cried with one accord   70
'Thou art King and God and Lord;
Anarchy, to Thee we bow,
Be Thy name made holy now!'

And Anarchy, the Skeleton,
Bowed and grinned to every one,
As well as if his education
Had cost ten millions to the Nation.

For he knew the Palaces
Of our Kings were rightly his;
His the sceptre, crown, and globe,   80
And the gold-inwoven robe.

So he sent his slaves before
To seize upon the Bank and Tower,
And was proceeding with intent
To meet his pensioned Parliament

When One fled past, a Maniac maid,
And her name was Hope, she said:
But she looked more like Despair,
And she cried out in the air—

'My father Time is weak and grey   90
With waiting for a better day—
See how idiot-like he stands
Fumbling with his palsied hands!

He has had child after child
And the dust of death is piled
Over every one but me—
Misery, o Misery!'

Then she lay down in the street
Right before the horses' feet,

Expecting with a patient eye   100
Murder, Fraud and Anarchy,

When between her and her foes
A mist, a light, an image rose,
Small at first, and weak and frail
Like the vapour of a vale,

Till as clouds grow on the blast
Like tower-crowned giants striding fast,
And glare with lightnings as they fly
And speak in thunder to the sky,

It grew—a Shape arrayed in mail   110
Brighter than the viper's scale,
And upborne on wings whose grain
Was as the light of sunny rain.

On its helm seen far away
A planet, like the Morning's lay;
And those plumes its light rained through
Like a shower of crimson dew;

With step as soft as wind it passed
O'er the heads of men—so fast
That they knew the presence there   120
And looked—but all was empty air.

As flowers beneath May's footstep waken,
As stars from Night's loose hair are shaken,
As waves arise when loud winds call,
Thoughts sprung where'er that step did fall.

And the prostrate multitude
Looked—and ankle-deep in blood
Hope, that maiden most serene,
Was walking with a quiet mien,

And Anarchy, the ghastly birth,   130
Lay dead earth upon the earth—

The Horse of Death tameless as wind
Fled, and with his hoofs did grind
To dust the murderers thronged behind.

A rushing light of clouds and splendour,
A sense awakening and yet tender
Was heard and felt—and at its close
These words of joy and fear arose

As if their own indignant Earth
Which gave the Sons of England birth   140
Had felt their blood upon her brow,
And shuddering with a mother's throe

Had turned every drop of blood
By which her face had been bedewed
To an accent unwithstood—
As if her heart cried out aloud:

'Men of England, Heirs of Glory,
Heroes of unwritten Story,
Nurslings of one mighty Mother,
Hopes of her and one another,   150

'Rise like Lions after slumber
In unvanquishable number,
Shake your chains to Earth like dew
Which in sleep had fallen on you—
Ye are many—they are few.

'What is Freedom?—ye can tell
That which slavery is, too well—
For its very name has grown
To an echo of your own.

' 'Tis to work and have such pay   160
As just keeps life from day to day
In your limbs, as in a cell
For the tyrants' use to dwell,

'So that ye for them are made
Loom and plough and sword and spade,

With or without your own will bent
To their defence and nourishment;

' 'Tis to see your children weak
With their mothers pine and peak
When the winter winds are bleak—   170
They are dying whilst I speak;

' 'Tis to hunger for such diet
As the rich man in his riot
Casts to the fat dogs that lie
Surfeiting beneath his eye;

' 'Tis to let the Ghost of Gold
Take from Toil a thousandfold
More than e'er its substance could
In the tyrannies of old—

'Paper coin, that forgery   180
Of the title deeds, which ye
Hold to something from the worth
Of the inheritance of Earth;

' 'Tis to be a slave in soul
And to hold no strong control
Over your own will, but be
All that others make of ye;

'And at length when ye complain
With a murmur weak and vain,
'Tis to see the tyrants' crew   190
Ride over your wives and you—
Blood is on the grass like dew.

'Then it is to feel revenge
Fiercely thirsting to exchange
Blood for blood, and wrong for wrong—
Do not thus when ye are stong.

'Birds find rest, in narrow nest
When weary of their wingèd quest,

Beasts find fare, in woody lair
When storm and snow are in the air;   200

'Horses, oxen, have a home
When from daily toil they come;
Household dogs, when the wind roars
Find a home within warm doors;

'Asses, swine, have litter spread
And with fitting food are fed;
All things have a home but one—
Thou, o Englishman, hast none!

'This is slavery—savage men
Or wild beasts within a den   210
Would endure not as ye do—
But such ills they never knew.

'What art thou, Freedom? o, could slaves
Answer from their living graves
This demand, tyrants would flee
Like a dream's dim imagery.

'Thou art not as imposters say
A Shadow soon to pass away,
A Superstition, and a name
Echoing from the cave of Fame: 220

'For the labourer thou art bread
And a comely table spread,
From his daily labour come,
In a neat and happy home;

'Thou art clothes and fire and food
For the trampled multitude—
No—in countries that are free
Such starvation cannot be
As in England now we see.

'To the rich thou art a check—   230
When his foot is on the neck

Of his victim, thou dost make
That he treads upon a snake.

'Thou art Justice—ne'er for gold
May thy righteous laws be sold
As laws are in England—thou
Shieldst alike both high and low.

'Thou art Wisdom—Freemen never
Dream that God will damn forever
All who think those things untrue   240
Of which Priests make such ado.

'Thou art Peace—never by thee
Would blood and treasure wasted be
As tyrants wasted them, when all
Leagued to quench thy flame in Gaul.

'What if English toil and blood
Was poured forth even as a flood?
It availed, o Liberty,
To dim, but not extinguish thee.

'Thou art Love—the rich have kissed   250
Thy feet, and like him following Christ
Give their substance to the free
And through the rough world follow thee,

'Or turn their wealth to arms, and make
War for thy belovèd sake
On wealth and war and fraud—whence they
Drew the power which is their prey.

'Science, Poetry and Thought
Are thy lamps; they make the lot
Of the dwellers in a cot   260
Such, they curse their Maker not.

'Spirit, Patience, Gentleness,
All that can adorn and bless
Art thou . . . let deeds not words express
Thine exceeding loveliness—

'Let a great Assembly be
Of the fearless and the free
On some spot of English ground
Where the plains stretch wide around.

'Let the blue sky overhead,   270
The green earth on which ye tread,
All that must eternal be
Witness the Solemnity.

'From the corners uttermost
Of the bounds of English coast,
From every hut, village and town
Where those who live and suffer, moan
For others' misery or their own—

'From the workhouse and the prison
Where pale as corpses newly risen   280
Women, children, young and old
Groan for pain and weep for cold—

'From the haunts of daily life
Where is waged the daily strife
With common wants and common cares
Which sows the human heart with tares—

'Lastly from the palaces
Where the murmur of distress
Echoes, like the distant sound
Of a wind alive around   290

'Those prison-halls of wealth and fashion
Where some few feel such compassion
For those who groan and toil and wail
As must make their brethren pale,

'Ye who suffer woes untold
Or to feel or to behold
Your lost country bought and sold
With a price of blood and gold—

'Let a vast Assembly be,
And with great solemnity   300

Declare with measured words that ye
Are, as God has made ye, free—

'Be your strong and simple words
Keen to wound as sharpened swords,
And wide as targes let them be
With their shade to cover ye.

'Let the tyrants pour around
With a quick and startling sound
Like the loosening of a sea
Troops of armed emblazonry.   310

'Let the charged artillery drive
Till the dead air seems alive
With the clash of clanging wheels
And the tramp of horses' heels.

'Let the fixèd bayonet
Gleam with sharp desire to wet
Its bright point in English blood—
Looking keen, as one for food.

'Let the horsemen's scimitars
Wheel and flash like sphereless stars   320
Thirsting to eclipse their burning
In a sea of death and mourning.

'Stand ye calm and resolute
Like a forest close and mute
With folded arms and looks which are
Weapons of unvanquished war,

'And let Panic who outspeeds
The career of armed steeds
Pass, a disregarded shade,
Through your phalanx undismayed.   330

'Let the Laws of your own land,
Good or ill, between ye stand
Hand to hand and foot to foot,
Arbiters of the dispute,

'The old laws of England—they
Whose reverend heads with age are grey,
Children of a wiser day,
And whose solemn voice must be
Thine own echo—Liberty!

'On those who first should violate   340
Such sacred heralds in their state
Rest the blood that must ensue . . .
And it will not rest on you.

'And if then the tyrants dare,
Let them ride among you there,
Slash and stab and maim and hew—
What they like, that let them do.

'With folded arms, and steady eyes,
And little fear, and less surprise,
Look upon them as they slay   350
Till their rage has died away.

'Then they will return with shame
To the place from which they came,
And the blood thus shed will speak
In hot blushes on their cheek:

'Every Woman in the land
Will point at them as they stand . . .
They will hardly dare to greet
Their acquaintance in the street.

'And the bold, true warriors   360
Who have hugged Danger in wars
Will turn to those who would be free,
Ashamed of such base company.

'And that slaughter, to the Nation
Shall steam up like inspiration,
Eloquent, oracular;
A volcano heard afar.

'And these words shall then become
Like oppression's thundered doom
Ringing through each heart and brain,   370
Heard again, again, again—

'Rise like lions after slumber
In unvanquishable number,
Shake your chains to earth like dew
Which in sleep had fallen on you—
Ye are many—they are few—'

ODE TO THE WEST WIND*

1.   O wild West Wind, thou breath of Autumn's being,
     Thou, from whose unseen presence the leaves dead
     Are driven, like ghosts from an enchanter fleeing,

     Yellow, and black, and pale, and hectic red,
     Pestilence-stricken multitudes: O thou,
     Who chariotest to their dark wintry bed

     The wingèd seeds, where they lie cold and low,
     Each like a corpse within its grave, until
     Thine azure sister of the Spring shall blow

     Her clarion o'er the dreaming earth, and fill   10
     (Driving sweet buds like flocks to feed in air)
     With living hues and odours plain and hill:

---

* This poem was conceived and chiefly written in a wood that skirts the
Arno, near Florence, and on a day when that tempestuous wind, whose
temperature is at once mild and animating, was collecting the vapours
which pour down the autumnal rains. They began, as I foresaw, at
sunset with a violent tempest of hail and rain, attended by that
magnificent thunder and lightning peculiar to the Cisalpine regions.
   The phenomenon alluded to at the conclusion of the third stanza is
well known to naturalists. The vegetation at the bottom of the sea, of
rivers, and of lakes, sympathises with that of the land in the change of
seasons, and is consequently influenced by the winds which announce
it.

Wild Spirit, which art moving everywhere;
Destroyer and Preserver; hear, O hear!

2. Thou on whose stream, 'mid the steep sky's commotion,
    Loose clouds like Earth's decaying leaves are shed,
    Shook from the tangled boughs of Heaven and Ocean,

    Angels of rain and lightning: there are spread
    On the blue surface of thine airy surge,
    Like the bright hair uplifted from the head   20

    Of some fierce Mænad, even from the dim verge
    Of the horizon to the zenith's height,
    The locks of the approaching storm. Thou dirge

    Of the dying year, to which this closing night
    Will be the dome of a vast sepulchre
    Vaulted with all thy congregated might

    Of vapours, from whose solid atmosphere
    Black rain, and fire, and hail will burst: O hear!

3. Thou who didst waken from his summer dreams
    The blue Mediterranean, where he lay,   30
    Lulled by the coil of his crystalline streams,

    Beside a pumice isle in Baiæ's bay,
    And saw in sleep old palaces and towers
    Quivering within the wave's intenser day,

    All overgrown with azure moss and flowers
    So sweet, the sense faints picturing them! Thou
    For whose path the Atlantic's level powers

    Cleave themselves into chasms, while far below
    The sea-blooms and the oozy woods which wear
    The sapless foliage of the ocean, know   40

Thy voice, and suddenly grow grey with fear,
And tremble and despoil themselves: O hear!

4.   If I were a dead leaf thou mightest bear;
     If I were a swift cloud to fly with thee;
     A wave to pant beneath thy power, and share

     The impulse of thy strength, only less free
     Than thou, O Uncontrollable! If even
     I were as in my boyhood, and could be

     The comrade of thy wanderings over Heaven,
     As then, when to outstrip thy skiey speed   50
     Scarce seemed a vision; I would ne'er have striven

     As thus with thee in prayer in my sore need.
     Oh! lift me as a wave, a leaf, a cloud!
     I fall upon the thorns of life! I bleed!

     A heavy weight of hours has chained and bowed
     One too like thee: tameless, and swift, and proud.

5.   Make me thy lyre, even as the forest is:
     What if my leaves are falling like its own!
     The tumult of thy mighty harmonies

     Will take from both a deep, autumnal tone,   60
     Sweet though in sadness. Be thou, Spirit fierce,
     My spirit! Be thou me, impetuous one!

     Drive my dead thoughts over the universe
     Like withered leaves to quicken a new birth!
     And, by the incantation of this verse,

     Scatter, as from an unextinguished hearth
     Ashes and sparks, my words among mankind!
     Be through my lips to unawakened Earth

     The trumpet of a prophecy! O Wind,
     If Winter comes, can Spring be far behind?   70

FROM PETER BELL THE THIRD

Part the third

HELL

Hell is a city much like London—
   A populous and a smoky city;
There are all sorts of people undone,
And there is little or no fun done;
   Small justice shown, and still less pity.

There is a Castle, and a Canning,
   A Cobbett, and a Castlereagh;
All sorts of caitiff corpses planning
All sorts of cozening for trepanning
   Corpses less corrupt than they.   10

There is a * * *, who has lost
   His wits, or sold them, none knows which;
He walks about a double ghost,
And though as thin as Fraud almost—
   Ever grows more grim and rich.

There is a Chancery Court; a King;
   A manufacturing mob; a set
Of thieves who by themselves are sent
Similar thieves to represent;
   An army; and a public debt—   20

Which last is a scheme of Paper money,
   And means—being interpreted—
'Bees, keep your wax—give us the honey,
And we will plant while skies are sunny,
   Flowers, which in winter serve instead.'

There is great talk of Revolution—
   And a great chance of Despotism—
German soldiers—camps—confusion—
Tumults—lotteries—rage—delusion—
   Gin—suicide—and methodism.   30

Taxes too, on wine and bread,
　　And meat, and beer, and tea, and cheese,
From which those patriots pure are fed,
Who gorge before they reel to bed
　　The tenfold essence of all these.

There are mincing women, mewing
　　(Like cats, who *amant miserè*,)
Of their own virtue, and pursuing
Their gentler sisters to that ruin,
　　Without which—what were chastity?   40

Lawyers—judges—old hobnobbers
　　Are there—bailiffs—chancellors—
Bishops—great and little robbers—
Rhymesters—pamphleteers—stock-jobbers—
　　Men of glory in the wars,—

Things whose trade is, over ladies
　　To lean, and flirt, and stare, and simper,
Till all that is divine in woman
Grows cruel, courteous, smooth, inhuman,
　　Crucified 'twixt a smile and whimper.   50

Thrusting, toiling, wailing, moiling,
　　Frowning, preaching—such a riot!
Each with never-ceasing labour,
Whilst he thinks he cheats his neighbour,
　　Cheating his own heart of quiet.

And all these meet at levees;—
　　Dinners convivial and political;—
Suppers of epic poets;—teas,
Where small talk dies in agonies;—
　　Breakfasts professional and critical;—   60

Lunches and snacks so aldermanic
　　That one would furnish forth ten dinners,
Where reigns a Cretan-tonguèd panic
Lest news Russ, Dutch, or Alemannic
　　Should make some losers, and some winners;—

At conversazioni—balls—
   Conventicles—and drawing-rooms—
Courts of law—committees—calls
Of a morning—clubs—book-stalls—
   Churches—masquerades—and tombs.   70

And this is Hell—and in this smother
   All are damnable and damned;
Each one damning, damns the other;
They are damned by one another,
   By none other are they damned.

'Tis a lie to say, 'God damns!'
   Where was Heaven's Attorney General
When they first gave out such flams?
Let there be an end of shams,
   They are mines of poisonous mineral.   80

Statesmen damn themselves to be
   Cursed; and lawyers damn their souls
To the auction of a fee;
Churchmen damn themselves to see
   God's sweet love in burning coals.

The rich are damned, beyond all cure,
   To taunt, and starve, and trample on
The weak and wretched; and the poor
Damn their broken hearts to endure
   Stripe on stripe, with groan on groan.   90

Sometimes the poor are damned indeed
   To take,— not means for being blest,—
But Cobbett's snuff, revenge; that weed
From which the worms that it doth feed
   Squeeze less than they before possessed.

And some few, like we know who,
   Damned—but God alone knows why—
To believe their minds are given
To make this ugly Hell a Heaven;
   In which faith they live and die.   100

Thus, as in a town plague-stricken,
   Each man be he sound or no
Must indifferently sicken;
As when day begins to thicken,
   None knows a pigeon from a crow,—

So good and bad, sane and mad,
   The oppressor and the oppressed;
Those who weep to see what others
Smile to inflict upon their brothers;
   Lovers, haters, worst and best;   110

All are damned—they breathe an air
   Thick, infected, joy-dispelling:
Each pursues what seems most fair,
Mining like moles through mind, and there
Scoop palace-caverns vast, where Care
   In thronèd state is ever dwelling.

Part the fourth

SIN

Lo, Peter in Hell's Grosvenor-square,
   A footman in the devil's service!
And the misjudging world would swear
That every man in service there   120
   To virtue would prefer vice.

But Peter, though now damned, was not
   What Peter was before damnation.
Men oftentimes prepare a lot
Which, ere it finds them, is not what
   Suits with their genuine station.

All things that Peter saw and felt
   Had a peculiar aspect to him;
And when they came within the belt
Of his own nature, seemed to melt,   130
   Like cloud to cloud, into him.

And so, the outward world uniting
   To that within him, he became
Considerably uninviting
To those, who meditation slighting,
   Were moulded in a different frame.

And he scorned them, and they scorned him;
   And he scorned all they did; and they
Did all that men of their own trim
Are wont to do to please their whim,—   140
   Drinking, lying, swearing, play.

Such were his fellow-servants; thus
   His virtue, like our own, was built
Too much on that indignant fuss
Hypocrite Pride stirs up in us
   To bully one another's guilt.

He had a mind which was somehow
   At once circumference and centre
Of all he might or feel or know;
Nothing went ever out, although   150
   Something did ever enter.

He had as much imagination
   As a pint-pot:—he never could
Fancy another situation,
From which to dart his contemplation,
   Than that wherein he stood.

Yet his was individual mind,
   And new created all he saw
In a new manner, and refined
Those new creations, and combined   160
   Them, by a master-spirit's law.

Thus—though unimaginative—
   An apprehension clear, intense,
Of his mind's work, had made alive
The things it wrought on; I believe,
   Wakening a sort of thought in sense.

But from the first 'twas Peter's drift
   To be a kind of moral eunuch,
He touched the hem of nature's shift,
Felt faint—and never dared uplift   170
   The closest, all-concealing tunic.

She laughed the while, with an arch smile,
   And kissed him with a sister's kiss,
And said—'My best Diogenes,
I love you well—but, if you please,
   Tempt not again my deepest bliss.

'Tis you are cold—for I, not coy,
   Yield love for love, frank, warm and true;
And Burns, a Scottish peasant boy—
His errors prove it—knew my joy   180
   More, learned friend, than you.

'*Bocca baciata non perde ventura*
   Anzi rinnuova come fa la luna:—
So thought Boccaccio, whose sweet words might cure a
Male prude, like you, from what you now endure, a
   Low-tide in soul, like a stagnant laguna.'

Then Peter rubbed his eyes severe,
   And smoothed his spacious forehead down
With his broad palm:—'twixt love and fear,
He looked, as he no doubt felt, queer;   190
   And in his dream sate down.

The Devil was no uncommon creature;
   A leaden-witted thief—just huddled
Out of the dross and scum of nature;
A toad-like lump of limb and feature,
   With mind, and heart, and fancy muddled.

He was that heavy, dull, cold thing
   The Spirit of Evil well may be:
A drone too base to have a sting;
Who gluts, and grimes his lazy wing,   200
   And calls lust, luxury.

Now he was quite the kind of wight
　　Round whom collect, at a fixed era,
Venison, turtle, hock and claret,—
Good cheer—and those who come to share it—
　　And best East Indian madeira!

It was his fancy to invite
　　Men of science, wit and learning,
Who came to lend each other light:—
He proudly thought that his gold's might   210
　　Had set those spirits burning.

And men of learning, science, wit,
　　Considered him as you and I
Think of some rotten tree, and sit
Lounging and dining under it,
　　Exposed to the wide sky.

And all the while, with loose fat smile
　　The willing wretch sat winking there,
Believing 'twas his power that made
That jovial scene—and that all paid   220
　　Homage to his unnoticed chair.

Though to be sure this place was Hell;
　　He was the Devil—and all they—
What though the claret circled well,
And wit, like ocean, rose and fell?—
　　Were damned eternally.

Part the fifth

GRACE

Among the guests who often stayed
　　Till the Devil's petits-soupers,
A man there came, fair as a maid,
And Peter noted what he said,   230
　　Standing behind his master's chair.

He was a mighty poet—and
    A subtle-souled psychologist;
All things he seemed to understand,
Of old or new—of sea or land—
    But his own mind—which was a mist.

This was a man who might have turned
    Hell into Heaven—and so in gladness
A Heaven unto himself have earned;
But he in shadows undiscerned   240
    Trusted,—and damned himself to madness.

He spoke of Poetry, and how
    'Divine it was—a light—a love—
A spirit which like wind doth blow
As it listeth, to and fro;
    A dew rained down from God above;

'A Power which comes and goes like dream,
    And which none can ever trace—
Heaven's light on Earth—Truth's brightest beam.'
And when he ceased there lay the gleam   250
    Of those words upon his face.

Now Peter when he heard such talk
    Would, heedless of a broken pate
Stand like a man asleep, or baulk
Some wishing guest of knife or fork,
    Or drop and break his master's plate.

At night he oft would start and wake
    Like a lover, and began
In a wild measure songs to make
On moor, and glen, and rocky lake,   260
    And on the heart of man;—

And on the universal sky;—
    And the wide earth's bosom green;—
And the sweet, strange mystery
Of what beyond these things may lie,
    And yet remain unseen.

For in his thought he visited
   The spots in which, ere dead and damned,
He his wayward life had led;
Yet knew not whence the thoughts were fed,   270
   Which thus his fancy crammed.

And these obscure rememberances
   Stirred such harmony in Peter,
That, whensoever he should please,
He could speak of rocks and trees
   In poetic metre.

For though it was without a sense
   Of memory, yet he remembered well
Many a ditch and quick-set fence;
Of lakes he had intelligence,   280
   He knew something of heath, and fell.

He had also dim recollections
   Of pedlars tramping on their rounds;
Milk-pans and pails; and odd collections
Of saws and proverbs; and reflections
   Old parsons make in burying-grounds.

But Peter's verse was clear, and came
   Announcing from the frozen hearth
Of a cold age, that none might tame
The soul of that diviner flame   290
   It augured to the Earth:

Like gentle rains, on the dry plains,
   Making that green which late was grey,
Or like the sudden moon, that stains
Some gloomy chamber's window panes
   With a broad light like day.

For language was in Peter's hand,
   Like clay, while he was yet a potter;
And he made songs for all the land,
Sweet both to feel and understand,   300
   As pipkins late to mountain cotter.

And Mr. —, the bookseller,
   Gave twenty pounds for some;—then scorning
A footman's yellow coat to wear,
Peter, too proud of heart, I fear,
   Instantly gave the Devil warning.

Whereat the Devil took offence,
   And swore in his soul a great oath then,
   'That for his damned impertinence,
He'd bring him to a proper sense   310
   Of what was due to gentlemen!'—

ODE TO HEAVEN

CHORUS OF SPIRITS

First Spirit
Palace-roof of cloudless nights!
Paradise of golden lights!
   Deep, immeasurable, vast,
Which art now, and which wert then;
   Of the present and the past,
Of the eternal where and when,
   Presence-chamber, temple, home,
   Ever-canopying dome
   Of acts and ages yet to come!

Glorious shapes have life in thee—   10
Earth, and all Earth's company,
   Living globes which ever throng
Thy deep chasms and wildernesses;
   And green worlds that glide along;
And swift stars with flashing tresses;
   And icy moons most cold and bright,
   And mighty suns, beyond the night,
   Atoms of intensest light!

Even thy name is as a God,
Heaven! for thou art the abode   20
   Of that Power which is the glass

Wherein man his nature sees;—
   Generations as they pass
Worship thee with bended knees.
    Their unremaining Gods and they
    Like a river roll away:
    Thou remainest such—alway!

Second Spirit
   Thou art but the mind's first chamber,
   Round which its young fancies clamber,
    Like weak insects in a cave   30
Lighted up by stalactites;
    But the portal of the grave,
Where a world of new delights
    Will make thy best glories seem
    But a dim and noonday gleam
    From the shadow of a dream!

Third Spirit
   Peace! the Abyss is wreathed with scorn
At your presumption, atom-born!
    What is Heaven? and what are ye
Who its brief expanse inherit?   40
    What are suns and spheres which flee
With the instinct of that spirit
    Of which ye are but a part?
    Drops which Nature's mighty heart
    Drives through thinnest veins. Depart!

What is Heaven? a globe of dew,
Filling in the morning new
    Some eyed flower whose young leaves waken
On an unimagined world.
    Constellated suns unshaken,   50
Orbits measureless, are furled
    In that frail and fading sphere,
    With ten millions gathered there
    To tremble, gleam, and disappear!

ENGLAND IN 1819

An old, mad, blind, despised and dying King;
Princes, the dregs of their dull race, who flow
Through public scorn,—mud from a muddy spring;
Rulers who neither see nor feel nor know,
But leechlike to their fainting Country cling
Till they drop, blind in blood, without a blow;
A people starved and stabbed on the untilled field;
An army whom liberticide and prey
Makes as a two-edged sword to all who wield;
Golden and sanguine laws which tempt and slay;   10
Religion Christless, Godless, a book sealed;
A senate, Time's worst statute, unrepealed,—
Are graves from which a glorious Phantom may
Burst, to illumine our tempestuous day.

LINES TO A CRITIC

1. Honey from silk-worms who can gather,
        Or silk from the yellow bee?
    The grass may grow in winter weather
        As soon as hate in me.

2. Hate men who cant, and men who pray,
        And men who rail, like thee;
    An equal passion to repay
        They are not coy—like me—.

3. Or seek some slave of power and gold,
        To be thy dear heart's mate—   10
    Thy love will move that bigot cold
        Sooner than me, thy hate.

4. A passion like the one I prove
        Cannot divided be;
    I hate thy want of truth and love—
        How should I then hate thee?

ODE TO LIBERTY

> Yet, Freedom, yet, thy banner torn but flying,
> Streams like a thunder-storm against the wind.
>
> *Byron*

1.   A glorious people vibrated again
        The lightning of the nations: Liberty,
    From heart to heart, from tower to tower, o'er Spain,
        Scattering contagious fire into the sky,
    Gleamed. My soul spurned the chains of its dismay,
            And in the rapid plumes of song
            Clothed itself, sublime and strong;
    As a young eagle soars the morning clouds among,
        Hovering in verse o'er its accustomed prey;
            Till from its station in the Heaven of fame   10
        The Spirit's whirlwind rapt it, and the ray
            Of the remotest sphere of living flame
    Which paves the void was from behind it flung,
        As foam from a ship's swiftness, when there came
        A voice out of the deep: I will record the same.

2.   The Sun and the serenest Moon sprang forth:
        The burning stars of the abyss were hurled
    Into the depths of Heaven. The dædal Earth,
        That island in the ocean of the world,
    Hung in its cloud of all-sustaining air: 20
            But this divinest universe
            Was yet a chaos and a curse,
    For thou wert not: but, Power from worst producing
        worse,
        The spirit of the beasts was kindled there,
            And of the birds, and of the watery forms,
    And there was war among them, and despair
            Within them, raging without truce or terms:
    The bosom of their violated nurse
        Groaned, for beasts warred on beasts, and worms on
          worms,
        And men on men; each heart was as a hell of storms. 30

3.   Man, the imperial shape, then multiplied
        His generations under the pavilion
    Of the Sun's throne: palace and pyramid,

Temple and prison, to many a swarming million
Were as to mountain-wolves their ruggèd caves.
    This human living multitude
      Was savage, cunning, blind, and rude,
For thou wert not; but o'er the populous solitude,
  Like one fierce cloud over a waste of waves,
    Hung Tyranny; beneath, sate deified   40
The Sister-Pest, congregator of slaves;
    Into the shadow of her pinions wide
Anarchs and priests, who feed on gold and blood
  Till with the stain their inmost souls are dyed,
  Drove the astonished herds of men from every side.

4. The nodding promontories, and blue isles,
    And cloud-like mountains, and dividuous waves
Of Greece, basked glorious in the open smiles
    Of favouring Heaven: from their enchanted caves
Prophetic echoes flung dim melody   50
    On the unapprehensive wild.
      The vine, the corn, the olive mild,
Grew savage yet, to human use unreconciled;
    And, like unfolded flowers beneath the sea,
      Like the man's thought dark in the infant's brain,
  Like aught that is which wraps what is to be,
    Art's deathless dreams lay veiled by many a vein
Of Parian stone; and, yet a speechless child,
    Verse murmured, and Philosophy did strain
  Her lidless eyes for thee; when o'er the Aegean main 60

5. Athens arose: a city such as Vision
    Builds from the purple crags and silver towers
Of battlemented cloud, as in derision
    Of kingliest masonry: the ocean-floors
Pave it; the evening sky pavilions it;
    Its portals are inhabited
      By thunder-zonèd winds, each head
Within its cloudy wings with sunfire garlanded;—
    A divine work! Athens, diviner yet,
      Gleamed with its crest of columns, on the will 70
    Of man, as on a mount of diamond, set;
      For thou wert, and thine all-creative skill

Peopled, with forms that mock the eternal dead
   In marble immortality, that hill
   Which was thine earliest throne and latest oracle.

6.   Within the surface of Time's fleeting river
     Its wrinkled image lies, as then it lay,
Immoveably unquiet, and for ever
     It trembles, but it cannot pass away!
The voices of its bards and sages thunder   80
         With an earth-awakening blast
         Through the caverns of the past;
   (Religion veils her eyes; Oppression shrinks aghast;)
     A wingèd sound of joy, and love, and wonder,
       Which soars where Expectation never flew,
   Rending the veil of space and time asunder!
     One ocean feeds the clouds, and streams, and dew;
One sun illumines Heaven; one Spirit vast
   With life and love makes chaos ever new,
   As Athens doth the world with thy delight renew.   90

7.   Then Rome was—and from thy deep bosom, fairest,
     Like a wolf-cub from a Cadmæan Mænad,*
She drew the milk of greatness, though thy dearest
     From that Elysian food was yet unweanèd;
And many a deed of terrible uprightness
         By thy sweet love was sanctified;
         And in thy smile, and by thy side,
Saintly Camillus lived, and firm Attilius died.
     But when tears stained thy robe of vestal whiteness,
       And gold profaned thy Capitolian throne,   100
     Thou didst desert, with spirit-wingèd lightness,
       The senate of the tyrants: they sunk prone,
Slaves of one tyrant: Palatinus sighed
   Faint echoes of Ionian song; that tone
   Thou didst delay to hear, lamenting to disown.

8.   From what Hyrcanian glen or frozen hill,
     Or piny promontory of the Arctic main,
Or utmost islet inaccessible,
     Didst thou lament the ruin of thy reign,

---

* See the Bacchæ of Euripides

Teaching the woods and waves, and desert rocks,   110
   And every Naiad's ice-cold urn,
   To talk in echoes sad and stern,
Of that sublimest lore which man had dared unlearn?
  For neither didst thou watch the wizard flocks
   Of the Scald's dreams, nor haunt the Druid's sleep.
  What if the tears rained through thy scattered locks
   Were quickly dried? for thou didst groan, not weep,
When from its sea of death, to kill and burn,
  The Galilean serpent forth did creep,
  And made thy world an undistinguishable heap.   120

9. A thousand years the Earth cried, 'Where art thou?'
   And then the shadow of thy coming fell
On Saxon Alfred's olive-cinctured brow:
  And many a warrior-peopled citadel,
Like rocks which fire lifts out of the flat deep,
   Arose in sacred Italy,
   Frowning o'er the tempestuous sea
Of kings, and priests, and slaves, in tower-crowned majesty;
  That multitudinous anarchy did sweep
   And burst around their walls, like idle foam,   130
  Whilst from the human spirit's deepest deep
   Strange melody with love and awe struck dumb
Dissonant arms; and Art, which cannot die,
  With divine wand traced on our earthly home
  Fit imagery to pave Heaven's everlasting dome.

10. Thou huntress swifter than the Moon! thou terror
   Of the world's wolves! thou bearer of the quiver,
Whose sunlike shafts pierce tempest-wingèd Error,
  As light may pierce the clouds when they dissever
In the calm regions of the orient day!   140
    Luther caught thy wakening glance—
    Like lightning, from his leaden lance
Reflected, it dissolved the visions of the trance
  In which, as in a tomb, the nations lay;
   And England's prophets hailed thee as their queen,
  In songs whose music cannot pass away,
   Though it must flow forever: not unseen

Before the spirit-sighted countenance
Of Milton didst thou pass, from the sad scene
Beyond whose night he saw, with a dejected mien.   150

11.   The eager Hours and unreluctant Years
As on a dawn-illumined mountain stood,
Trampling to silence their loud hopes and fears,
Darkening each other with their multitude,
And cried aloud, 'Liberty!' Indignation
Answered Pity from her cave;
Death grew pale within the grave,
And Desolation howled to the Destroyer, 'Save!'
When, like Heaven's Sun girt by the exhalation
Of its own glorious light, thou didst arise,   160
Chasing thy foes from nation unto nation
Like shadows: as if day had cloven the skies
At dreaming midnight o'er the western wave,
Men started, staggering with a glad surprise,
Under the lightnings of thine unfamiliar eyes.

12.   Thou Heaven of earth! what spells could pall thee then
In ominous eclipse? A thousand years
Bred from the slime of deep Oppression's den
Dyed all thy liquid light with blood and tears,
Till thy sweet stars could weep the stain away;   170
How like Bacchanals of blood
Round France, the ghastly vintage, stood
Destruction's sceptred slaves, and Folly's mitred brood!
When one, like them, but mightier far than they,
The Anarch of thine own bewildered powers,
Rose: armies mingled in obscure array,
Like clouds with clouds, darkening the sacred bowers
Of serene Heaven. He, by the past pursued,
Rests with those dead but unforgotten Hours,
Whose ghosts scare victor kings in their ancestral towers.
180

13.   England yet sleeps; was she not called of old?
Spain calls her now, as with its thrilling thunder
Vesuvius wakens Etna, and the cold
Snow-crags by its reply are cloven in sunder:

O'er the lit waves every Aeolian isle
    From Pithecusa to Pelorus
    Howls, and leaps, and glares in chorus:
They cry, 'Be dim, ye lamps of heaven suspended o'er us.'
    Her chains are threads of gold,—she need but smile
      And they dissolve; but Spain's were links
        of steel,   190
    Till bit to dust by Virtue's keenest file.
      Twins of a single destiny! appeal
To the eternal years enthroned before us
    In the dim West: impress, as from a seal,
    All ye have thought and done! Time cannot dare conceal.

14.   Tomb of Arminius! render up thy dead
      Till, like a standard from a watch-tower's staff,
His soul may stream over the tyrant's head;
      Thy victory shall be his epitaph,
Wild Bacchanal of truth's mysterious wine;   200
      King-deluded Germany,
        His dead spirit lives in thee.
Why do we fear or hope? thou art already free!
    And thou, lost Paradise of this divine
      And glorious world! thou flowery wilderness!
Thou island of eternity! thou shrine
      Where Desolation, clothed with loveliness,
Worships the thing thou wert! O Italy,
    Gather thy blood into thy heart: repress
    The beasts who make their dens thy sacred palaces.   210

15.   O that the free would stamp the impious name
      Of KING into the dust! or write it there,
So that this blot upon the page of fame
    Were as a serpent's path, which the light air
Erases, and the flat sands close behind!
      Ye the oracle have heard:
      Lift the victory-flashing sword,
And cut the snaky knots of this foul gordian word,
    Which, weak itself as stubble, yet can bind
      Into a mass, irrefragably firm,   220
    The axes and the rods which awe mankind;
      The sound has poison in it, 'tis the sperm

Of what makes life foul, cankerous, and abhorred;
   Disdain not thou, at thine appointed term,
   To set thine armèd heel on this reluctant worm.

16.   O that the wise from their bright minds would kindle
     Such lamps within the dome of this dim world,
That the pale name of PRIEST might shrink and dwindle
     Into the hell from which it first was hurled,
A scoff of impious pride from fiends impure;   230
       Till human thoughts might kneel alone,
       Each before the judgement-throne
Of its own aweless soul, or of the Power unknown!
    O that the words which make the thoughts obscure
      From which they spring, as clouds of glimmering dew
    From a white lake blot Heaven's blue portraiture,
      Were stripped of their thin masks and various hue
And frowns and smiles and splendours not their own,
     Till in the nakedness of false and true
     They stand before their Lord, each to receive its due.
                   240

17.   He who taught man to vanquish whatsoever
     Can be between the cradle and the grave
Crowned him the King of Life: O vain endeavour!—
     If on his own high will, a willing slave,
He has enthroned the oppression and the oppressor.
       What if Earth can clothe and feed
       Amplest millions at their need,
And power in thought be as the tree within the seed?
     Or what if Art, an ardent intercessor,
      Diving on fiery wings to Nature's throne,   250
    Checks the great Mother stooping to caress her,
      And cries: 'Give me, thy child, dominion
Over all height and depth'?—if Life can breed
     New wants, and Wealth from those who toil and groan
     Rend, of thy gifts and hers, a thousandfold for one.

18.   Come thou! but lead out of the inmost cave
     Of man's deep spirit, as the morning-star
Beckons the Sun from the Eoan wave,
     Wisdom. I hear the pennons of her car

Self-moving, like cloud charioted by flame;   260
   Comes she not, and come ye not,
   Rulers of eternal thought,
To judge, with solemn truth, life's ill-apportioned lot?
  Blind Love, and equal Justice, and the Fame
   Of what has been, the Hope of what will be?
  O Liberty! if such could be thy name
   Wert thou disjoined from these, or they from thee:
If thine or theirs were treasures to be bought
  By blood or tears, have not the wise and free
  Wept tears, and blood like tears?—The solemn
   harmony   270

19. Paused, and the Spirit of that mighty singing
   To its abyss was suddenly withdrawn;
  Then, as a wild swan, when sublimely winging
   Its path athwart the thunder-smoke of dawn,
  Sinks headlong through the aërial golden light
    On the heavy-sounding plain,
    When the bolt has pierced its brain;
  As summer clouds dissolve, unburthened of their rain;
   As a far taper fades with fading night,
    As a brief insect dies with dying day,—   280
   My song, its pinions disarrayed of might,
    Drooped; o'er it closed the echoes far away
  Of the great voice which did its flight sustain,
   As waves which lately paved his watery way
   Hiss round a drowner's head in their tempestuous play.

THE CLOUD

I bring fresh showers for the thirsting flowers,
  From the seas and the streams;
I bear light shade for the leaves when laid
  In their noon-day dreams.
From my wings are shaken the dews that waken
  The sweet buds every one,
When rocked to rest on their mother's breast,
  As she dances about the sun.
I wield the flail of the lashing hail,
  And whiten the green plains under,   10

And then again I dissolve it in rain,
    And laugh as I pass in thunder.

I sift the snow on the mountains below,
    And their great pines groan aghast;
And all the night 'tis my pillow white,
    While I sleep in the arms of the blast.
Sublime on the towers of my skiey bowers,
    Lightning my pilot sits,
In a cavern under is fettered the thunder,
    It struggles and howls at fits;   20
Over earth and ocean, with gentle motion,
    This pilot is guiding me,
Lured by the love of the genii that move
    In the depths of the purple sea;
Over the rills, and the crags, and the hills,
    Over the lakes and the plains,
Wherever he dream, under mountain or stream,
    The Spirit he loves remains;
And I all the while bask in Heaven's blue smile,
    Whilst he is dissolving in rains.   30

The sanguine sunrise, with his meteor eyes,
    And his burning plumes outspread,
Leaps on the back of my sailing rack,
    When the morning star shines dead;
As on the jag of a mountain crag
    Which an earthquake rocks and swings,
An eagle alit one moment may sit
    In the light of its golden wings;
And when sunset may breathe, from the lit sea beneath,
    Its ardours of rest and of love,   40
And the crimson pall of eve may fall
    From the depths of Heaven above,
With wings folded I rest, on mine aëry nest,
    As still as a brooding dove.

That orbèd maiden with white fire laden,
    Whom mortals call the moon,
Glides glimmering o'er my fleece-like floor,
    By the midnight breezes strewn;
And wherever the beat of her unseen feet,

Which only the angels hear,   50
May have broken the woof of my tent's thin roof,
    The stars peep behind her, and peer;
And I laugh to see them whirl and flee
    Like a swarm of golden bees,
When I widen the rent in my wind-built tent,
    Till the calm rivers, lakes, and seas,
Like strips of the sky fallen through me on high,
    Are each paved with the moon and these.

I bind the sun's throne with a burning zone,
    And the moon's with a girdle of pearl;   60
The volcanoes are dim, and the stars reel and swim,
    When the whirlwinds my banner unfurl.
From cape to cape, with a bridge-like shape,
    Over a torrent sea,
Sunbeam-proof, I hang like a roof—
    The mountains its columns be.
The triumphal arch through which I march
    With hurricane, fire, and snow,
When the powers of the air are chained to my chair,
    Is the million-coloured bow;   70
The sphere-fire above its soft colours wove,
    While the moist earth was laughing below.

I am the daughter of Earth and Water,
    And the nursling of the sky;
I pass through the pores of the oceans and shores;
    I change, but I cannot die—
For after the rain, when never a stain
    The pavilion of Heaven is bare,
And the winds and sunbeams, with their convex gleams,
    Build up the blue dome of air,   80
I silently laugh at my own cenotaph,
    And out of the caverns of rain,
Like a child from the womb, like a ghost from the tomb,
    I arise and unbuild it again.

FROM THE SENSITIVE PLANT

Whether the Sensitive Plant, or that
Which within its boughs like a Spirit sat

Ere its outward form had known decay,
Now felt this change, I cannot say.

Whether that Lady's gentle mind,
No longer with the form combined
Which scattered love, as stars do light,
Found sadness, where it left delight,

I dare not guess; but in this life
Of error, ignorance and strife,   10
Where nothing is, but all things seem,
And we the shadows of the dream,

It is a modest creed, and yet
Pleasant if one considers it,
To own that death itself must be,
Like all the rest, a mockery.

That garden sweet, that Lady fair,
And all sweet shapes and odours there,
In truth have never passed away:
'Tis we, 'tis ours, are changed; not they.   20

For love, and beauty, and delight,
There is no death nor change: their might
Exceeds our organs, which endure
No light, being themselves obscure.

AN EXHORTATION

Chameleons feed on light and air:
    Poets' food is love and fame:
If in this wide world of care
    Poets could but find the same
With as little toil as they,
    Would they ever change their hue
    As the light chameleons do,
        Suiting it to every ray
        Twenty times a day?

Poets are on this cold earth   10
   As chameleons might be,
Hidden from their early birth
   In a cave beneath the sea;
Where light is, chameleons change:
   Where love is not, Poets do:
   Fame is love disguised—if few
     Find either, never think it strange
     That Poets range.

Yet dare not stain with wealth or power
   A Poet's free and heavenly mind: 20
If bright chameleons should devour
   Any food but beams and wind,
They would grow as earthly soon
   As their brother lizards are.—
   Children of a sunnier star,
     Spirits from beyond the moon,
     O, refuse the boon!

SONG

Rarely, rarely, comest thou,
   Spirit of Delight!
Wherefore hast thou left me now
   Many a day and night?
Many a weary night and day
'Tis since thou art fled away.

How shall ever one like me
   Win thee back again?
With the joyous and the free
   Thou wilt scoff at pain.   10
Spirit false! that hast forgot
All but those who need thee not.

As a lizard with the shade
   Of a trembling leaf,
Thou with sorrow art dismayed;

  Even the sighs of grief
Reproach thee, that thou art not near,
And reproach thou wilt not hear.

Let me set my mournful ditty
    To a merry measure;   20
Thou wilt never come for pity,
    Thou wilt come for pleasure;
Pity then will cut away
Those cruel wings, and thou wilt stay.

I love all that thou lovest,
    Spirit of Delight!
The fresh Earth in new leaves dressed,
    And the starry night;
Autumn evening, and the morn
When the golden mists are born.   30

I love snow, and all the forms
    Of the radiant frost;
I love waves and winds and storms—
    Every thing almost
Which is Nature's, and may be
Untainted by man's misery.

I love tranquil solitude,
    And such society
As is quiet, wise and good;
    Between thee and me   40
    What difference?—but thou dost possess
The things I seek, not love them less.

I love Love—though he has wings,
    And like light can flee—
But above all other things,
    Spirit, I love thee—
Thou art Love and Life! O come,
Make once more my heart thy home.

TO A SKY-LARK

     Hail to thee, blithe Spirit!
        Bird thou never wert,
     That from Heaven, or near it,
        Pourest thy full heart
In profuse strains of unpremeditated art.

     Higher still and higher
        From the earth thou springest
     Like a cloud of fire;
        The blue deep thou wingest,
And singing still dost soar, and soaring ever singest.   10

     In the golden lightning
        Of the sunken Sun,
     O'er which clouds are bright'ning,
        Thou dost float and run;
Like an unbodied joy whose race is just begun.

     The pale purple even
        Melts around thy flight;
     Like a star of Heaven
        In the broad day-light
Thou art unseen,—but yet I hear thy shrill delight,   20

     Keen as are the arrows
        Of that silver sphere
     Whose intense lamp narrows
        In the white dawn clear,
Until we hardly see—we feel that it is there.

     All the earth and air
        With thy voice is loud,
     As when night is bare
        From one lonely cloud
The moon rains out her beams, and Heaven is overflowed.   30

     What thou art we know not;
        What is most like thee?
     From rainbow clouds there flow not
        Drops so bright to see,
As from thy presence showers a rain of melody.

Like a Poet hidden
        In the light of thought,
    Singing hymns unbidden
        Till the world is wrought
To sympathy with hopes and fears it heeded not: 40

Like a high-born maiden
        In a palace tower,
    Soothing her love-laden
        Soul in secret hour
With music sweet as love, which overflows her bower:

Like a glow-worm golden
        In a dell of dew,
    Scattering unbeholden
        Its aërial hue
Among the flowers and grass which screen it from the view: 50

Like a rose embowered
        In its own green leaves,
    By warm winds deflowered,
        Till the scent it gives
Makes faint with too much sweet those heavy-wingèd thieves:

Sound of vernal showers
        On the twinkling grass,
    Rain-awakened flowers,
        All that ever was
Joyous and clear and fresh, thy music doth surpass.   60

Teach us, Sprite or Bird,
        What sweet thoughts are thine;
    I have never heard
        Praise of love or wine
That panted forth a flood of rapture so divine:

Chorus Hymenæal
        Or triumphal chaunt
    Matched with thine, would be all
        But an empty vaunt,
A thing wherein we feel there is some hidden want.   70

What objects are the fountains
    Of thy happy strain?
What fields or waves or mountains?
    What shapes of sky or plain?
What love of thine own kind? what ignorance of pain?

With thy clear keen joyance
    Languor cannot be—
Shadow of annoyance
    Never came near thee:
Thou lovest—but ne'er knew love's sad satiety.   80

Waking or asleep,
    Thou of death must deem
Things more true and deep
    Than we mortals dream,
Or how could thy notes flow in such a crystal stream?

We look before and after
    And pine for what is not:
Our sincerest laughter
    With some pain is fraught;
Our sweetest songs are those that tell of saddest thought.   90

Yet if we could scorn
    Hate and pride and fear;
If we were things born
    Not to shed a tear,
I know not how thy joy we ever should come near.

Better than all measures
    Of delightful sound—
Better than all treasures
    That in books are found—
Thy skill to poet were, thou scorner of the ground!   100

Teach me half the gladness
    That thy brain must know,
Such harmonious madness
    From my lips would flow,
The world should listen then—as I am listening now.

LETTER TO MARIA GISBORNE

The spider spreads her webs, whether she be
In poet's tower, cellar or barn or tree;
The silk-worm in the dark green mulberry leaves
His winding sheet and cradle ever weaves;
So I, a thing whom moralists call worm,
Sit spinning still round this decaying form
From the fine threads of rare and subtle thought—
No net of words in garish colours wrought
To catch the idle buzzers of the day—
But a soft cell where, when that fades away,   10
Memory may clothe in wings my living name
And feed it with the asphodels of fame,
Which in those hearts that must remember me
Grow, making love an immortality.

Whoever should behold me now, I wist,
Would think I were a mighty mechanist,
Bent with sublime Archimedean art
To breathe a soul into the iron heart
Of some machine portentous, or stange gin,
Which, by the force of figured spells, might win   20
Its way over the sea, and sport therein;
For round the walls are hung dread engines, such
As Vulcan never wrought for Jove to clutch
Ixion or the Titans;—or the quick
Wit of that man of God, St. Dominic,
To convince Atheist, Turk or heretic;
Or those in philanthropic council met
Who thought to pay some interest for the debt
They owed to Jesus Christ for their salvation,
By giving a faint foretaste of damnation   30
To Shakespeare, Sidney, Spenser, and the rest
Who made our land an island of the blest,
When lamplike Spain, who now relumes her fire
On Freedom's hearth, grew dim with Empire—
With thumbscrews, wheels, with tooth and spike and jag,
Which fishers found under the utmost crag
Of Cornwall, and the storm-encompassed isles,
Where to the sky the rude sea rarely smiles
Unless in treacherous wrath, as on the morn

When the exulting elements, in scorn,   40
Satiated with destroyed destruction, lay
Sleeping in beauty on their mangled prey,
As panthers sleep;—and other strange and dread
Magical forms the brick floor overspread—
Proteus transformed to metal did not make
More figures or more strange; nor did he take
Such shapes of unintelligible brass,
Or heap himself in such a horrid mass
Of tin and iron not to be understood,
And forms of unimaginable wood,   50
To puzzle Tubal Cain and all his brood:
Great screws, and cones, and wheels, and groovèd blocks,
The elements of what will stand the shocks
Of wave and wind and time.—Upon the table
More knacks and quips there be than I am able
To catalogize in this verse of mine:—
A pretty bowl of wood, not full of wine
But quicksilver, that dew which the gnomes drink
When at their subterranean toil they swink,
Pledging the demons of the earthquake, who   60
Reply to them in lava, cry halloo!
And call out to the cities o'er their head—
Roofs, towers, and shrines, the dying and the dead,
Crash through the chinks of earth—and then all quaff
Another rouse, and hold their ribs and laugh.
This quicksilver no gnome has drunk—within
The walnut bowl it lies, veinèd and thin,
In colour like the wake of light that stains
The Tuscan deep, when from the moist moon rains
The inmost shower of its white fire—the breeze   70
Is still—blue heaven smiles over the pale seas.
And in this bowl of quicksilver—for I
Yield to the impulse of an infancy
Outlasting manhood—I have made to float
A rude idealism of a paper boat:
A hollow screw with cogs—Henry will know
The thing I mean, and laugh at me, if so
He fears not I should do more mischief—next
Lie bills and calculations much perplexed,
With steam boats, frigates and machinery quaint   80
Traced over them in blue and yellow paint.

Then comes a range of mathematical
Instruments, for plans nautical and statical;
A heap of rosin, a queer broken glass
With ink in it; a china cup that was
What it will never be again, I think,
A thing from which sweet lips were wont to drink
The liquor doctors rail at—and which I
Will quaff in spite of them—and when we die
We'll toss up who died first of drinking tea,   90
And cry out, 'Heads or tails?' where'er we be.
Near that a dusty paint box, some odd hooks,
A half-burnt match, an ivory block, three books
Where conic sections, spherics, logarithms,
To great Laplace from Saunderson and Sims
Lie heaped in their harmonious disarray
Of figures—disentangle them who may.
Baron de Tott's memoirs beside them lie,
And some odd volumes of old chemistry.
Near those a most inexplicable tin thing   100
With lead in the middle—I'm conjecturing
How to make Henry understand—but no,
I'll leave, as Spenser says, with many mo,
This secret in the pregnant womb of time,
Too vast a matter for so weak a rhyme.

And here like some weird Archimage sit I,
Plotting dark spells and devilish enginery,
The self-impelling steam wheels of the mind
Which pump up oaths from clergymen, and grind
The gentle spirit of our meek reviews   110
Into a powdery foam of salt abuse,
Ruffling the dull wave of their self-content—
I sit, and smile or sigh, as is my bent,
But not for them—Libeccio rushes round
With an inconstant and an idle sound,
I heed him more than them—the thundersmoke
Is gathering on the mountains, like a cloak
Folded athwart their shoulders broad and bare;
The ripe corn under the undulating air
Undulates like an ocean;—and the vines   120
Are trembling wide in all their trellised lines—
The murmur of the awakening sea doth fill

The empty pauses of the blast—the hill
Looks hoary through the white electric rain—
And from the glens beyond, in sullen strain
The interrupted thunder howls; above
One chasm of heaven smiles, like the eye of Love,
O'er the unquiet world;—while such things are,
How could one worth your friendship heed this war
Of worms? the shriek of the world's carrion jays,   130
Their censure, or their wonder, or their praise?

You are not here! . . . the quaint witch Memory sees
In vacant chairs your absent images,
And points where once you sat, and now should be
But are not—I demand if ever we
Shall meet as then we met,—and she replies,
Veiling in awe her second-sighted eyes,
'I know the past alone—but summon home
My sister Hope,—she speaks of all to come.'
But I, an old diviner, who know well   140
Every false verse of that sweet oracle,
Turned to the sad enchantress once again,
And sought a respite from my gentle pain
In citing every passage o'er and o'er
Of our communion—how on the sea shore
We watched the ocean and the sky together
Under the roof of blue Italian weather;
How I ran home through last year's thunderstorm,
And felt the transverse lightning linger warm
Upon my cheek—and how we often made   150
Feasts for each other, where good will outweighed
The frugal luxury of our country cheer,
As well it might, were it less firm and clear
Than ours must ever be;—and how we spun
A shroud of talk to hide us from the sun
Of this familiar life, which seems to be
But is not,—or is but quaint mockery
Of all we would believe; or sadly blame
The jarring and inexplicable frame
Of this wrong world—and then anatomize   160
The purposes and thoughts of men whose eyes
Were closed in distant years—or widely guess
The issue of the earth's great business,

When we shall be, as we no longer are,
Like babbling gossips safe, who hear the war
Of winds, and sigh, but tremble not—or how
You listened to some interrupted flow
Of visionary rhyme, in joy and pain
Struck from the inmost fountains of my brain
With little skill perhaps—or how we sought   170
Those deepest wells of passion and of thought
Wrought by wise poets in the waste of years,
Staining their sacred waters with our tears,
Quenching a thirst ever to be renewed!
Or how I, wisest lady! then indued
The language of a land which now is free
And winged with thoughts of truth and majesty
Flits round the tyrant's sceptre like a cloud,
And bursts the peopled prisons, cries aloud
'My name is Legion!'—that majestic tongue   180
Which Calderon over the desert flung
Of ages and of nations; and which found
An echo in our hearts, and with the sound
Startled oblivion;—thou wert then to me
As is a nurse, when inarticulately
A child would talk as its grown parents do.
If living winds the rapid clouds pursue,
If hawks chase doves through the aetherial way,
Huntsmen the innocent deer, and beasts their prey,
Why should not we rouse with the spirit's blast   190
Out of the forest of the pathless past
These recollected pleasures?

                                        You are now
In London, that great sea, whose ebb and flow
At once is deaf and loud, and on the shore
Vomits its wrecks, and still howls on for more.
Yet in its depth what treasures!—You will see
That which was Godwin,—greater none than he
Though fallen—and fallen on evil times—to stand
Among the spirits of our age and land,
Before the dread tribunal of *to come*   200
The foremost—while Rebuke cowers, pale and dumb.
You will see Coleridge—he who sits obscure
In the exceeding lustre and the pure

Intense irradiation of a mind,
Which, with its own internal lightning blind,
Flags wearily through darkness and despair—
A cloud-encircled meteor of the air,
A hooded eagle among blinking owls.—
You will see Hunt—one of those happy souls
Who are the salt of the earth, and without whom   210
This world would smell like what it is—a tomb;
Who is, what others seem;—his room no doubt
Is still adorned with many a cast from Shout,
With graceful flowers, tastefully placed about;
And coronals of bay from ribbons hung,
And brighter wreaths in neat disorder flung,
The gifts of the most learn'd among some dozens
Of female friends, sisters-in-law and cousins.
And there is he with his eternal puns,
Which beat the dullest brain for smiles, like duns   220
Thundering for money at a poet's door;
Alas, it is no use to say 'I'm poor!'
Or oft in graver mood, when he will look
Things wiser than were ever read in book,
Except in Shakespeare's wisest tenderness.—
You will see Hogg—and I cannot express
His virtues, though I know that they are great,
Because he locks, then barricades, the gate
Within which they inhabit;—of his wit
And wisdom, you'll cry out when you are bit.   230
He is a pearl within an oyster shell,
One of the richest of the deep. And there
Is English Peacock with his mountain Fair,
Turned into a Flamingo,—that shy bird
That gleams i' the Indian air. Have you not heard
When a man marries, dies, or turns Hindoo,
His best friends hear no more of him?—but you
Will see him and will like him too, I hope,
With the milk-white Snowdonian Antelope
Matched with this Cameleopard.—His fine wit   240
Makes such a wound, the knife is lost in it;
A strain too learnèd for a shallow age,
Too wise for selfish bigots; let his page
Which charms the chosen spirits of the time
Fold itself up for the serener clime

Of years to come, and find its recompense
In that just expectation.—Wit and sense,
Virtue and human knowledge, all that might
Make this dull world a business of delight,
Are all combined in Horace Smith.—And these,   250
With some exceptions which I need not tease
Your patience by descanting on, are all
You and I know in London—

                I recall
My thoughts, and bid you look upon the night.
As water does a sponge, so the moonlight
Fills the void, hollow, universal air—
What see you?—unpavilioned heaven is fair,
Whether the moon, into her chamber gone,
Leaves midnight to the golden stars, or wan
Climbs with diminished beams the azure steep;   260
Or whether clouds sail o'er the inverse deep,
Piloted by the many-wandering blast,
And the rare stars rush through them dim and fast:—
All this is beautiful in every land.—
But what see you beside?—a shabby stand
Of hackney coaches—a brick house or wall
Fencing some lordly court, white with the scrawl
Of our unhappy politics; or worse—
A wretched woman reeling by, whose curse
Mixed with the watchman's, partner of her trade,   270
You must accept in place of serenade—
Or yellow-haired Pollonia murmuring
To Henry some unutterable thing.
I see a chaos of green leaves and fruit
Built round dark caverns, even to the root
Of the living stems which feed them—in whose bowers
There sleep in their dark dew the folded flowers;
Beyond, the surface of the unsickled corn
Trembles not in the slumbering air, and borne
In circles quaint, and ever-changing dance,   280
Like wingèd stars the fire-flies flash and glance
Pale in the open moonshine, but each one
Under the dark trees seems a little sun,
A meteor tamed, a fixed star gone astray
From the silver regions of the Milky Way;—

Afar the Contadino's song is heard,
Rude, but made sweet by distance—and a bird
Which cannot be the nightingale, and yet
I know none else that sings so sweet as it
At this late hour;—and then all is still—   290
Now, Italy or London—which you will!

    Next winter you must pass with me; I'll have
My house by that time turned into a grave
Of dead despondence and low-thoughted care,
And all the dreams which our tormentors are.
Oh, that Hunt, Hogg, Peacock and Smith were there,
With every thing belonging to them fair!
We will have books, Spanish, Italian, Greek;
And ask one another week to make another week
As like his father as I'm unlike mine,   300
Which is not his fault, as you may divine.
Though we eat little flesh and drink no wine,
Yet let's be merry: we'll have tea and toast,
Custards for supper, and an endless host
Of syllabubs and jellies and mince-pies,
And other such lady-like luxuries—
Feasting on which, we will philosophize!
And we'll have fires out of the Grand Duke's wood
To thaw the six weeks' winter in our blood.
And then we'll talk;—what shall we talk about?   310
Oh! there are themes enough for many a bout
Of thought-entangled descant;—as to nerves,
With cones and parallelograms and curves
I've sworn to strangle them if once they dare
To bother me—when you are with me there,
And they shall never more sip laudanum
From Helicon or Himeros;—well, come,
And in despite of God and of the devil,
We'll make our friendly philosophic revel
Outlast the leafless time;—till buds and flowers   320
Warn the obscure inevitable hours
Sweet meeting by sad parting to renew—
'Tomorrow to fresh woods and pastures new.'

FROM HOMER'S HYMN TO MERCURY

1. Sing, Muse, the son of Maia and of Jove,
      The herald-child, king of Arcadia
    And all its pastoral hills, whom in sweet love
      Having been interwoven, modest May
    Bore Heaven's dread Supreme. An antique grove
      Shadowed the cavern where the lovers lay
    In the deep night, unseen by Gods or men;
    And white-armed Juno slumbered sweetly then.

2. Now, when the joy of Jove had its fulfilling
      And Heaven's tenth moon chronicled her relief,   10
    She gave to light a babe all babes excelling,
      A schemer subtle beyond all belief,
    A shepherd of thin dreams, a cow-stealing,
      A night-watching and door-waylaying thief,
    Who 'mongst the Gods was soon about to thieve
    And other glorious actions to achieve.

3. The babe was born at the first peep of day,
      He began playing on the lyre at noon,
    And the same evening did he steal away
      Apollo's herds—the fourth day of the moon,   20
    On which him bore the venerable May.
      From her immortal limbs he leaped full soon,
    Nor long could in his sacred cradle keep,
    But out to seek Apollo's herds would creep.

4. Out of the lofty cavern wandering
      He found a tortoise, and cried out: 'A treasure!'
    (For Mercury first made the tortoise sing).
      The beast before the portal at his leisure
    The flowery herbage was depasturing,
      Moving his feet in a deliberate measure   30
    Over the turf. Jove's profitable son
    Eyeing him laughed, and laughing thus begun:

5. 'A useful god-send are you to me now,
      King of the dance, companion of the feast,
    Lordly in all your nature! Welcome, you
      Excellent plaything! Where, sweet mountain-beast,

Got you that speckled shell? Thus much I know,
   You must come home with me and be my guest;
You will give joy to me, and I will do
All that is in my power to honour you.   40

6. 'Better to be at home than out of door,
     So come with me; and though it has been said
That you alive defend from magic power,
     I know you will sing sweetly when you're dead.'
Thus having spoken, the quaint infant bore,
     Lifting it from the grass on which it fed
And grasping it in his delighted hold,
His treasured prize into the cavern old.

7. Then scooping with a chisel of grey steel
     He bored the life and soul out of the beast.—   50
Not swifter a swift thought of woe or weal
     Darts through the tumult of a human breast
Which thronging cares annoy, not swifter wheel
     The flashes of its torture and unrest
Out of the dizzy eyes, than Maia's son
All that he did devise hath featly done.

8. And through the tortoise's hard stony skin
     At proper distances small holes he made,
And fastened the cut stems of reeds within,
     And with a piece of leather overlaid   60
The open space, and fixed the cubits in,
Fitting the bridge to both, and stretched o'er all
Symphonious chords of sheep-gut rhythmical.

9. When he had wrought the lovely instrument,
     He tried the chords and made division meet,
Preluding with the plectrum; and there went
     Up from beneath his hand a tumult sweet
Of mighty sounds, and from his lips he sent
     A strain of unpremeditated wit,
Joyous and wild and wanton, such you may   70
Hear among revellers on a holiday.

10.   He sung how Jove and May of the bright sandal
          Dallied in love not quite legitimate,
      And his own birth, still scoffing at the scandal
          And naming his own name, did celebrate;
      His mother's cave and servant maids he planned all
          In plastic verse, her household stuff and state,
      Perennial pot, trippet and brazen pan—
      But singing he conceived another plan.

11.   Seized with a sudden fancy for fresh meat,   80
          He in his sacred crib deposited
      The hollow lyre, and from the cavern sweet
          Rushed, with great leaps up to the mountain's head,
      Revolving in his mind some subtle feat
          Of thievish craft, such as a swindler might
      Devise in the lone season of dun night.

12.   Lo! the great sun under the Ocean's bed has
          Driven steeds and chariot—the child meanwhile strode
      O'er the Pierian mountains clothed in shadows,
          Where the immortal oxen of the God   90
      Are pastured in the flowering unmown meadows,
          And safely stalled in a remote abode.
      The archer Argicide, elate and proud,
      Drove fifty from the herd, lowing aloud.

13.   He drove them wandering o'er the sandy way,
          But, being ever mindful of his craft,
      Backward and forward drove he them astray,
          So that the tracks which seemed before were aft;
      His sandals then he threw to the Ocean spray,
          And for each foot he wrought a kind of raft   100
      Of tamarisk and tamarisk-like sprigs,
      And bound them in a lump with withy twigs.

14.   And on his feet he tied these sandals light,
          The trail of whose wide leaves might not betray
      His track; and then, a self-sufficing wight,
          Like a man hastening on some distant way,
      He from Pieria's mountain bent his flight;
      But an old man perceived the infant pass
      Down green Onchestus heaped like beds with grass.

15.   The old man stood dressing his sunny vine: 110
          'Halloo! old fellow with the crooked shoulder!
      You grub those stumps? Before they will bear wine
          Methinks even you must grow a little older.
      Attend, I pray, to this advice of mine:
          As you would 'scape what might appal a bolder—
      Seeing, see not—and hearing, hear not—and—
      If you have understanding, understand.'

16.   So saying, Hermes roused the oxen vast.
          O'er shadowy mountain and resounding dell
      And flower-paven plains, great Hermes passed;   120
          Till the black night divine, which favouring fell
      Around his steps, grew grey, and morning fast
          Wakened the world to work, and from her cell
      Sea-strewn, the Pallantean Moon sublime
      Into her watch-tower just began to climb.

17.   Now to Alpheus he had driven all
          The broad-foreheaded oxen of the Sun:
      They came unwearied to the lofty stall
          And to the water troughs which ever run
      Through the fresh fields; and when with rushgrass tall,   130
          Lotus and all sweet herbage, every one
      Had pastured been, the great God made them move
      Towards the stall in a collected drove.

18.   A mighty pile of wood the God then heaped
          And, having soon conceived the mystery
      Of fire, from two smooth laurel branches stripped
          The bark and rubbed them in his palms;—on high
      Suddenly forth the burning vapour leaped,
          And the divine child saw delightedly.—
      Mercury first found out for human weal   140
      Tinder-box, matches, fire-irons, flint and steel.

19.   And fine dry logs and roots innumerous
          He gathered in a delve upon the ground—
      And kindled them—and instantaneous
          The strength of the fierce flame was breathed around:
      And whilst the might of glorious Vulcan thus

Wrapped the great pile with glare and roaring sound,
Hermes dragged forth two heifers, moaning loud,
Close to the fire—such might was in the God.

20.   And on the earth upon their backs he threw   150
      The panting beasts, and rolled them o'er and o'er,
And bored their lives out. Without more ado
      He cut up fat and flesh, and down before
The fire, on spits of wood, he placed the two,
      Toasting their flesh and ribs, and all the gore
Pursed in the bowels; and while this was done,
He stretched their hides over a craggy stone.

21.   We mortals let an ox grow old, and then
      Cut it up after long consideration—
But joyous-minded Hermes from the glen   160
      Drew the fat spoils to [a] more open station
Of flat smooth space, and portioned them; and when
      He had by lot assigned to each a ration
Of the twelve Gods, his mind became aware
Of all the joys which in religion are,

22.   For the sweet savour of the roasted meat
      Tempted him though immortal. Nathelesse
He checked his haughty will and did not eat,
      Though what it cost him words can scarce express,
And every wish to put such morsels sweet   170
      Down his most sacred throat he did repress;
But soon within the lofty-portalled stall
He placed the fat and flesh and bones and all.

23.   And every trace of the fresh butchery
      And cooking the God soon made disappear,
As if it all had vanished through the sky.
      He burned the hoofs and horns and head and hair—
The insatiate fire devoured them hungrily—
      And when he saw that every thing was clear,
He quenched the coals and trampled the black dust,   180
And in the stream his bloody sandals tossed.

24.   All night he worked in the serene moonshine—
      But when the light of day was spread abroad
He sought his natal mountain-peaks divine.

> On his long wandering, neither man nor God
> Had met him, since he killed Apollo's kine,
>   Nor housedog had barked at him on his road;
> Now he obliquely through the key-hole passed,
> Like a thin mist or an autumnal blast.

TWO SONGS FOR *MIDAS*

SONG OF APOLLO

The sleepless Hours who watch me as I lie
    Curtained with star-enwoven tapestries
From the broad moonlight of the open sky,
    Fanning the busy dreams from my dim eyes,—
Waken me when their mother, the grey Dawn,
Tells them that dreams and that the moon is gone.

Then I arise; and climbing Heaven's blue dome,
    I walk over the mountains and the waves,
Leaving my robe upon the ocean foam;
    My footsteps pave the clouds with fire; the caves   10
Are filled with my bright presence, and the air
Leaves the green Earth to my embraces bare.

The sunbeams are my shafts with which I kill
    Deceit, that loves the night and fears the day;
All men who do, or even imagine ill
    Fly me; and from the glory of my ray
Good minds and open actions take new might,
Until diminished by the reign of night.

I feed the clouds, the rainbows and the flowers
    With their ætherial colours; the moon's globe   20
And the pure stars in their eternal bowers
    Are cinctured with my power as with a robe;
Whatever lamps on Earth or Heaven may shine
Are portions of one spirit; which is mine.

I stand at noon upon the peak of Heaven;
    Then with unwilling steps, I linger down
Into the clouds of the Atlantic even;

For grief that I depart they weep and frown—
What look is more delightful, than the smile
With which I soothe them from the Western isle?   30

I am the eye with which the Universe
    Beholds itself, and knows it is divine;
All harmony of instrument and verse,
    All prophecy and medicine are mine,
All light of art or nature:—to my song
Victory and praise, in its own right, belong.

SONG OF PAN

From the forests and highlands
    We come, we come,
From the river-girt islands
    Where loud waves were dumb,
        Listening my sweet pipings.
            The wind in the reeds and the rushes,
            The bees on the bells of thyme,
            The birds in the myrtle bushes,
            The cicadæ above in the lime,
                And the lizards below in the grass,   10
Were silent as even old Tmolus was,
            Listening my sweet pipings.

Liquid Peneus was flowing,
    And all dark Tempe lay
In Pelion's shadow, outgrowing
    The light of the dying day,
        Speeded with my sweet pipings.
            The sileni and sylvans and fauns
            And the nymphs of the woods and the waves
            To the edge of the moist river-lawns   20
            And the brink of the dewy caves,
                And all that did then attend and follow
Were as silent for love, as you now, Apollo,
            For envy of my sweet pipings.

I sang of the dancing stars,
   I sang of the dædal Earth,
And of Heaven, and the giant wars,
    And Love and Death and Birth;
     And then I changed my pipings,
     Singing how, down the vales of Mænalus   30
     I pursued a maiden and clasped a reed.
     Gods and men, we are all deluded thus!—
     It breaks on our bosom and then we bleed.
     They wept as I think both ye now would,
If envy or age had not frozen your blood,
     At the sorrow of my sweet pipings.

THE TWO SPIRITS: AN ALLEGORY

First Spirit
   O thou, who plumed with strong desire
   Would float above the Earth—beware!
   A shadow tracks thy flight of fire—
      Night is coming!
   Bright are the regions of the air,
   And when winds and beams [ ]
   It were delight to wander there—
      Night is coming!

Second Spirit
   The deathless stars are bright above;
   If I should cross the shade of night   10
   Within my heart is the lamp of love,
      And that is day!
   And the moon will smile with gentle light
   On my golden plumes where'er they move;
   The meteors will linger around my flight,
      And make night day.

First Spirit
   But if the whirlwinds of darkness waken
   Hail and lightning and stormy rain—
   See, the bounds of the air are shaken—
      Night is coming!   20

And swift the clouds of the hurricane
Yon declining sun have overtaken,
The clash of the hail sweeps o'er the plain—
    Night is coming!

Second Spirit
I see the glare and I hear the sound—
I'll sail on the flood of the tempest dark
With the calm within and light around
    Which make night day;
And thou, when the gloom is deep and stark,
Look from thy dull earth slumberbound—   30
My moonlike flight thou then mayst mark
    On high, far away.

————————————

Some say there is a precipice
Where one vast pine hangs frozen to ruin
O'er piles of snow and chasms of ice
    Mid Alpine mountains;
And that the languid storm pursuing
That wingèd shape forever flies
Round those hoar branches, aye renewing
    Its aëry fountains.   40

Some say when the nights are dry [and] clear
And the death-dews sleep on the morass,
Sweet whispers are heard by the traveller,
    Which make night day;
And a shape like his early love doth pass
Upborne by her wild and glittering hair,
And when he awakes on the fragrant grass
    He finds night day.

SONNET TO THE REPUBLIC OF BENEVENTO

Nor happiness, nor majesty, nor fame,
Nor peace nor strength, nor skill in arms or arts,
Shepherd those herds whom Tyranny makes tame:
Verse echoes not one beating of their hearts;
History is but the shadow of their shame;

Art veils her glass, or from the pageant starts
As to oblivion their blind millions fleet,
Staining that Heaven with obscene imagery
Of their own likeness.—What are numbers, knit
By force or custom? Man, who man would be,   10
Must rule the empire of himself; in it
Must be supreme, establishing his throne
On vanquished will; quelling the anarchy
Of hopes and fears; being himself alone.

GOODNIGHT

Goodnight? ah no, the night is ill
    Which severs those it should unite;
Let us remain together still,
    Then it will be *good* night.

How can I call the lone night good,
    Though thy sweet wishes wing its flight?
Be it not said, thought, understood;
    Then it will be, *good night.*

To hearts which near each other move
    From evening close to morning light   10
The night is good; because, my love,
    They never *say* goodnight.

Fragment: TO THE MOON

    Art thou pale for weariness
Of climbing Heaven, and gazing on the earth,
    Wandering companionless
Among the stars that have a different birth,—
And ever changing, like a joyless eye
That finds no object worth its constancy?

EPIPSYCHIDION:

Verses addressed to the noble and unfortunate lady

EMILIA V

NOW IMPRISONED IN THE CONVENT OF

L'anima amante si slancia fuori del creato, e si crea nell'infinito un Mondo tutto per essa, diverso assai da questo oscuro e pauroso baratro.

Her own words

ADVERTISEMENT

The Writer of the following Lines died at Florence, as he was preparing for a voyage to one of the wildest of the Sporades, which he had bought, and where he had fitted up the ruins of an old building, and where it was his hope to have realised a scheme of life, suited perhaps to that happier and better world of which he is now an inhabitant, but hardly practicable in this. His life was singular; less on account of the romantic vicissitudes which diversified it, than the ideal tinge which it received from his own character and feelings. The present Poem, like the Vita Nuova of Dante, is sufficiently intelligible to a certain class of readers without a matter-of-fact history of the circumstances to which it relates; and to a certain other class it must ever remain incomprehensible, from a defect of a common organ of perception for the ideas of which it treats. Not but that, *gran vergogna sarebbe a colui, che rimasse cosa sotto veste di figura, o di colore rettorico: e domandato non sapesse denudare le sue parole da cotal veste, in guisa che avessero verace intendimento.*

The present poem appears to have been intended by the Writer as the dedication to some longer one. The stanza on the opposite page is almost a literal translation from Dante's famous Canzone

Voi, ch'intendendo, il terzo ciel movete, &c.

The presumptuous application of the concluding lines to his own composition will raise a smile at the expense of my unfortunate friend: be it a smile not of contempt, but pity.

S.

My Song, I fear that thou wilt find but few
Who fitly shall conceive thy reasoning,
Of such hard matter dost thou entertain;

Whence, if by misadventure, chance should bring
Thee to base company (as chance may do),
Quite unaware of what thou dost contain,
I prithee, comfort thy sweet self again,
My last delight! tell them that they are dull,
And bid them own that thou art beautiful.

EPIPSYCHIDION

Sweet Spirit! Sister of that orphan one,
Whose empire is the name thou weepest on,
In my heart's temple I suspend to thee
These votive wreaths of withered memory.

　　Poor captive bird! who, from thy narrow cage,
Pourest such music, that it might assuage
The rugged hearts of those who prisoned thee,
Were they not deaf to all sweet melody;
This song shall be thy rose: its petals pale
Are dead, indeed, my adored Nightingale!   10
But soft and fragrant is the faded blossom,
And it has no thorn left to wound thy bosom.

　　High, spirit-wingèd Heart! who dost for ever
Beat thine unfeeling bars with vain endeavour,
Till those bright plumes of thought, in which arrayed
It over-soared this low and worldly shade,
Lie shattered; and thy panting, wounded breast
Stains with dear blood its unmaternal nest!
I weep vain tears: blood would less bitter be,
Yet poured forth gladlier, could it profit thee.   20

　　Seraph of Heaven! too gentle to be human,
Veiling beneath that radiant form of Woman
All that is insupportable in thee
Of light, and love, and immortality!
Sweet Benediction in the eternal Curse!
Veiled Glory of this lampless Universe!
Thou Moon beyond the clouds! Thou living Form
Among the Dead! Thou Star above the Storm!

Thou Wonder, and thou Beauty, and thou Terror!
Thou Harmony of Nature's art! Thou Mirror   30
In whom, as in the splendour of the Sun,
All shapes look glorious which thou gazest on!
Ay, even the dim words which obscure thee now
Flash, lightning-like, with unaccustomed glow;
I pray thee that thou blot from this sad song
All of its much mortality and wrong
With those clear drops, which start like sacred dew
From the twin lights thy sweet soul darkens through,
Weeping, till sorrow becomes ecstacy:
Then smile on it, so that it may not die.   40

I never thought before my death to see
Youth's vision thus made perfect. Emily,
I love thee; though the world by no thin name
Will hide that love, from its unvalued shame.
Would we two had been twins of the same mother!
Or, that the name my heart lent to another
Could be a sister's bond for her and thee,
Blending two beams of one eternity!
Yet were one lawful and the other true,
These names, though dear, could paint not, as is due,   50
How beyond refuge I am thine. Ah me!
I am not thine: I am part of *thee*.

Sweet Lamp! my moth-like Muse has burnt its wings;
Or, like a dying swan who soars and sings,
Young Love should teach Time, in his own grey style,
All that thou art. Art thou not void of guile,
A lovely soul formed to be blest and bless?
A well of sealed and secret happiness,
Whose waters like blithe light and music are,
Vanquishing dissonance and gloom? A Star   60
Which moves not in the moving Heavens, alone?
A smile amid dark frowns? a gentle tone
Amid rude voices? a belovèd light?
A Solitude, a Refuge, a Delight?
A lute, which those whom love has taught to play
Make music on, to soothe the roughest day
And lull fond grief asleep? a buried treasure?
A cradle of young thoughts of wingless pleasure?

A violet-shrouded grave of Woe?—I measure
The world of fancies, seeking one like thee,   70
And find—alas! mine own infirmity.

She met me, Stranger, upon life's rough way,
And lured me towards sweet Death; as Night by Day,
Winter by Spring, or Sorrow by swift Hope,
Led into light, life, peace. An antelope,
In the suspended impulse of its lightness,
Were less ethereally light: the brightness
Of her divinest presence trembles through
Her limbs, as underneath a cloud of dew
Embodied in the windless Heaven of June   80
Amid the splendour-wingèd stars, the Moon
Burns, inextinguishably beautiful:
And from her lips, as from a hyacinth full
Of honey-dew, a liquid murmur drops,
Killing the sense with passion; sweet as stops
Of planetary music heard in trance.
In her mild lights the starry spirits dance,
The sun-beams of those wells which ever leap
Under the lightnings of the soul—too deep
For the brief fathom-line of thought or sense.   90
The glory of her being, issuing thence,
Stains the dead, blank, cold air with a warm shade
Of unentangled intermixture, made
By Love, of light and motion: one intense
Diffusion, one serene Omnipresence,
Whose flowing outlines mingle in their flowing,
Around her cheeks and utmost fingers glowing
With the unintermitted blood, which there
Quivers, (as in a fleece of snow-like air
The crimson pulse of living morning quiver,)   100
Continuously prolonged, and ending never,
Till they are lost, and in that Beauty furled
Which penetrates and clasps and fills the world;
Scarce visible from extreme loveliness.
Warm fragrance seems to fall from her light dress,
And her loose hair; and where some heavy tress
The air of her own speed has disentwined,
The sweetness seems to satiate the faint wind;
And in the soul a wild odour is felt,

Beyond the sense, like fiery dews that melt   110
Into the bosom of a frozen bud.——
See where she stands! a mortal shape indued
With love and life and light and deity,
And motion which may change but cannot die;
An image of some bright Eternity;
A shadow of some golden dream; a Splendour
Leaving the third sphere pilotless; a tender
Reflection of the eternal Moon of Love
Under whose motions life's dull billows move;
A Metaphor of Spring and Youth and Morning;   120
A Vision like incarnate April, warning,
With smiles and tears, Frost the Anatomy
Into his summer grave.

                Ah, woe is me!
What have I dared? where am I lifted? how
Shall I descend, and perish not? I know
That Love makes all things equal: I have heard
By mine own heart this joyous truth averred:
The spirit of the worm beneath the sod
In love and worship, blends itself with God.

     Spouse! Sister! Angel! Pilot of the Fate   130
Whose course has been so starless! O too late
Belovèd! O too soon adored, by me!
For in the fields of immortality
My spirit should at first have worshipped thine,
A divine presence in a place divine;
Or should have moved beside it on this earth,
A shadow of that substance, from its birth;
But not as now:—I love thee; yes, I feel
That on the fountain of my heart a seal
Is set, to keep its waters pure and bright   140
For thee, since in those *tears* thou hast delight.
We—are we not formed, as notes of music are,
For one another, though dissimilar;
Such difference without discord, as can make
Those sweetest sounds in which all spirits shake
As trembling leaves in a continuous air?

    Thy wisdom speaks in me, and bids me dare
Beacon the rocks on which high hearts are wrecked.
I never was attached to that great sect   150
Whose doctrine is, that each one should select
Out of the crowd a mistress or a friend,
And all the rest, though fair and wise, commend
To cold oblivion, though it is in the code
Of modern morals, and the beaten road
Which those poor slaves with weary footsteps tread,
Who travel to their home among the dead
By the broad highway of the world, and so
With one chained friend, perhaps a jealous foe,
The dreariest and the longest journey go.   160

    True Love in this differs from gold and clay,
That to divide is not to take away.
Love is like understanding, that grows bright,
Gazing on many truths; 'tis like thy light,
Imagination! which from earth and sky,
And from the depths of human phantasy,
As from a thousand prisms and mirrors, fills
The Universe with glorious beams, and kills
Error, the worm, with many a sun-like arrow
Of its reverberated lightning. Narrow
The heart that loves, the brain that contemplates,   170
The life that wears, the spirit that creates
One object, and one form, and builds thereby
A sepulchre for its eternity.

    Mind from its object differs most in this:
Evil from good; misery from happiness;
The baser from the nobler; the impure
And frail, from what is clear and must endure.
If you divide suffering and dross, you may
Diminish till it is consumed away;
If you divide pleasure and love and thought,   180
Each part exceeds the whole; and we know not
How much, while any yet remains unshared,
Of pleasure may be gained, of sorrow spared:
This truth is that deep well, whence sages draw
The unenvied light of hope; the eternal law
By which those live, to whom this world of life

Is as a garden ravaged, and whose strife
Tills for the promise of a later birth
The wilderness of this Elysian earth.

There was a Being whom my spirit oft   190
Met on its visioned wanderings, far aloft,
In the clear golden prime of my youth's dawn,
Upon the fairy isles of sunny lawn,
Amid the enchanted mountains, and the caves
Of divine sleep, and on the air-like waves
Of wonder-level dream, whose tremulous floor
Paved her light steps;—on an imagined shore,
Under the grey beak of some promontory
She met me, robed in such exceeding glory
That I beheld her not. In solitudes   200
Her voice came to me through the whispering woods,
And from the fountains, and the odours deep
Of flowers, which, like lips murmuring in their sleep
Of the sweet kisses which had lulled them there,
Breathed but of *her* to the enamoured air;
And from the breezes whether low or loud,
And from the rain of every passing cloud,
And from the singing of the summer-birds,
And from all sounds, all silence. In the words
Of antique verse and high romance,—in form   210
Sound, colour—in whatever checks that Storm
Which with the shattered present chokes the past;
And in that best philosophy, whose taste
Makes this cold common hell, our life, a doom
As glorious as a fiery martyrdom;
Her Spirit was the harmony of truth.—

Then, from the caverns of my dreamy youth
I sprang, as one sandalled with plumes of fire,
And towards the loadstar of my one desire,
I flitted, like a dizzy moth, whose flight   220
Is as a dead leaf's in the owlet light,
When it would seek in Hesper's setting sphere
A radiant death, a fiery sepulchre,
As if it were a lamp of earthly flame.—
But She, whom prayers or tears then could not tame,

Passed, like a God throned on a wingèd planet,
Whose burning plumes to tenfold swiftness fan it,
Into the dreary cone of our life's shade;
And as a man with mighty loss dismayed,
I would have followed, though the grave between   230
Yawned like a gulf whose spectres are unseen:
When a voice said:—'O Thou of hearts the weakest,
'The phantom is beside thee whom thou seekest.'
Then I—'Where?' the world's echo answered 'Where!'
And in that silence, and in my despair,
I questioned every tongueless wind that flew
Over my tower of mourning, if it knew
Whither 'twas fled, this soul out of my soul;
And murmured names and spells which have control
Over the sightless tyrants of our fate;   240
But neither prayer nor verse could dissipate
The night which closed on her; nor uncreate
That world within this Chaos, mine and me,
Of which she was the veiled Divinity,
The world I say of thoughts that worshipped her:
And therefore I went forth, with hope and fear
And every gentle passion sick to death,
Feeding my course with expectation's breath,
Into the wintry forest of our life;
And struggling through its error with vain strife,   250
And stumbling in my weakness and my haste,
And half bewildered by new forms, I passed
Seeking among those untaught foresters
If I could find one form resembling hers,
In which she might have masked herself from me.
There,—One, whose voice was venomed melody,
Sate by a well, under blue night-shade bowers;
The breath of her false mouth was like faint flowers,
Her touch was as electric poison,—flame
Out of her looks into my vitals came,   260
And from her living cheeks and bosom flew
A killing air, which pierced like honey-dew
Into the core of my green heart, and lay
Upon its leaves; until, as hair grown grey
O'er a young brow, they hid its unblown prime
With ruins of unseasonable time.

In many mortal forms I rashly sought
The shadow of that idol of my thought.
And some were fair—but beauty dies away:
Others were wise—but honeyed words betray: 270
And One was true—oh! why not true to me?
Then, as a hunted deer that could not flee,
I turned upon my thoughts, and stood at bay,
Wounded and weak and panting; the cold day
Trembled, for pity of my strife and pain;
When, like a noon-day dawn, there shone again
Deliverance. One stood on my path who seemed
As like the glorious shape which I had dreamed,
As is the Moon, whose changes ever run
Into themselves, to the eternal Sun;   280
The cold chaste Moon, the Queen of Heaven's bright isles,
Who makes all beautiful on which she smiles;
That wandering shrine of soft yet icy flame
Which ever is transformed, yet still the same,
And warms not but illumines. Young and fair
As the descended Spirit of that sphere,
She hid me, as the Moon may hide the night
From its own darkness, until all was bright
Between the Heaven and Earth of my calm mind,
And, as a cloud charioted by the wind,   290
She led me to a cave in that wild place,
And sate beside me, with her downward face
Illumining my slumbers, like the Moon
Waxing and waning o'er Endymion.
And I was laid asleep, spirit and limb,
And all my being became bright or dim
As the Moon's image in a summer sea,
According as she smiled or frowned on me;
And there I lay, within a chaste cold bed:
Alas, I then was nor alive nor dead:—   300
For at her silver voice came Death and Life,
Unmindful each of their accustomed strife,
Masked like twin babes, a sister and a brother,
The wandering hopes of one abandoned mother,
And through the cavern without wings they flew,
And cried 'Away, he is not of our crew.'
I wept, and though it be a dream, I weep.

What storms then shook the ocean of my sleep,
Blotting that Moon, whose pale and waning lips
Then shrank as in the sickness of eclipse;—   310
And how my soul was as a lampless sea,
And who was then its Tempest; and when She,
The Planet of that hour, was quenched, what frost
Crept o'er those waters, till from coast to coast
The moving billows of my being fell
Into a death of ice, immoveable;—
And then—what earthquakes made it gape and split,
The white Moon smiling all the while on it,
These words conceal:—if not, each word would be
The key of staunchless tears. Weep not for me!   320

    At length, into the obscure Forest came
The Vision I had sought through grief and shame.
Athwart that wintry wilderness of thorns
Flashed from her motion splendour like the Morn's,
And from her presence life was radiated
Through the grey earth and branches bare and dead;
So that her way was paved, and roofed above
With flowers as soft as thoughts of budding love;
And music from her respiration spread
Like light,—all other sounds were penetrated   330
By the small, still, sweet spirit of that sound,
So that the savage winds hung mute around;
And odours warm and fresh fell from her hair
Dissolving the dull cold in the frore air:
Soft as an Incarnation of the Sun,
When light is changed to love, this glorious One
Floated into the cavern where I lay,
And called my Spirit, and the dreaming clay
Was lifted by the thing that dreamed below
As smoke by fire, and in her beauty's glow   340
I stood, and felt the dawn of my long night
Was penetrating me with living light:
I knew it was the Vision veiled from me
So many years—that it was Emily.

    Twin Spheres of light who rule this passive Earth,
This world of love, this *me*; and into birth
Awaken all its fruits and flowers, and dart

Magnetic might into its central heart;
And lift its billows and its mists, and guide
By everlasting laws, each wind and tide   350
To its fit cloud, and its appointed cave;
And lull its storms, each in the craggy grave
Which was its cradle, luring to faint bowers
The armies of the rainbow-wingèd showers;
And, as those married lights, which from the towers
Of Heaven look forth and fold the wandering globe
In liquid sleep and splendour, as a robe;
And all their many-mingled influence blend,
If equal, yet unlike, to one sweet end;—
So ye, bright regents, with alternate sway   360
Govern my sphere of being, night and day!
Thou, not disdaining even a borrowed might;
Thou, not eclipsing a remoter light;
And, through the shadow of the seasons three,
From Spring to Autumn's sere maturity,
Light it into the Winter of the tomb,
Where it may ripen to a brighter bloom.
Thou too, O Comet beautiful and fierce,
Who drew the heart of this frail Universe
Towards thine own; till, wrecked in that convulsion,   370
Alternating attraction and repulsion,
Thine went astray and that was rent in twain;
Oh, float into our azure heaven again!
Be there love's folding-star at thy return;
The living Sun will feed thee from its urn
Of golden fire; the Moon will veil her horn
In thy last smiles; adoring Even and Morn
Will worship thee with incense of calm breath
And lights and shadows; as the star of Death
And Birth is worshipped by those sisters wild   380
Called Hope and Fear—upon the heart are piled
Their offerings,—of this sacrifice divine
A World shall be the altar.

                    Lady mine,
Scorn not these flowers of thought, the fading birth
Which from its heart of hearts that plant puts forth
Whose fruit, made perfect by thy sunny eyes,
Will be as of the trees of Paradise.

    The day is come, and thou wilt fly with me.
To whatsoe'er of dull mortality
Is mine, remain a vestal sister still;   390
To the intense, the deep, the imperishable,
Not mine but me, henceforth be thou united
Even as a bride, delighting and delighted.
The hour is come:—the destined Star has risen
Which shall descend upon a vacant prison.
The walls are high, the gates are strong, thick set
The sentinels—but true love never yet
Was thus constrained: it overleaps all fence:
Like lightning, with invisible violence
Piercing its continents; like Heaven's free breath,   400
Which he who grasps can hold not; liker Death,
Who rides upon a thought, and makes his way
Through temple, tower, and palace, and the array
Of arms: more strength has Love than he or they;
For it can burst his charnel, and make free
The limbs in chains, the heart in agony,
The soul in dust and chaos.

                  Emily,
A ship is floating in the harbour now,
A wind is hovering o'er the mountain's brow;
There is a path on the sea's azure floor,   410
No keel has ever ploughed that path before;
The halcyons brood around the foamless isles;
The treacherous Ocean has forsworn its wiles;
The merry mariners are bold and free:
Say, my heart's sister, wilt thou sail with me?
Our bark is as an albatross, whose nest
Is a far Eden of the purple East;
And we between her wings will sit, while Night
And Day, and Storm, and Calm, pursue their flight,
Our ministers, along the boundless Sea,   420
Treading each other's heels, unheededly.
It is an isle under Ionian skies,
Beautiful as a wreck of Paradise,
And, for the harbours are not safe and good,
This land would have remained a solitude
But for some pastoral people native there,
Who from the Elysian, clear, and golden air

Draw the last spirit of the age of gold,
Simple and spirited; innocent and bold.
The blue Aegean girds this chosen home,   430
With ever-changing sound and light and foam
Kissing the sifted sands, and caverns hoar;
And all the winds wandering along the shore
Undulate with the undulating tide:
There are thick woods where sylvan forms abide;
And many a fountain, rivulet, and pond,
As clear as elemental diamond,
Or serene morning air; and far beyond,
The mossy tracks made by the goats and deer
(Which the rough shepherd treads but once a year,)   440
Pierce into glades, caverns, and bowers, and halls
Built round with ivy, which the waterfalls
Illumining, with sound that never fails
Accompany the noon-day nightingales;
And all the place is peopled with sweet airs;
The light clear element which the isle wears
Is heavy with the scent of lemon-flowers,
Which floats like mist laden with unseen showers,
And falls upon the eye-lids like faint sleep;
And from the moss violets and jonquils peep,   450
And dart their arrowy odour through the brain
Till you might faint with that delicious pain;
And every motion, odour, beam, and tone,
With that deep music is in unison,
Which is a soul within the soul—they seem
Like echoes of an antenatal dream.—
It is an isle 'twixt Heaven, Air, Earth, and Sea
Cradled, and hung in clear tranquillity;
Bright as that wandering Eden Lucifer,
Washed by the soft blue Oceans of young air.   460
It is a favoured place. Famine or Blight,
Pestilence, War and Earthquake, never light
Upon its mountain-peaks; blind vultures, they
Sail onward far upon their fatal way:
The wingèd storms, chaunting their thunder-psalm
To other lands, leave azure chasms of calm
Over this isle or weep themselves in dew,
From which its fields and woods ever renew
Their green and golden immortality.

And from the sea there rise, and from the sky   470
There fall, clear exhalations, soft and bright,
Veil after veil, each hiding some delight,
Which Sun or Moon or zephyr draw aside,
Till the isle's beauty, like a naked bride
Glowing at once with love and loveliness,
Blushes and trembles at its own excess:
Yet, like a buried lamp, a Soul no less
Burns in the heart of this delicious isle,
An atom of th'Eternal, whose own smile
Unfolds itself, and may be felt not seen   480
O'er the grey rocks, blue waves, and forests green,
Filling their bare and void interstices.—
But the chief marvel of the wilderness
Is a lone dwelling, built by whom or how
None of the rustic island-people know:
'Tis not a tower of strength, though with its height
It overtops the woods; but, for delight,
Some wise and tender Ocean-King, ere crime
Had been invented, in the world's young prime,
Reared it, a wonder of that simple time,   490
An envy of the isles, a pleasure-house
Made sacred to his sister and his spouse.
It scarce seems now a wreck of human art,
But as it were Titanic; in the heart
Of Earth having assumed its form, then grown
Out of the mountain, from the living stone,
Lifting itself in caverns light and high:
For all the antique and learnèd imagery
Has been erased, and in the place of it
The ivy and the wild-vine interknit   500
The volumes of their many-twining stems;
Parasite flowers illume with dewy gems
The lampless halls, and when they fade, the sky
Peeps through their winter-woof of tracery
With Moon-light patches, or star atoms keen,
Or fragments of the day's intense serene,—
Working mosaic on their Parian floors.
And, day and night, aloof, from the high towers
And terraces, the Earth and Ocean seem
To sleep in one another's arms, and dream   510

Of waves, flowers, clouds, woods, rocks, and all that we
Read in their smiles, and call reality.

This isle and house are mine, and I have vowed
Thee to be lady of the solitude.—
And I have fitted up some chambers there
Looking towards the golden Eastern air,
And level with the living winds, which flow
Like waves above the living waves below.—
I have sent books and music there, and all
Those instruments with which high spirits call   520
The future from its cradle, and the past
Out of its grave, and make the present last
In thoughts and joys which sleep, but cannot die,
Folded within their own eternity.
Our simple life wants little, and true taste
Hires not the pale drudge Luxury, to waste
The scene it would adorn, and therefore still,
Nature, with all her children, haunts the hill.
The ring-dove, in the embowering ivy, yet
Keeps up her love-lament, and the owls flit   530
Round the evening tower, and the young stars glance
Between the quick bats in their twilight dance;
The spotted deer bask in the fresh moon-light
Before our gate, and the slow, silent night
Is measured by the pants of their calm sleep.
Be this our home in life, and when years heap
Their withered hours, like leaves, on our decay,
Let us become the over-hanging day,
The living soul of this Elysian isle,
Conscious, inseparable, one. Meanwhile   540
We two will rise, and sit, and walk together,
Under the roof of blue Ionian weather,
And wander in the meadows, or ascend
The mossy mountains, where the blue heavens bend
With lightest winds, to touch their paramour;
Or linger, where the pebble-paven shore,
Under the quick, faint kisses of the sea
Trembles and sparkles as with ecstasy,—
Possessing and possessed by all that is
Within that calm circumference of bliss,   550
And by each other, till to love and live

Be one:—or, at the noontide hour, arrive
Where some old cavern hoar seems yet to keep
The moonlight of the expired night asleep,
Through which the awakened day can never peep;
A veil for our seclusion, close as Night's,
Where secure sleep may kill thine innocent lights;
Sleep, the fresh dew of languid love, the rain
Whose drops quench kisses till they burn again.
And we will talk, until thought's melody   560
Become too sweet for utterance, and it die
In words, to live again in looks, which dart
With thrilling tone into the voiceless heart,
Harmonizing silence without a sound.
Our breath shall intermix, our bosoms bound,
And our veins beat together; and our lips
With other eloquence than words, eclipse
The soul that burns between them and the wells
Which boil under our being's inmost cells,
The fountains of our deepest life, shall be   570
Confused in passion's golden purity,
As mountain-springs under the morning Sun.
We shall become the same, we shall be one
Spirit within two frames, oh! wherefore two?
One passion in twin-hearts, which grows and grew,
Till, like two meteors of expanding flame,
Those spheres instinct with it become the same,
Touch, mingle, are transfigured; ever still
Burning, yet ever inconsumable:
In one another's substance finding food,   580
Like flames too pure and light and unimbued
To nourish their bright lives with baser prey,
Which point to Heaven and cannot pass away:
One hope within two wills, one will beneath
Two overshadowing minds, one life, one death,
One Heaven, one Hell, one immortality,
And one annihilation. Woe is me!
The wingèd words on which my soul would pierce
Into the height of love's rare Universe,
Are chains of lead around its flight of fire.—   590
I pant, I sink, I tremble, I expire!

Weak Verses, go, kneel at your Sovereign's feet,
And say:—'We are the masters of thy slave;
'What wouldest thou with us and ours and thine?'
Then call your sisters from Oblivion's cave,
All singing loud: 'Love's very pain is sweet,
But its reward is in the world divine
Which, if not here, it builds beyond the grave.'
So shall ye live when I am there. Then haste
Over the hearts of men, until ye meet   600
Marina, Vanna, Primus, and the rest,
And bid them love each other and be blest:
And leave the troop which errs, and which reproves,
And come and be my guest,—for I am Love's.

LINES WRITTEN ON HEARING THE NEWS OF THE DEATH OF NAPOLEON

What! alive and so bold, o Earth?
    Art thou not overbold?
    What! leapest thou forth as of old
In the light of thy morning mirth,
The last of the flock of the starry fold?
Ha! leapest thou forth as of old?
Are not the limbs still when the ghost is fled,
And canst thou move, Napoleon being dead?

How! is not thy quick heart cold?
    What spark is alive on thy hearth?   10
How! is not *his* death-knell knolled?
    And livest *thou* still, Mother Earth?
Thou wert warming thy fingers old
O'er the embers covered and cold
Of that most fiery spirit, when it fled—
What, Mother, do you laugh now he is dead?

'Who has known me of old,' replied Earth,
    'Or who has my story told?
    It is thou who art overbold.'
And the lightning of scorn laughed forth   20

As she sung, 'To my bosom I fold
All my sons when their knell is knolled,
And so with living motion all are fed,
And the quick spring like weeds out of the dead.

'Still alive and still bold,' shouted Earth,
    'I grow bolder and still more bold.
    The dead fill me ten thousandfold
Fuller of speed, and splendour, and mirth.
I was cloudy, and sullen, and cold,
Like a frozen chaos uprolled,   30
Till by the spirit of the mighty dead
My heart grew warm. I feed on whom I fed.

'Aye, alive and still bold,' muttered Earth.
    'Napoleon's fierce spirit rolled,
    In terror and blood and gold,
A torrent of ruin to death from his birth.
Leave the millions who follow to mould
The metal before it be cold;
And weave into his shame, which like the dead
Shrouds me, the hopes that from his glory fled.'   40

ADONAIS

An Elegy on the death of John Keats, author of Endymion,
Hyperion, etc.

Ἀστὴρ πρὶν μὲν ἔλαμπες ἐνὶ ζωοῖσιν Ἐῶος.
    νῦν δὲ θανὼν λάμπεις Ἕσπερος ἐν φθιμένοις.

Plato

PREFACE

Φάρμακον ἦλθε, Βίων, ποτὶ σὸν στόμα, φάρμακον εἶδες.
πῶς τευ τοῖς χείλεσσι ποτέδραμε, κοὐκ ἐγλυκάνθη;
τίς δὲ βροτὸς τοσσοῦτον ἀνάμερος, ἢ κεράσαι τοι,
ἢ δοῦναι λαλέοντι τὸ φάρμακον; ἔκφυγεν ᾠδάν.

Moschus, Epitaph. Bion

It is my intention to subjoin to the London edition of this poem a
criticism upon the claims of its lamented object to be classed among

the writers of the highest genius who have adorned our age. My known repugnance to the narrow principles of taste on which several of his earlier compositions were modelled proves at least that I am an impartial judge. I consider the fragment of *Hyperion* as second to nothing that was ever produced by a writer of the same years.

John Keats died at Rome of a consumption, in his twenty-fourth year, on the [twenty-third] of [February] 1821; and was buried in the romantic and lonely cemetery of the Protestants in that city, under the pyramid which is the tomb of Cestius, and the massy walls and towers, now mouldering and desolate, which formed the circuit of ancient Rome. The cemetry is an open space among the ruins, covered in winter with violets and daisies. It might make one in love with death, to think that one should be buried in so sweet a place.

The genius of the lamented person to whose memory I have dedicated these unworthy verses was not less delicate and fragile than it was beautiful; and where cankerworms abound, what wonder if its young flower was blighted in the bud? The savage criticism on his *Endymion*, which appeared in the *Quarterly Review*, produced the most violent effect on his susceptible mind; the agitation thus originated ended in the rupture of a blood-vessel in the lungs; a rapid consumption ensued, and the succeeding acknowledgements from more candid critics of the true greatness of his powers were ineffectual to heal the wound thus wantonly inflicted.

It may be well said that these wretched men know not what they do. They scatter their insults and their slanders without heed as to whether the poisoned shaft lights on a heart made callous by many blows or one like Keats's composed of more penetrable stuff. One of their associates is, to my knowledge, a most base and unprincipled calumniator. As to *Endymion*, was it a poem, whatever might be its defects, to be treated contemptuously by those who had celebrated, with various degrees of complacency and panegyric, *Paris*, and *Woman*, and a *Syrian Tale*, and Mrs. Lefanu, and Mr. Barrett, and Mr. Howard Payne, and a long list of the illustrious obscure? Are these the men who in their venal good nature presumed to draw a parallel between the Rev. Mr. Milman and Lord Byron? What gnat did they strain at here, after having swallowed all those camels? Against what woman taken in adultery dares the foremost of these literary prostitutes to cast his opprobrious stone? Miserable man! you, one of the meanest, have wantonly defaced one of the noblest specimens of the workmanship of God. Nor shall it be your excuse, that, murderer as you are, you have spoken daggers, but used none.

The circumstances of the closing scene of poor Keats's life were not made known to me until the *Elegy* was ready for the press. I am given to understand that the wound which his sensitive spirit had received from the criticism of *Endymion* was exasperated by the bitter sense of unrequited benefits; the poor fellow seems to have been hooted from the stage of life, no less by those on whom he had wasted the promise of his genius, than those on whom he had lavished his fortune and his care. He was accompanied to Rome, and attended in his last illness by Mr. Severn, a young artist of the highest promise, who, I have been informed, 'almost risked his own life, and sacrificed every prospect to unwearied attendance upon his dying friend.' Had I known these circumstances before the completion of my poem, I should have been tempted to add my feeble tribute of applause to the more solid recompense which the virtuous man finds in the recollection of his own motives. Mr. Severn can dispense with a reward from 'such stuff as dreams are made of.' His conduct is a golden augury of the success of his future career—may the unextinguished Spirit of his illustrious friend animate the creations of his pencil, and plead against Oblivion for his name!

ADONAIS

1. I weep for Adonais—he is dead!
    O, weep for Adonais! though our tears
    Thaw not the frost which binds so dear a head!
    And thou, sad Hour, selected from all years
    To mourn our loss, rouse thy obscure compeers,
    And teach them thine own sorrow, say: with me
    Died Adonais; till the Future dares
    Forget the Past, his fate and fame shall be
    An echo and a light unto eternity!

2. Where wert thou, mighty Mother, when he lay,   10
    When thy Son lay, pierced by the shaft which flies
    In darkness? where was lorn Urania
    When Adonais died? With veilèd eyes,

Mid listening Echoes, in her Paradise
She sate, while one, with soft enamoured breath,
Rekindled all the fading melodies
With which, like flowers that mock the corse beneath,
He had adorned and hid the coming bulk of death.

3. O, weep for Adonais—he is dead!
    Wake, melancholy Mother, wake and weep!   20
    Yet wherefore? Quench within their burning bed
    Thy fiery tears, and let thy loud heart keep
    Like his, a mute and uncomplaining sleep;
    For he is gone, where all things wise and fair
    Descend;—oh, dream not that the amorous Deep
    Will yet restore him to the vital air;
    Death feeds on his mute voice, and laughs at our despair.

4. Most musical of mourners, weep again!
    Lament anew, Urania!—He died,
    Who was the Sire of an immortal strain,   30
    Blind, old, and lonely, when his country's pride
    The priest, the slave, and the liberticide
    Trampled and mocked with many a loathèd rite
    Of lust and blood; he went, unterrified,
    Into the gulf of death; but his clear Sprite
    Yet reigns o'er earth; the third among the sons of light.

5. Most musical of mourners, weep anew!
    Not all to that bright station dared to climb;
    And happier they their happiness who knew,
    Whose tapers yet burn through that night of time   40
    In which suns perished; others more sublime,
    Struck by the envious wrath of man or God,
    Have sunk, extinct in their refulgent prime;
    And some yet live, treading the thorny road
    Which leads, through toil and hate, to Fame's serene abode.

6. But now, thy youngest, dearest one, has perished—
    The nursling of thy widowhood, who grew,
    Like a pale flower by some sad maiden cherished,
    And fed with true love tears, instead of dew;
    Most musical of mourners, weep anew!   50
    Thy extreme hope, the loveliest and the last,

The bloom, whose petals nipped before they blew
Died on the promise of the fruit, is waste;
The broken lily lies—the storm is overpast.

7.   To that high Capital, where kingly Death
Keeps his pale court in beauty and decay,
He came; and bought, with price of purest breath,
A grave among the eternal.—Come away!
Haste, while the vault of blue Italian day
Is yet his fitting charnel-roof! while still   60
He lies, as if in dewy sleep he lay;
Awake him not! surely he takes his fill
Of deep and liquid rest, forgetful of all ill.

8.   He will awake no more, oh, never more!—
Within the twilight chamber spreads apace
The shadow of white Death, and at the door
Invisible Corruption waits to trace
His extreme way to her dim dwelling-place;
The eternal Hunger sits, but pity and awe
Soothe her pale rage, nor dares she to deface   70
So fair a prey, till darkness, and the law
Of change, shall o'er his sleep the mortal curtain draw.

9.   O, weep for Adonais!—The quick Dreams,
The passion-wingèd Ministers of thought,
Who were his flocks, whom near the living streams
Of his young spirit he fed, and whom he taught
The love which was its music, wander not,—
Wander no more, from kindling brain to brain,
But droop there, whence they sprung; and mourn their lot
Round the cold heart, where, after their sweet pain, 80
They ne'er will gather strength, or find a home again.

10. And one with trembling hands clasps his cold head,
And fans him with her moonlight wings, and cries,
'Our love, our hope, our sorrow, is not dead;
See, on the silken fringe of his faint eyes,
Like dew upon a sleeping flower, there lies
A tear some Dream has loosened from his brain.'

Lost Angel of a ruined Paradise!
She knew not 'twas her own; as with no stain
She faded, like a cloud which had outwept its rain.   90

11.   One from a lucid urn of starry dew
        Washed his light limbs as if embalming them;
        Another clipped her profuse locks, and threw
        The wreath upon him, like an anadem,
        Which frozen tears instead of pearls begem;
        Another in her wilful grief would break
        Her bow and wingèd reeds, as if to stem
        A greater loss with one which was more weak;
        And dull the barbèd fire against his frozen cheek.

12.   Another Splendour on his mouth alit,   100
        That mouth, whence it was wont to draw the breath
        Which gave it strength to pierce the guarded wit,
        And pass into the panting heart beneath
        With lightning and with music: the damp death
        Quenched its caress upon his icy lips;
        And, as a dying meteor stains a wreath
        Of moonlight vapour, which the cold night clips,
        It flushed through his pale limbs, and passed to its eclipse.

13.   And others came ... Desires and Adorations,
        Wingèd Persuasions and veiled Destinies,   110
        Splendours, and Glooms, and glimmering Incarnations
        Of hopes and fears, and twilight Phantasies;
        And Sorrow, with her family of Sighs,
        And Pleasure, blind with tears, led by the gleam
        Of her own dying smile instead of eyes,
        Came in slow pomp;—the moving pomp might seem
        Like pageantry of mist on an autumnal stream.

14.   All he had loved, and moulded into thought,
        From shape, and hue, and odour, and sweet sound,
        Lamented Adonais. Morning sought   120
        Her eastern watch-tower, and her hair unbound,
        Wet with the tears which should adorn the ground,
        Dimmed the aërial eyes that kindle day;

Afar the melancholy thunder moaned,
Pale Ocean in unquiet slumber lay,
And the wild winds flew round, sobbing in their dismay.

15.   Lost Echo sits amid the voiceless mountains,
      And feeds her grief with his remembered lay,
      And will no more reply to winds or fountains,
      Or amorous birds perched on the young green spray,   130
      Or herdsman's horn, or bell at closing day,
      Since she can mimic not his lips, more dear
      Than those for whose disdain she pined away
      Into a shadow of all sounds:—a drear
      Murmur, between their songs, is all the woodmen hear.

16.   Grief made the young Spring wild, and she threw down
      Her kindling buds, as if she Autumn were,
      Or they dead leaves; since her delight is flown,
      For whom should she have waked the sullen year?
      To Phoebus was not Hyacinth so dear   140
      Nor to himself Narcissus, as to both
      Thou, Adonais: wan they stand and sere
      Amid the faint companions of their youth,
      With dew all turned to tears; odour, to sighing ruth.

17.   Thy spirit's sister, the lorn nightingale
      Mourns not her mate with such melodious pain;
      Not so the eagle, who like thee could scale
      Heaven, and could nourish in the sun's domain
      Her mighty youth with morning, doth complain,
      Soaring and screaming round her empty nest,   150
      As Albion wails for thee: the curse of Cain
      Light on his head who pierced thy innocent breast,
      And scared the angel soul that was its earthly guest!

18.   Ah, woe is me! Winter is come and gone,
      But grief returns with the revolving year;
      The airs and streams renew their joyous tone;
      The ants, the bees, the swallows reappear;
      Fresh leaves and flowers deck the dead Season's bier;
      The amorous birds now pair in every brake,

And build their mossy homes in field and brere;   160
And the green lizard, and the golden snake,
Like unimprisoned flames, out of their trance awake.

19.   Through wood and stream and field and hill and Ocean
A quickening life from the Earth's heart has burst
As it has ever done, with change and motion,
From the great morning of the world when first
God dawned on Chaos; in its stream immersed,
The lamps of Heaven flash with a softer light;
All baser things pant with life's sacred thirst;
Diffuse themselves; and spend in love's delight   170
The beauty and the joy of their renewèd might.

20.   The leprous corpse touched by this spirit tender
Exhales itself in flowers of gentle breath;
Like incarnations of the stars, when splendour
Is changed to fragrance, they illumine death
And mock the merry worm that wakes beneath;
Nought we know, dies. Shall that alone which knows
Be as a sword consumed before the sheath
By sightless lightning?—the intense atom glows
A moment, then is quenched in a most cold repose.   180

21.   Alas! that all we loved of him should be,
But for our grief, as if it had not been,
And grief itself be mortal! Woe is me!
Whence are we, and why are we? of what scene
The actors or spectators? Great and mean
Meet massed in death, who lends what life must borrow.
As long as skies are blue, and fields are green,
Evening must usher night, night urge the morrow,
Month follow month with woe, and year wake year
    to sorrow.

22.   *He* will awake no more, oh, never more!   190
'Wake thou,' cried Misery, 'childless Mother, rise
Out of thy sleep, and slake, in thy heart's core,
A wound more fierce than his with tears and sighs.'
And all the Dreams that watched Urania's eyes,
And all the Echoes whom their sister's song

Had held in holy silence, cried: 'Arise!'
Swift as a Thought by the snake Memory stung,
From her ambrosial rest the fading Splendour sprung.

23. She rose like an autumnal Night, that springs
     Out of the East, and follows wild and drear   200
     The golden Day, which, on eternal wings,
     Even as a ghost abandoning a bier,
     Has left the Earth a corpse. Sorrow and fear
     So struck, so roused, so rapt Urania;
     So saddened round her like an atmosphere
     Of stormy mist; so swept her on her way
     Even to the mournful place where Adonais lay.

24. Out of her secret Paradise she sped,
     Through camps and cities rough with stone, and steel,
     And human hearts, which to her aery tread   210
     Yielding not, wounded the invisible
     Palms of her tender feet where'er they fell:
     And barbèd tongues, and thoughts more sharp than they,
     Rent the soft Form they never could repel,
     Whose sacred blood, like the young tears of May,
     Paved with eternal flowers that undeserving way.

25. In the death-chamber for a moment Death,
     Shamed by the presence of that living Might,
     Blushed to annihilation, and the breath
     Revisited those lips, and life's pale light   220
     Flashed through those limbs, so late her dear delight.
     'Leave me not wild and drear and comfortless,
     As silent lightning leaves the starless night!
     Leave me not!' cried Urania: her distress
     Roused Death: Death rose and smiled, and met
         her vain caress.

26. 'Stay yet awhile! speak to me once again;
     Kiss me, so long but as a kiss may live;
     And in my heartless breast and burning brain
     That word, that kiss, shall all thoughts else survive,
     With food of saddest memory kept alive,   230
     Now thou art dead, as if it were a part

Of thee, my Adonais! I would give
All that I am to be as thou now art!
But I am chained to Time, and cannot thence depart!

27. 'Oh gentle child, beautiful as thou wert,
Why didst thou leave the trodden paths of men
Too soon, and with weak hands though mighty heart
Dare the unpastured dragon in his den?
Defenceless as thou wert, oh where was then
Wisdom the mirrored shield, or scorn the spear?   240
Or hadst thou waited the full cycle, when
Thy spirit should have filled its crescent sphere,
The monsters of life's waste had fled from thee like deer.

28. 'The herded wolves, bold only to pursue;
The obscene ravens, clamorous o'er the dead;
The vultures to the conqueror's banner true
Who feed where Desolation first has fed,
And whose wings rain contagion;—how they fled,
When like Apollo, from his golden bow,
The Pythian of the age one arrow sped   250
And smiled!—The spoilers tempt no second blow,
They fawn on the proud feet that spurn them lying low.

29. 'The sun comes forth, and many reptiles spawn;
He sets, and each ephemeral insect then
Is gathered into death without a dawn,
And the immortal stars awake again;
So is it in the world of living men:
A godlike mind soars forth, in its delight
Making earth bare and veiling heaven, and when
It sinks, the swarms that dimmed or shared its light   260
Leave to its kindred lamps the spirit's awful night.'

30. Thus ceased she: and the mountain shepherds came,
Their garlands sere, their magic mantles rent;
The Pilgrim of Eternity, whose fame
Over his living head like Heaven is bent,
An early but enduring monument,
Came, veiling all the lightnings of his song

In sorrow; from her wilds Ierne sent
The sweetest lyrist of her saddest wrong,
And love taught grief to fall like music from his tongue.

                                                            270

31.   Midst others of less note, came one frail Form,
        A phantom among men; companionless
        As the last cloud of an expiring storm
        Whose thunder is its knell; he, as I guess,
        Had gazed on Nature's naked loveliness,
        Actaeon-like, and now he fled astray
        With feeble steps o'er the world's wilderness,
        And his own thoughts, along that rugged way,
        Pursued, like raging hounds, their father and their prey.

32.   A pardlike Spirit beautiful and swift—   280
        A Love in desolation masked;—a Power
        Girt round with weakness;—it can scarce uplift
        The weight of the superincumbent hour;
        It is a dying lamp, a falling shower,
        A breaking billow;—even whilst we speak
        Is it not broken? On the withering flower
        The killing sun smiles brightly: on a cheek
        The life can burn in blood, even while the heart may break.

33.   His head was bound with pansies overblown,
        And faded violets, white, and pied, and blue;   290
        And a light spear topped with a cypress cone,
        Round whose rude shaft dark ivy tresses grew
        Yet dripping with the forest's noonday dew,
        Vibrated, as the ever-beating heart
        Shook the weak hand that grasped it; of that crew
        He came the last, neglected and apart;
        A herd-abandoned deer struck by the hunter's dart.

34.   All stood aloof, and at his partial moan
        Smiled through their tears; well knew that gentle band
        Who in another's fate now wept his own—   300
        As in the accents of an unknown land
        He sung new sorrow; sad Urania scanned
        The Stranger's mien, and murmured: 'Who art thou?'

He answered not, but with a sudden hand
Made bare his branded and ensanguined brow,
Which was like Cain's or Christ's—Oh! that it should be so!

35. What softer voice is hushed over the dead?
Athwart what brow is that dark mantle thrown?
What form leans sadly o'er the white death-bed,
In mockery of monumental stone,   310
The heavy heart heaving without a moan?
If it be He, who gentlest of the wise,
Taught, soothed, loved, honoured the departed one,
Let me not vex, with inharmonious sighs,
The silence of that heart's accepted sacrifice.

36. Our Adonais has drunk poison—oh!
What deaf and viperous murderer could crown
Life's early cup with such a draught of woe?
The nameless worm would now itself disown:
It felt, yet could escape, the magic tone   320
Whose prelude held all envy, hate, and wrong,
But what was howling in one breast alone,
Silent with expectation of the song,
Whose master's hand is cold, whose silver lyre unstrung.

37. Live thou, whose infamy is not thy fame!
Live! fear no heavier chastisement from me,
Thou noteless blot on a remembered name!
But be thyself, and know thyself to be!
And ever at thy season be thou free
To spill the venom when thy fangs o'erflow: 330
Remorse and Self-contempt shall cling to thee;
Hot Shame shall burn upon thy secret brow,
And like a beaten hound tremble thou shalt—as now.

38. Nor let us weep that our delight is fled
Far from these carrion kites that scream below;
He wakes or sleeps with the enduring dead;
Thou canst not soar where he is sitting now.—
Dust to the dust! but the pure spirit shall flow
Back to the burning fountain whence it came,

A portion of the Eternal, which must glow   340
Through time and change, unquenchably the same,
Whilst thy cold embers choke the sordid hearth of shame.

39. Peace, peace! he is not dead, he doth not sleep—
He hath awakened from the dream of life—
'Tis we, who lost in stormy visions, keep
With phantoms an unprofitable strife,
And in mad trance, strike with our spirit's knife
Invulnerable nothings.—*We* decay
Like corpses in a charnel; fear and grief
Convulse us and consume us day by day,   350
And cold hopes swarm like worms within our living clay.

40. He has outsoared the shadow of our night;
Envy and calumny and hate and pain,
And that unrest which men miscall delight,
Can touch him not and torture not again;
From the contagion of the world's slow stain
He is secure, and now can never mourn
A heart grown cold, a head grown grey in vain;
Nor, when the spirit's self has ceased to burn,
With sparkless ashes load an unlamented urn.   360

41. He lives, he wakes—'tis Death is dead, not he;
Mourn not for Adonais.—Thou young Dawn
Turn all thy dew to splendour, for from thee
The spirit thou lamentest is not gone;
Ye caverns and ye forests, cease to moan!
Cease ye faint flowers and fountains, and thou Air
Which like a mourning veil thy scarf hadst thrown
O'er the abandoned Earth, now leave it bare
Even to the joyous stars which smile on its despair!

42. He is made one with Nature: there is heard   370
His voice in all her music, from the moan
Of thunder, to the song of night's sweet bird;
He is a presence to be felt and known
In darkness and in light, from herb and stone,
Spreading itself where'er that Power may move
Which has withdrawn his being to its own;
Which wields the world with never wearied love,
Sustains it from beneath, and kindles it above.

43.   He is a portion of the loveliness
      Which once he made more lovely: he doth bear   380
      His part, while the one Spirit's plastic stress
      Sweeps through the dull dense world, compelling there
      All new successions to the forms they wear;
      Torturing th'unwilling dross that checks its flight
      To its own likeness, as each mass may bear;
      And bursting in its beauty and its might
      From trees and beasts and men into the Heavens' light.

44.   The splendours of the firmament of time
      May be eclipsed, but are extinguished not;
      Like stars to their appointed height they climb,   390
      And death is a low mist which cannot blot
      The brightness it may veil. When lofty thought
      Lifts a young heart above its mortal lair,
      And love and life contend in it, for what
      Shall be its earthly doom, the dead live there
      And move like winds of light on dark and stormy air.

45.   The inheritors of unfulfilled renown
      Rose from their thrones, built beyond mortal thought,
      Far in the Unapparent. Chatterton
      Rose pale, his solemn agony had not   400
      Yet faded from him; Sidney as he fought
      And as he fell and as he lived and loved
      Sublimely mild, a Spirit without spot,
      Arose; and Lucan, by his death approved:
      Oblivion as they rose shrank like a thing reproved.

46.   And many more, whose names on Earth are dark,
      But whose transmitted effluence cannot die
      So long as fire outlives the parent spark,
      Rose, robed in dazzling immortality.
      'Thou art become as one of us,' they cry,   410
      'It was for thee yon kingless sphere has long
      Swung blind in unascended majesty,
      Silent alone amid an Heaven of song.
      Assume thy wingèd throne, thou Vesper of our throng!'

47.   Who mourns for Adonais? oh, come forth
      Fond wretch! and know thyself and him aright.
      Clasp with thy panting soul the pendulous Earth;

As from a centre, dart thy spirit's light
Beyond all worlds, until its spacious might
Satiate the void circumference: then shrink   420
Even to a point within our day and night;
And keep thy heart light lest it make thee sink
When hope has kindled hope, and lured thee to the brink;

48.   Or go to Rome, which is the sepulchre,
O, not of him, but of our joy: 'tis nought
That ages, empires, and religions there
Lie buried in the ravage they have wrought;
For such as he can lend,—they borrow not
Glory from those who made the world their prey;
And he is gathered to the kings of thought   430
Who waged contention with their time's decay,
And of the past are all that cannot pass away.

49.   Go thou to Rome,—at once the Paradise,
The grave, the city, and the wilderness;
And where its wrecks like shattered mountains rise,
And flowering weeds, and fragrant copses dress
The bones of Desolation's nakedness
Pass, till the Spirit of the spot shall lead
Thy footsteps to a slope of green access
Where, like an infant's smile, over the dead,   440
A light of laughing flowers along the grass is spread.

50.   And grey walls moulder round, on which dull Time
Feeds, like slow fire upon a hoary brand:
And one keen pyramid with wedge sublime,
Pavilioning the dust of him who planned
This refuge for his memory, doth stand
Like flame transformed to marble; and beneath,
A field is spread, on which a newer band
Have pitched in Heaven's smile their camp of death,
Welcoming him we lose with scarce extinguished breath.
                                                               450

51.   Here pause: these graves are all too young as yet
To have outgrown the sorrow which consigned
Its charge to each; and if the seal is set,
Here, on one fountain of a mourning mind,

Break it not thou! too surely shalt thou find
Thine own well full, if thou returnest home,
Of tears and gall. From the world's bitter wind
Seek shelter in the shadow of the tomb.
What Adonais is, why fear we to become?

52. The One remains, the many change and pass;   460
Heaven's light forever shines, Earth's shadows fly;
Life, like a dome of many-coloured glass,
Stains the white radiance of Eternity,
Until Death tramples it to fragments.—Die,
If thou wouldst be with that which thou dost seek!
Follow where all is fled!—Rome's azure sky,
Flowers, ruins, statues, music, words, are weak
The glory they transfuse with fitting truth to speak.

53. Why linger, why turn back, why shrink, my Heart?
Thy hopes are gone before: from all things here   470
They have departed; thou shouldst now depart!
A light is passed from the revolving year,
And man, and woman; and what still is dear
Attracts to crush, repels to make thee wither.
The soft sky smiles,—the low wind whispers near:
'Tis Adonais calls! oh, hasten thither,
No more let Life divide what Death can join together.

54. That Light whose smiles kindles the Universe,
That Beauty in which all things work and move,
That Benediction which the eclipsing Curse   480
Of birth can quench not, that sustaining Love
Which through the web of being blindly wove
By man and beast and earth and air and sea,
Burns bright or dim, as each are mirrors of
The fire for which all thirst, now beams on me,
Consuming the last clouds of cold mortality.

55. The breath whose might I have invoked in song
Descends on me; my spirit's bark is driven
Far from the shore, far from the trembling throng
Whose sails were never to the tempest given;   490
The massy earth and spherèd skies are riven!
I am borne darkly, fearfully, afar;

Whilst burning through the inmost veil of Heaven,
The soul of Adonais, like a star,
Beacons from the abode where the Eternal are.

THE AZIOLA

'Do you not hear the aziola cry?
Methinks she must be nigh—'
   Said Mary as we sate
In dusk, ere stars were lit or candles brought—
   And I who thought
This Aziola was some tedious woman
Asked, 'Who is Aziola?'—how elate
I felt to know that it was nothing human,
No mockery of myself to fear or hate!
   And Mary saw my soul,   10
And laughed and said—'Disquiet yourself not,
   'Tis nothing but a little downy owl.'

Sad aziola, many an eventide
   Thy music I had heard
By wood and stream, meadow and mountainside,
   And fields and marshes wide,
Such as nor voice, nor lute, nor wind, nor bird
   The soul ever stirred—
Unlike and far sweeter than them all.
Sad aziola, from that moment I   20
Loved thee and thy sad cry.

FROM: HELLAS: TWO CHORUSES

1.   Worlds on worlds are rolling ever
       From creation to decay,
    Like the bubbles on a river
       Sparkling, bursting, borne away.
         But *they* are still immortal
          Who, through Birth's orient portal
    And Death's dark chasm hurrying to and fro,

      Clothe their unceasing flight
      In the brief dust and light
Gathered around their chariots as they go;   10
      New shapes they still may weave,
      New gods, new laws receive,
Bright or dim are they as the robes they last
      On Death's bare ribs had cast.

      A Power from the unknown God,
      A Promethean conqueror, came;
Like a triumphal path he trod
      The thorns of death and shame.
      A mortal shape to him
      Was like the vapour dim   20
Which the orient planet animates with light;
      Hell, Sin, and Slavery came
      Like bloodhounds mild and tame,
Nor preyed, until their Lord had taken flight;
      The moon of Mahomet
      Arose, and it shall set
While blazoned as on Heaven's immortal noon
      The cross leads generations on.

      Swift as the radiant shapes of sleep
      From one whose dreams are Paradise   30
Fly, when the fond wretch wakes to weep
      And Day peers forth with her blank eyes,
      So fleet, so faint, so fair,
      The Powers of earth and air
Fled from the folding-star of Bethlehem:
      Apollo, Pan, and Love,
      And even Olympian Jove
Grew weak, for killing Truth had glared on them;
      Our hills and seas and streams,
      Dispeopled of their dreams,   40
Their waters turned to blood, their dew to tears,
      Wailed for the golden years.

2.   The world's great age begins anew,
      The golden years return,
      The earth doth like a snake renew

Her winter weeds outworn;
Heaven smiles, and faiths and empires gleam
Like wrecks of a dissolving dream.

A brighter Hellas rears its mountains
    From waves serener far,
A new Peneus rolls his fountains
    Against the morning-star;   10
Where fairer Tempes bloom, there sleep
Young Cyclads on a sunnier deep.

A loftier Argo cleaves the main
    Fraught with a later prize;
Another Orpheus sings again,
    And loves, and weeps, and dies;
A new Ulysses leaves once more
Calypso for his native shore.

O, write no more the tale of Troy,
    If earth Death's scroll must be!   20
Nor mix with Laian rage the joy
    Which dawns upon the free;
Although a subtler Sphinx renew
Riddles of death Thebes never knew.

Another Athens shall arise,
    And to remoter time
Bequeath, like sunset to the skies,
    The splendour of its prime;
And leave, if nought so bright may live,
All earth can take or Heaven can give.   30

Saturn and Love their long repose
    Shall burst, more bright and good
Than all who fell, than One who rose,
    Than many unsubdued;
Not gold, not blood, their altar dowers,
But votive tears and symbol flowers.

O cease! must hate and death return?
    Cease! must men kill and die?
Cease! drain not to its dregs the urn

Of bitter prophecy. 40
The world is weary of the past,
O might it die or rest at last!

THE FLOWER THAT SMILES TODAY

The flower that smiles today
   Tomorrow dies;
All that we wish to stay
   Tempts and then flies;
What is this world's delight?
Lightning, that mocks the night,
   Brief even as bright.—

Virtue, how frail it is!—
   Friendship, how rare!—
Love, how it sells poor bliss 10
   For proud despair!
But these, though soon they fall,
Survive their joy, and all
   Which ours we call.—

Whilst skies are blue and bright,
   Whilst flowers are gay,
Whilst eyes that change ere night
   Make glad the day;
Whilst yet the calm hours creep,
Dream thou—and from thy sleep 20
   Then wake to weep.

TO NIGHT

Swiftly walk o'er the western wave,
   Spirit of Night!
Out of the misty eastern cave
Where, all the long and lone daylight
Thou wovest dreams of joy and fear,
Which make thee terrible and dear,
   Swift be thy flight!

Wrap thy form in a mantle grey,
    Star-inwrought!
Blind with thine hair the eyes of Day,   10
Kiss her until she be wearied out—
Then wander o'er city and sea and land,
Touching all with thine opiate wand—
    Come, long-sought!

When I arose and saw the dawn
    I sighed for thee;
When light rode high, and the dew was gone,
And noon lay heavy on flower and tree,
And the weary Day turned to his rest,
Lingering like an unloved guest,   20
    I sighed for thee.

Thy brother Death came, and cried,
    'Wouldst thou me?'
Thy sweet child Sleep, the filmy-eyed,
Murmured like a noontide bee,
'Shall I nestle near thy side?
Wouldst thou me?' and I replied,
    'No, not thee!'

Death will come when thou art dead,
    Soon, too soon—   30
    Sleep will come when thou art fled;
Of neither would I ask the boon
I ask of thee, belovèd Night—
Swift be thine approaching flight,
    Come soon, soon!

FRAGMENT: ROSE LEAVES, WHEN THE ROSE IS DEAD

Rose leaves, when the rose is dead,
Are heaped for the beloved's bed,
And so thy thoughts, when thou art gone,
Love itself shall slumber on.

Music, when soft voices die,
Vibrates in the memory,—
Odours, when sweet violets sicken,
Live within the sense they quicken—

O WORLD, O LIFE, O TIME

O World, O Life, O Time,
    On whose last steps I climb,
Trembling at that where I had stood before—
    When will return the glory of your prime?
        No more, O never more!

Out of the day and night
    A joy has taken flight—
Fresh spring and summer [   ] and winter hoar
    Move my faint heart with grief, but with delight
        No more, O never more!   10

WHEN PASSION'S TRANCE IS OVERPAST

When passion's trance is overpast,
If tenderness and truth could last
Or live, whilst all wild feelings keep
Some mortal slumber, dark and deep,
I should not weep, I should not weep!

It were enough to feel, to see
Thy soft eyes gazing tenderly,
And dream the rest—and burn and be
The secret food of fires unseen,
Could thou but be what thou hast been.   10

After the slumber of the year
The woodland violets reappear;
All things revive in field or grove
And sky and sea, but two, which move
And form all others—life and love.

ONE WORD IS TOO OFTEN PROFANED

1. One word is too often profaned
        For me to profane it,
    One feeling too falsely disdained
        For thee to disdain it;
    One hope is too like despair
        For prudence to smother,
    And pity from thee more dear
        Than that from another.

2. I can give not what men call love;
        But wilt thou accept not   10
    The worship the heart lifts above
        And the Heavens reject not,—
    The desire of the moth for the star,
        Of the night for the morrow,
    The devotion to something afar
        From the sphere of our sorrow?

TO EDWARD WILLIAMS

1. The serpent is shut out from Paradise—
    The wounded deer must seek the herb no more
    In which its heart's cure lies—
    The widowed dove must cease to haunt a bower
    Like that from which its mate, with feignèd sighs,
    Fled in the April hour—
    I too, must seldom seek again
    Near happy friends a mitigated pain.

2. Of hatred I am proud,—with scorn content;
    Indifference, which once hurt me, is now grown   10
    Itself indifferent.
    But, not to speak of love, Pity alone
    Can break a spirit already more than bent.
    The miserable one
    Turns the mind's poison into food:
    Its medicine is tears,—its evil, good.

3.   Therefore, if now I see you seldomer,
     Dear friends, dear *friend*, know that I only fly
     Your looks, because they stir
     Griefs that should sleep, and hopes that cannot die.   20
     The very comfort which they minister
     I scarce can bear; yet I
     (So deeply is the arrow gone)
     Should quickly perish if it were withdrawn.

4.   When I return to my cold home, you ask
     Why I am not as I have lately been?
     You spoil me for the task
     Of acting a forced part in life's dull scene,—
     Of wearing on my brow the idle mask
     Of author, great or mean,   30
     In the world's carnival. I sought
     Peace thus, and but in you I found it not.

5.   Full half an hour today I tried my lot
     With various flowers, and every one still said,
     'She loves me, loves me not.'
     And if this meant a Vision long since fled—
     If it meant Fortune, Fame, or Peace of thought—
     If it meant—(but I dread
     To speak what you may know too well)—
     Still there was truth in the sad oracle.   40

6.   The crane o'er seas and forests seeks her home.
     No bird so wild but has its quiet nest
     When it no more would roam.
     The sleepless billows on the Ocean's breast
     Break like a bursting heart, and die in foam
     And thus, at length, find rest.
     Doubtless there is a place of peace
     Where *my* weak heart and all its throbs will cease.

7.   I asked her yesterday if she believed
     That I had resolution,—one who *had*   50
     Would ne'er have thus relieved
     His heart with words, but what his judgment bade
     Would do, and leave the scorner unrelieved.—

These verses were too sad
To send to you, but that I know,
Happy yourself, you feel another's woe.

TO JANE: THE RECOLLECTION
Feb. 2, 1822

Now the last day of many days,
All beautiful and bright as thou,
The loveliest and the last, is dead.
Rise Memory, and write its praise!
Up to thy wonted work! come, trace
The epitaph of glory fled;
For now the Earth has changed its face,
A frown is on the Heaven's brow.

1. We wandered to the pine forest
        That skirts the ocean foam;   10
    The lightest wind was in its nest,
        The Tempest in its home;
    The whispering waves were half asleep,
        The clouds were gone to play,
    And on the bosom of the deep
        The smile of Heaven lay;
    It seemed as if the hour were one
        Sent from beyond the skies,
    Which scattered from above the sun
        A light of Paradise.   20

2. We paused amid the pines that stood
        The giants of the waste,
    Tortured by storms to shapes as rude
        As serpents interlaced,
    And soothed by every azure breath
        That under Heaven is blown
    To harmonies and hues beneath,
        As tender as its own;
    Now all the tree-tops lay asleep
        Like green waves on the sea,   30
    As still as in the silent deep
        The Ocean woods may be.

3.   How calm it was! the silence there
         By such a chain was bound
      That even the busy woodpecker
         Made stiller with her sound
      The inviolable quietness;
         The breath of peace we drew
      With its soft motion made not less
         The calm that round us grew.—   40
      There seemed from the remotest seat
         Of the white mountain-waste,
      To the soft flower beneath our feet
         A magic circle traced,
      A spirit interfused around,
         A thrilling silent life,
      To momentary peace it bound
         Our mortal nature's strife;—
      And still I felt the centre of
         The magic circle there   50
      Was one fair form that filled with love
         The lifeless atmosphere.

4.   We paused beside the pools that lie
         Under the forest bough—
      Each seemed as 'twere, a little sky
         Gulfed in a world below;
      A firmament of purple light
         Which in the dark earth lay
      More boundless than the depth of night
         And purer than the day,   60
      In which the lovely forests grew
         As in the upper air,
      More perfect, both in shape and hue,
         Than any spreading there;
      There lay the glade, the neighbouring lawn,
         And through the dark green wood
      The white sun twinkling like the dawn
         Out of a speckled cloud.

5.   Sweet views, which in our world àbove
         Can never well be seen,   70
      Were imaged in the water's love
         Of that fair forest green;

And all was interfused beneath
  With an Elysian glow,
An atmosphere without a breath,
  A softer day below—
Like one beloved, the scene had lent
  To the dark water's breast,
Its every leaf and lineament
  With more than truth exprest;   80
Until an envious wind crept by,
  Like an unwelcome thought
Which from the mind's too faithful eye
  Blots one dear image out.—
Though thou art ever fair and kind
  And forests ever green,
Less oft is peace in —'s mind
  Than calm in water seen.

FROM GOETHE'S FAUST: PROLOGUE IN HEAVEN

The Lord *and the* Host *of* Heaven: to them Mephistopheles. *Enter three* Archangels.
Raphael.
The Sun makes music as of old
  Amid the rival spheres of Heaven,
On its predestined circle rolled
  With thunder speed: the Angels even
Draw strength from gazing on its glance,
  Though none its meaning fathom may;—
The world's unwithered countenance
  Is bright as at Creation's day.

Gabriel.
And swift and swift, with rapid lightness,
  The adornèd Earth spins silently,   10
Alternating Elysian brightness
  With deep and dreadful night; the sea
Foams in broad billows from its deep
  Up to the rocks, and rocks and Ocean,
Onward, with spheres which never sleep,
  Are hurried in eternal motion.

Michael.
    And tempests in contention roar
      From land to sea, from sea to land;
    And, raging, weave a chain of power,
      Which girds the earth, as with a band.—   20
    A flashing desolation there,
      Flames before the thunder's way;
    But thy servants, Lord, revere
      The gentle changes of thy day.

Chorus of the Three.
    The Angels draw strength from thy glance,
      Though no one comprehend thee may;—
    Thy world's unwithered countenance
      Is bright as on Creation's day.

Enter Mephistopheles.
    Mephistopheles.   As thou, O Lord, once more art kind enough
    To interest thyself in our affairs,   30
    And ask, 'How goes it with you there below?'
    And as indulgently at other times
    Thou tookedst not my visits in ill part,
    Thou seest me here once more among thy household.
    Though I should scandalize this company,
    You will excuse me if I do not talk
    In the high style which they think fashionable;
    My pathos certainly would make you laugh too,
    Had you not long since given over laughing.
    Nothing know I to say of suns and worlds;   40
    I observe only how men plague themselves;—
    The little God o'the world keeps the same stamp,
    As wonderful as on Creation's day.—
    A little better would he live, hadst thou
    Not given him a glimpse of Heaven's light
    Which he calls reason, and employs it only
    To live more beastlily than any beast.
    With reverence of your Lordship be it spoken,
    He's like one of those long-legged grasshoppers,
    Who flits and jumps about, and sings for ever   50
    The same old song i'the grass. There let him lie,
    Burying his nose in every heap of dung.

The Lord.   Have you no more to say? Do you come here
     Always to scold and cavil and complain?
     Seems nothing ever right to you on Earth?
Mephistopheles.   No, Lord; I find all there, as ever, bad at heart.
     Even I am sorry for man's days of sorrow;
     I could myself almost give up the pleasure
     Of plaguing the poor things.
The Lord.   Knowest thou Faust?   60
Mephistopheles.   The Doctor?
The Lord.   Ay; my servant Faust.
Mephistopheles.   In truth,
     He serves you in a fashion quite his own;
     And the fool's meat and drink are not of earth.
     His aspirations bear him on so far
     That he is half aware of his own folly;
     For he demands from Heaven its fairest star
     And from the earth the highest joy it bears,
     Yet all things far and all things near are vain
     To calm the deep emotions of his breast.
The Lord.   Though he now serves me in a cloud of error,   70
     I will soon lead him forth to the clear day.
     When trees look green, full well the gardener knows
     That fruits and blooms will deck the coming year.
Mephistopheles.   What will you bet?—now, I am sure of winning. . .
     Only, observe you give me full permission
     To lead him softly on my path.
The Lord.   As long
     As he shall live upon the earth, so long
     Is nothing unto thee forbidden — Man
     Must err till he has ceased to struggle.
Mephistopheles.   Thanks.
     And that is all I ask; for willingly   80
     I never make acquaintance with the dead.
     The full fresh cheeks of youth are food for me,
     And if a corpse knocks, I am not at home.
     For I am like a cat — I like to play
     A little with the mouse before I eat it.
The Lord.   Well, well, it is permitted thee! Draw thou
     His spirit from its springs; as thou find'st power,
     Seize him and lead him on thy downward path;
     And stand ashamed when failure teaches thee
     That a good man, even in his darkest longings,   90

Is well aware of the right way.
Mephistopheles.   Well and good.
  I am not in much doubt about my bet,
  And if I lose, then 'tis your turn to crow;
  Enjoy your triumph then with a full breast.
  Ay; dust shall he devour, and that with pleasure,
  Like my old paramour, the famous Snake.
The Lord.   Pray come here when it suits you; for I never
  Had much dislike for people of your sort.
  And, among all the spirits who rebelled,
  The knave was ever the least tedious to me.   100
  The active spirit of man soon sleeps, and soon
  He seeks unbroken quiet; therefore I
  Have given him the Devil for a companion,
  Who may provoke him to some sort of work,
  And must create forever.—But ye, pure
  Children of God, enjoy eternal beauty!
  Let that which ever operates and lives
  Clasp you within the limits of its love;
  And seize with sweet and melancholy thoughts
  The floating phantoms of its loveliness.   110
          Heaven closes, the Archangels exeunt.
Mephistopheles.   From time to time I visit the old fellow,
  And I take care to keep on good terms with him.
  Civil enough is this same God Almighty,
  To talk so freely with the Devil himself.

FRAGMENT: THE TRIUMPH OF LIFE

Swift as a spirit hastening to his task
  Of glory and of good, the Sun sprang forth
Rejoicing in his splendour, and the mask

  Of darkness fell from the awakened Earth.
The smokeless altars of the mountain snows
  Flamed above crimson clouds, and at the birth

Of light, the Ocean's orison arose
  To which the birds tempered their matin lay.
All flowers in field or forest which unclose

Their trembling eyelids to the kiss of day,   10
Swinging their censers in the element,
   With orient incense lit by the new ray

Burned slow and inconsumably, and sent
   Their odorous sighs up to the smiling air,
And in succession due, did Continent,

   Isle, Ocean, and all things that in them wear
The form and character of mortal mould
   Rise as the Sun their father rose, to bear

Their portion of the toil which he of old
   Took as his own and then imposed on them;   20
But I, whom thoughts which must remain untold

   Had kept as wakeful as the stars that gem
The cone of night, now they were laid asleep,
   Stretched my faint limbs beneath the hoary stem

Which an old chestnut flung athwart the steep
   Of a green Apennine: before me fled
The night; behind me rose the day; the Deep

   Was at my feet, and Heaven above my head;
When a strange trance over my fancy grew
   Which was not slumber, for the shade it spread   30

Was so transparent that the scene came through
   As clear as when a veil of light is drawn
O'er evening hills, they glimmer; and I knew

   That I had felt the freshness of that dawn,
Bathed in the same cold dew my brow and hair,
   And sate as thus upon that slope of lawn

Under the self same bough, and heard as there
   The birds, the fountains and the Ocean hold
Sweet talk in music through the enamoured air.

   And then a Vision on my brain was rolled. . .   40
                    ———————

As in that trance of wondrous thought I lay
   This was the tenour of my waking dream:
Methought I sate beside a public way

   Thick strewn with summer dust, and a great stream
Of people there was hurrying to and fro
   Numerous as gnats upon the evening gleam,

All hastening onward, yet none seemed to know
   Whither he went, or whence he came, or why
He made one of the multitude, yet so

   Was borne amid the crowd as through the sky   50
One of the million leaves of summer's bier.—
   Old age and youth, manhood and infancy,

Mixed in one mighty torrent did appear,
   Some flying from the thing they feared and some
Seeking the object of another's fear,

   And others as with steps towards the tomb
Pored on the trodden worms that crawled beneath,
   And others mournfully within the gloom

Of their own shadow walked, and called it death . . .
   And some fled from it as it were a ghost,   60
Half fainting in the affliction of vain breath.

   But more, with motions which each other crossed,
Pursued or shunned the shadows the clouds threw
   Or birds within the noonday aether lost,

Upon that path where flowers never grew;
   And weary with vain toil and faint for thirst
Heard not the fountains whose melodious dew

   Out of their mossy cells forever burst,
Nor felt the breeze which from the forest told
   Of grassy paths, and wood lawns interspersed   70

With overarching elms and caverns cold,
   And violet banks where sweet dreams brood, but they
Pursued their serious folly as of old . . .

   And as I gazed methought that in the way
The throng grew wilder, as the woods of June
   When the south wind shakes the extinguished day—

And a cold glare, intenser than the noon
   But icy cold, obscured with   light
The Sun as he the stars. Like the young moon

   When on the sunlit limits of the night   80
Her white shell trembles amid crimson air,
   And whilst the sleeping tempest gathers might

Doth, as a herald of its coming, bear
   The ghost of her dead mother, whose dim form
Bends in dark aether from her infant's chair,

   So came a chariot on the silent storm
Of its own rushing splendour, and a Shape
   So sate within as one whom years deform

Beneath a dusky hood and double cape
   Crouching within the shadow of a tomb,   90
And o'er what seemed the head, a cloud like crape

   Was bent, a dun and faint aetherial gloom
Tempering the light; upon the chariot's beam
   A Janus-visaged Shadow did assume

The guidance of that wonder-wingèd team.
   The shapes which drew it in thick lightnings
Were lost: I heard alone on the air's soft stream

   The music of their ever-moving wings.
All the four faces of that charioteer
   Had their eyes banded . . . little profit brings   100

Speed in the van and blindness in the rear,
   Nor then avail the beams that quench the Sun,
Or that his banded eyes could pierce the sphere

Of all that is, has been, or will be done.—
So ill was the car guided, but it passed
   With solemn speed majestically on . . .

The crowd gave way, and I arose aghast,
   Or seemed to rise, so mighty was the trance,
And saw like clouds upon the thunder-blast

   The million with fierce song and maniac dance   110
Raging around; such seemed the jubilee
   As when to greet some conqueror's advance

Imperial Rome poured forth her living sea
   From senate-house and prison and theatre,
When Freedom left those who upon the free

   Had bound a yoke which soon they stooped to bear.
Nor wanted here the true similitude
   Of a triumphal pageant, for where'er

The chariot rolled, a captive multitude
   Was driven; all those who had grown old in power   120
Or misery,—all who have their age subdued,

   By action or by suffering, and whose hour
Was drained to its last sand in weal or woe,
   So that the trunk survived both fruit and flower;

All those whose fame or infamy must grow
   Till the great winter lay the form and name
Of their green earth with them forever low,

   —All but the sacred few who could not tame
Their spirits to the Conqueror, but as soon
   As they had touched the world with living flame   130

Fled back like eagles to their native noon,
   Or those who put aside the diadem
Of earthly thrones or gems, till the last one

   Were there;—for they of Athens and Jerusalem
Were neither mid the mighty captives seen,
   Nor mid the ribald crowd that followed them

Or fled before . . . Now swift, fierce and obscene
   The wild dance maddens in the van, and those
Who lead it, fleet as shadows on the green,

   Outspeed the chariot and without repose   140
Mix with each other in tempestuous measure
   To savage music . . . Wilder as it grows,

They, tortured by the agonizing pleasure,
   Convulsed, and on the rapid whirlwinds spun
Of that fierce spirit, whose unholy leisure

   Was soothed by mischief since the world begun,
Throw back their heads and loose their streaming hair,
   And in their dance round her who dims the Sun

Maidens and youths fling their wild arms in air
   As their feet twinkle; they recede, and now   150
Bending within each other's atmosphere

   Kindle invisibly; and as they glow,
Like moths by light attracted and repelled,
   Oft to their bright destruction come and go,

Till—like two clouds into one vale impelled
   That shake the mountains when their lightnings mingle,
And die in rain,—the fiery band which held

   Their natures, snaps . . . ere the shock cease to tingle,
One falls and then another in the path
   Senseless, nor is the desolation single,—   160

Yet ere I can say *where*, the chariot hath
   Passed over them; nor other trace I find
But as of foam after the Ocean's wrath

   Is spent upon the desert shore.—Behind,
Old men, and women foully disarrayed
   Shake their grey hair in the insulting wind,

Limp in the dance and strain with limbs decayed
   To reach the car of light which leaves them still
Farther behind and deeper in the shade.

But not the less with impotence of will   170
They wheel, though ghastly shadows interpose
　　Round them and round each other, and fulfill

Their part and to the dust whence they arose
　　Sink, and corruption veils them as they lie,
And frost in these performs what fire in those.

　　Struck to the heart by this sad pageantry,
Half to myself I said, 'And what is this?
　　Whose shape is that within the car? and why'—

I would have added—'is all here amiss?'
　　But a voice answered: 'Life' . ... I turned and knew   180
(O Heaven have mercy on such wretchedness!)

　　That what I thought was an old root which grew
To strange distortion out of the hill side
　　Was indeed one of that deluded crew,

And that the grass which methought hung so wide
　　And white, was but his thin discoloured hair,
And that the holes it vainly sought to hide

　　Were or had been eyes.—'If thou canst forbear
To join the dance, which I had well forborne,'
　　Said the grim Feature, of my thought aware,   190

'I will unfold that which to this deep scorn
　　Led me and my companions, and relate
The progress of the pageant since the morn;

　　'If thirst of knowledge doth not thus abate,
Follow it even to the night, but I
　　Am weary' . . . Then like one who with the weight

Of his own words is staggered, wearily
　　He paused, and ere he could resume, I cried,
'First who art thou?'. . . 'Before thy memory

　　'I feared, loved, hated, suffered, did, and died,   200
And if the spark with which Heaven lit my spirit
　　Earth had with purer nutriment supplied,

'Corruption would not now thus much inherit
    Of what was once Rousseau—nor this disguise
Stain that within which still disdains to wear it.—

    'If I have been extinguished, yet there rise
A thousand beacons from the spark I bore.'
    'And who are those chained to the car?' 'The wise,

'The great, the unforgotten: they who wore
    Mitres and helms and crowns, or wreaths of light,   210
Signs of thought's empire over thought; their lore

    'Taught them not this—to know themselves; their might
Could not repress the mutiny within,
    And for the morn of truth they feigned, deep night

'Caught them ere evening.' 'Who is he with chin
    Upon his breast, and hands crossed on his chain?'
'The child of a fierce hour; he sought to win

    'The world, and lost all it did contain
Of greatness, in its hope destroyed; and more
    Of fame and peace than Virtue's self can gain   220

'Without the opportunity which bore
    Him on its eagle's pinion to the peak
From which a thousand climbers have before

    'Fall'n as Napoleon fell.'—I felt my cheek
Alter to see the great form pass away
    Whose grasp had left the giant world so weak

That every pigmy kicked it as it lay—
    And much I grieved to think how power and will
In opposition rule our mortal day—

    And why God made irreconcilable   230
Good and the means of good; and for despair
    I half disdained mine eye's desire to fill

With the spent vision of the times that were
    And scarce have ceased to be . . . 'Dost thou behold,'
Said then my guide, 'those spoilers spoiled, Voltaire,

   'Frederick, and Kant, Catharine, and Leopold,
Each hoary anarch, demagogue and sage
   Whose name the fresh world thinks already old,

'For in the battle Life and they did wage
   She remained conqueror—I was overcome   240
By my own heart alone, which neither age

   'Nor tears nor infamy nor now the tomb
Could temper to its object.'—'Let them pass',
   I cried, '—the world and its mysterious doom

'Is not so much more glorious than it was
   That I desire to worship those who drew
New figures on its false and fragile glass

   'As the old faded.'—'Figures ever new
Rise on the bubble, paint them how you may;
   We have but thrown, as those before us threw,   250

'Our shadows on it as it passed away.
   But mark, how chained to the triumphal chair
The mighty phantoms of an elder day—

   'All that is mortal of great Plato there
Expiates the joy and woe his master knew not—
   That star that ruled his doom was far too fair,

'And Life, where long that flower of Heaven grew not,
   Conquered the heart by love which gold or pain
Or age or sloth or slavery could subdue not;

   And near walk the   twain,   260
The tutor and his pupil, whom Dominion
   Followed as tame as vulture in a chain.—

'The world was darkened beneath either pinion
   Of him whom from the flock of conquerors
Fame singled as her thunderbearing minion;

   'The other long outlived both woes and wars,
Throned in the thoughts of men, and still had kept
   The jealous keys of truth's eternal doors

'If Bacon's spirit had not leapt
   Like lightning out of darkness; he compelled   270
The Proteus shape of Nature's as it slept

   'To wake and to unbar the caves that held
The treasure of the secrets of its reign.—
   See the great bards of old, who inly quelled

'The passions which they sung, as by their strain
   May well be known: their living melody
Tempers its own contagion to the vein

   'Of those who are infected with it—I
Have suffered what I wrote, or viler pain!—

   'And so my words were seeds of misery,   280
Even as the deeds of others.'—'Not as theirs,'
   I said—he pointed to a company

In which I recognized amid the heirs
   Of Caesar's crime, from him to Constantine,
The Anarchs old whose force and murderous snares

   Had founded many a sceptre-bearing line
And spread the plague of blood and gold abroad,
   And Gregory and John and men divine

Who rose like shadows between Man and God
   Till that eclipse, still hanging under Heaven,   290
Was worshipped by the world o'er which they strode

   For the true Sun it quenched.—'Their power was given
But to destroy,' replied the leader; 'I
   Am one of those who have created, even

'If it be but a world of agony.'—
   'Whence camest thou and whither goest thou?
How did thy course begin,' I said, 'and why?

   'Mine eyes are sick of this perpetual flow
Of people, and my heart of one sad thought.—
   Speak.'—'Whence I came, partly I seem to know,   300

'And how and by what paths I have been brought
   To this dread pass, methinks even thou mayst guess;
Why this should be, my mind can compass not,

'Whither the conqueror hurries me, still less.
But follow thou, and from spectator turn
   Actor or victim in this wretchedness,

'And what thou wouldst be taught I then may learn
   From thee. Now listen . . . In the April prime
When all the forest tips began to burn

'With kindling green, touched by the azure clime   310
Of the young year, I found myself asleep
   Under a mountain, which from unknown time

'Had yawned into a cavern high and deep,
   And from it came a gentle rivulet
Whose water like clear air in its calm sweep

'Bent the soft grass and kept for ever wet
The stems of the sweet flowers, and filled the grove
   With sound which whoso hear must needs forget

'All pleasure and all pain, all hate and love,
   Which they had known before that hour of rest: 320
A sleeping mother then would dream not of

'The only child who died upon her breast
At eventide, a king would mourn no more
   The crown of which his brow was dispossessed

'When the sun lingered o'er the Ocean floor
   To gild his rival's new prosperity:
Thou wouldst forget thus vainly to deplore

'Ills, which if ills, can find no cure from thee,
The thought of which no other sleep will quell,
   Nor other music blot from memory—   330

'So sweet and deep is the oblivious spell.
   Whether my life had been before that sleep
The Heaven which I imagine, or a Hell

'Like this harsh world in which I wake to weep,
I know not. I arose and for a space
   The scene of woods and waters seemed to keep,

'Though it was now broad day, a gentle trace
   Of light diviner than the common Sun
Sheds on the common Earth, but all the place

  'Was filled with many sounds woven into one   340
Oblivious melody, confusing sense
   Amid the gliding waves and shadows dun;

'And as I looked, the bright omnipresence
   Of morning through the orient cavern flowed,
And the Sun's image radiantly intense

  'Burned on the waters of the well that glowed
Like gold, and threaded all the forest maze
   With winding paths of emerald fire—there stood

'Amid the Sun, as he amid the blaze
   Of his own glory, on the vibrating   350
Floor of the fountain, paved with flashing rays,

  'A Shape all light, which with one hand did fling
Dew on the earth, as if she were the Dawn,
   Whose invisible rain forever seemed to sing

'A silver music on the mossy lawn,
   And still before her on the dusky grass
Iris her many-coloured scarf had drawn.—

  'In her right hand she bore a crystal glass
Mantling with bright Nepenthe;—the fierce splendour
   Fell from her as she moved under the mass   360

'Of the deep cavern, and with palms so tender
   Their tread broke not the mirror of its billow,
Glided along the river, and did bend her

  'Head under the dark boughs, till like a willow
Her fair hair swept the bosom of the stream
   That whispered with delight to be their pillow.—

'As one enamoured is upborne in dream
   O'er lily-paven lakes mid silver mist
To wondrous music, so this Shape might seem

'Partly to tread the waves with feet which kissed   370
The dancing foam, partly to glide along
   The airs that roughened the moist amethyst,

'Or the slant morning beams that fell among
   The trees, or the soft shadows of the trees;
And her feet ever to the ceaseless song

'Of leaves and winds and waves and birds and bees
And falling drops moved in a measure new
   Yet sweet, as on the summer evening breeze

'Up from the lake a shape of golden dew
   Between two rocks, athwart the rising moon,   380
Dances i'the wind, where eagle never flew.—

'And still her feet, no less than the sweet tune
To which they moved, seemed as they moved, to blot
   The thoughts of him who gazed on them; and soon

'All that was, seemed as if it had been not,
   As if the gazer's mind was strewn beneath
Her feet like embers, and she, thought by thought,

'Trampled its fires into the dust of death,
As Day upon the threshold of the east
   Treads out the lamps of night, until the breath   390

'Of darkness reillumines even the least
   Of Heaven's living eyes—like Day she came,
Making the night a dream; and ere she ceased

'To move, as one between desire and shame
Suspended, I said: "If, as it doth seem,
   Thou comest from the realm without a name

'Into this valley of perpetual dream,
   Show whence I came, and where I am, and why—
Pass not away upon the passing stream."'

' "Arise and quench thy thirst," was her reply.   400
And as a shut lily, stricken by the wand
    Of dewy morning's vital alchemy,

'I rose; and, bending at her sweet command,
    Touched with faint lips the cup she raised,
And suddenly my brain became as sand

'Where the first wave had more than half erased
The track of deer on desert Labrador,
    Whilst the empty wolf from which they fled amazed

'Leaves his stamp visibly upon the shore
    Until the second bursts—so on my sight   410
Burst a new Vision never seen before;

'And the fair Shape waned in the coming light,
As veil by veil the silent splendour drops
    From Lucifer, amid the chrysolite

'Of sunrise, ere it strike the mountain tops—
    And as the presence of that fairest planet,
Although unseen, is felt by one who hopes

'That his day's path may end as he began it
In that star's smile, whose light is like the scent
    Of a jonquil when evening breezes fan it,   420

'Or the soft note in which his dear lament
    The Brescian shepherd breathes, or the caress
That turned his weary slumber to content—

'So knew I in that light's severe excess
The presence of that Shape which on the stream
    Moved, as I moved along the wilderness,

'More dimly than a day-appearing dream,
    The ghost of a forgotten form of sleep,
A light from Heaven whose half-extinguished beam

'Through the sick day in which we wake to weep   430
Glimmers, forever sought, forever lost.—
    So did that shape its obscure tenour keep

'Beside my path, as silent as a ghost;
    But the new Vision, and its cold bright car,
With solemn speed and stunning music crossed

    'The forest, and as if from some dread war
Triumphantly returning, the loud million
    Fiercely extolled the fortune of her star.

'A moving arch of victory the vermilion
    And green and azure plumes of Iris had   440
Built high over her wind-winged pavilion,

    'And underneath, aetherial glory clad
The wilderness, and far before her flew
    The tempest of the splendour which forbade

'Shadow to fall from leaf or stone;—the crew
    Seemed in that light like atomies that dance
Within a sunbeam.—Some upon the new

    'Embroidery of flowers that did enhance
The grassy vesture of the desert, played,
    Forgetful of the chariot's swift advance;   450

'Others stood gazing till within the shade
    Of the great mountain its light left them dim.—
Others outspeeded it, and others made

    'Circles around it like the clouds that swim
Round the high moon in a bright sea of air;
    And more did follow, with exulting hymn,

'The chariot and the captives fettered there;
    But all like bubbles on an eddying flood
Fell into the same track at last and were

    'Borne onward.—I among the multitude   460
Was swept; me sweetest flowers delayed not long,
    Me not the shadow nor the solitude,

'Me not the falling stream's Lethean song,
    Me, not the phantom of that early form
Which moved upon its motion,—but among

'The thickest billows of the living storm
I plunged, and bared my bosom to the clime
   Of that cold light, whose airs too soon deform.—

'Before the chariot had begun to climb
   The opposing steep of that mysterious dell,   470
Behold a wonder worthy of the rhyme

   'Of him whom from the lowest depths of Hell
Through every Paradise and through all glory
   Love led serene, and who returned to tell

'In words of hate and awe the wondrous story
   How all things are transfigured, except Love;
For deaf as is a sea which wrath makes hoary

   'The world can hear not the sweet notes that move
The sphere whose light is melody to lovers—
   A wonder worthy of his rhyme: the grove   480

'Grew dense with shadows to its inmost covers,
   The earth was grey with phantoms, and the air
Was peopled with dim forms, as when there hovers

   'A flock of vampire-bats before the glare
Of the tropic sun, bringing ere evening
   Strange night upon some Indian isle,—thus were

'Phantoms diffused around, and some did fling
   Shadows of shadows, yet unlike themselves,
Behind them; some like eaglets on the wing

   'Were lost in the white blaze; others like elves   490
Danced in a thousand unimagined shapes
   Upon the sunny streams and grassy shelves;

'And others sate chattering like restless apes
   On vulgar hands and over shoulders leaped;
Some made a cradle of the ermined capes

   'Of kingly mantles; some upon the tiar
Of pontiffs sate like vultures; others played
   Within the crown which girt with empire

'A baby's or an idiot's brow, and made
   Their nests in it; the old anatomies   500
Sate hatching their bare brood under the shade

   'Of demons' wings, and laughed from their dead eyes
To reassume the delegated power
   Arrayed in which these worms did monarchize

'Who make this earth their charnel.—Others more
   Humble, like falcons sate upon the fist
Of common men, and round their heads did soar,

   'Or like small gnats and flies as thick as mist
On evening marshes thronged about the brow
   Of lawyer, statesman, priest and theorist;   510

'And others like discoloured flakes of snow
   On fairest bosoms and the sunniest hair
Fell, and were melted by the youthful glow

   'Which they extinguished; for like tears, they were
A veil to those from whose faint lids they rained
   In drops of sorrow.—I became aware

'Of whence those forms proceeded which thus stained
   The track in which we moved; after brief space
From every form the beauty slowly waned,

   'From every firmest limb and fairest face   520
The strength and freshness fell like dust, and left
   The action and the shape without the grace

'Of life; the marble brow of youth was cleft
   With care, and in the eyes where once hope shone
Desire like a lioness bereft

   'Of its last cub, glared ere it died; each one
Of that great crowd sent forth incessantly
   These shadows, numerous as the dead leaves blown

'In Autumn evening from a poplar tree.—
   Each, like himself and like each other were,   530
At first, but soon distorted, seemed to be

'Obscure clouds moulded by the casual air;
And of this stuff the car's creative ray
   Wrought all the busy phantoms fluttering there

'As the Sun shapes the clouds—thus, on the way,
   Mask after mask fell from the countenance
And form of all, and long before the day

   'Was old, the joy which waked like Heaven's glance
The sleepers in the oblivious valley, died,
   And some grew weary of the ghastly dance   540

'And fell, as I have fallen, by the wayside,
   Those soonest from whose forms most shadows passed
And least of strength and beauty did abide.'—

   'Then, what is Life?' I said . . . the cripple cast
His eye upon the car which now had rolled
   Onward, as if that look must be the last,

And answered: 'Happy those for whom the fold
   Of

TO JANE

   The keen stars were twinkling
And the fair moon was rising among them,
     Dear Jane.
   The guitar was tinkling
But the notes were not sweet till you sung them
     Again.—

   As the moon's soft splendour
O'er the faint cold starlight of Heaven
     Is thrown—
   So your voice most tender   10
To the strings without soul had then given
     Its own.

The stars will awaken,
Though the moon sleep a full hour later,
        Tonight;
    No leaf will be shaken
While the dews of your melody scatter
        Delight.

    Though the sound overpowers,
Sing again, with your dear voice revealing   20
        A tone
    Of some world far from ours,
Where music and moonlight and feeling
        Are one.

FRAGMENT: LINES WRITTEN IN THE BAY OF LERICI

Bright wanderer, fair coquette of Heaven,
To whom alone it has been given
To change and be adored for ever,
Envy not this dim world, for never
But once within its shadow grew
One fair as [thou], but far more true.—
She left me at the silent time
When the moon had ceased to climb
The azure dome of Heaven's steep,
And like an albatross asleep,   10
Balanced on her wings of light,
Hovered in the purple night,
Ere she sought her Ocean nest
In the chambers of the west.—
She left me, and I stayed alone
Thinking over every tone,
Which though now silent to the ear
The enchanted heart could hear
Like notes which die when born, but still
Haunt the echoes of the hill: 20
And feeling ever—o too much—
The soft vibrations of her touch,

As if her gentle hand even now
Lightly trembled on my brow;
And thus although she absent were
Memory gave me all of her
That even fancy dares to claim.—
Her presence had made weak and tame
All passions, and I lived alone
In the time which is our own;   30
The past and future were forgot
As they had been, and would be, not.—
But soon, the guardian angel gone,
The demon reassumed his throne
In my faint heart . . . I dare not speak
My thoughts; but thus disturbed and weak
I sate and watched the vessels glide
Along the Ocean bright and wide,
Like spirit-wingèd chariots sent
O'er some serenest element   40
To ministrations strange and far;
As if to some Elysian star
They sailed for drink to medicine
Such sweet and bitter pain as mine.—
And the wind that winged their flight
From the land came fresh and light,
And the scent of sleeping flowers
And the coolness of the hours
Of dew, and the sweet warmth of day
Was scattered o'er the twinkling bay;   50
And the fisher with his lamp
And spear, about the low rocks damp
Crept, and struck the fish who came
To worship the delusive flame:
Too happy, they whose pleasure sought
Extinguishes all sense and thought
Of the regret that pleasure [   ],
Seeking life alone, not peace.

NOTES

Abbreviations: ·*D.P.* = *Defence of Poetry*; *H.I.B.* = *Hymn to Intellectual Beauty*; *J.M.* = *Julian and Maddalo*; *L.* = *Letters*; *M.A.* = *Mask of Anarchy*; *O.L.* = *Ode to Liberty*; *O.W.W.* = *Ode to the West Wind*; *P.U.* = *Prometheus Unbound*; *T.L.* = *Triumph of Life*. Prose references are to the edition by D. L. Clark (Albuquerque, New Mexico, 1966).

Hymn to Intellectual Beauty. Written late June 1816 (conceived during a voyage round Lake Geneva with Lord Byron). Published in *The Examiner* (19 January 1817) and with *Rosalind and Helen* (1819). This heterodox hymn substitutes an abstract ideal for the received notion of divinity, and Love, Hope and Self-esteem for the orthodox virtues; yet its language and poetic conventions are those of religious and visionary poetry. The mysterious Power to which Shelley dedicates himself is recognized through intuition, revelation and faith; it is manifested not in the beauty of the natural world but in the mind of man (hence it is an *intellectual* beauty). Yet the divine can only be adumbrated through images drawn from the sensible world and Shelley, like all religious poets, employs analogies from nature. The poem owes something to Spenser's 'An Hymne to Heavenly Beautie' and to Wordsworth's Immortality Ode.

27. *God and ghosts*: originally printed as *Demon, Ghost* (which is less blasphemously specific).
37. *Self-esteem*: a proper valuation of one's own true worth (as opposed to self-contempt).
58. Cf. Wordsworth's 'To the Small Celandine', ii. 17-18.
60. The moment of religious revelation; this ecstasy is closely allied to those of poetic inspiration and of sexual pleasure.
67. Cf. 'Il Penseroso' l. 87.
70. *dark slavery*: subjection to poisonous names and false notions of divinity (whose consequences are social and political as much as spiritual).
84. A significant variation both on the usual injunction to fear God and keep his commandments and on Christ's 'Thou shalt love the Lord thy God with all thy heart . . . and thy neighbour as thyself'. The new emphasis is on self-knowledge and self-control as a realistic basis for charity and social concern.

Mont Blanc. Written July 1816, dated 23 July by Shelley (the day of the expedition rather than of the completed poem). Published in *History of a Six Weeks' Tour* (1817). For the background, see Shelley's letter to

Peacock (*L.* i. 495-502). Shelley's poem should be read in the context of Coleridge's 'Hymn before Sun-rise in the Vale of Chamouni' (1802; 1809) which celebrates God in his mountain-creation. Coleridge exclaimed: 'Who *would* be, who *could* be an Atheist in this valley of wonders!' On 23 July Shelley described himself in the hotel register at Chamonix as a lover of mankind, a democrat and an atheist; this was a calculated response to the customary attitude represented by Coleridge. Shelley believed that man must learn from nature not to subject himself to false and crippling notions of divinity, which had political as well as spiritual consequences (cf. *P.U.*). Consequently, the poem is centred on the relations between the perceiving mind and the external universe. Shelley suggests that man has imposed his own fantasies on the natural scene, whose only moral significance is its complete detachment from the will of a creator God.

1-11.   The river Arve flowing through its ravine supplies a metaphor for the relations between subject and object; with great compression, Shelley begins by describing mind in terms of the natural scene, which is not described in its own right till 11.

6.   *half its own*: because it renders and receives (see 38-40).

27.   *strange sleep*: apparent immobility in which 'thou [the ravine] dost lie'.

36ff.   The collaborative relationship between the external world and the perceiving mind. *separate fantasy*: cf. 'All was as much our own as if we had been the creators of such impressions in the minds of others, as now occupied our own' (*L.* i. 497).

43.   *that*: generally interpreted as the legion of wild thoughts. *thou*: the ravine.

47-8.   The sense is ambiguous, perhaps deliberately so. *Either* these images are derived from a Universe of Things outside the poet, perhaps from a Universal Mind — in which case the existence of the ravine in Shelley's mind depends on the permissive grace of a mysterious force; *or* they are maintained in existence by Shelley's own mind.

53.   *unfurled*: spread out (thus cutting off Shelley's vision).

71-4.   References to widely held theories on the volcanic origin of mountains.

76ff.   There are two ways of interpreting the data of this natural scene: one leads to *awful doubt* (perhaps a belief in dark divinities such as the Ahrimanes of the Zoroastrian system or perhaps a fear that everything is merely random), the other leads to a calm *faith* that the fierce presence of the mountain is unconnected with the designs of any divinity. Thus, the message of the mountain, if properly understood, can help to repeal those repressive systems of politics and religion (*codes of fraud and woe*) which depend on false notions of deity. *But for such faith* (79) is puzzling and may be the result of a mistake in copying; it has been suggested, though not very convincingly, that Shelley intended *But* as an adverb meaning 'only'. *But for* appears in the MS. draft which originally read *In such a faith*, as did the intermediate copy in Shelley's hand.

86.   *daedal*: artful, carefully wrought.
96ff.   Essentially the Epicurean doctrine expounded by Lucretius in *De Rerum Natura*. The natural scene can teach the attentive observer that no divinity is present in this creation; if it does exist, it dwells apart, as unconcerned as the mountain peak.
142-4.   The concluding emphasis is on the power of the human mind; but Shelley ends characteristically with a question rather than a statement.

Verses Written on Receiving a Celandine in a Letter from England.   Written July 1816. This poem records Shelley's disillusionment with the defection of Wordsworth from the ranks of the radicals. Wordsworth accepted a Government post as Distributor of Stamps in 1813 (hence the *impious gold* of 39), celebrated the Battle of Waterloo and invoked Carnage as *God's daughter* (43-8). Wordsworth had addressed three poems to the Small Celandine; Shelley makes ironical use of the pattern of the third which discovers in the Celandine an emblem of the human condition involuntarily subject to the process of ageing. The poem also acknowledges the true greatness of Wordsworth which was a positive influence on *H.I.B.* and 'Mont Blanc' (written in June and July 1816). For a later view of Wordsworth, see *Peter Bell the Third.*
2.   *blue*: the Celandine is, in fact, yellow.
5-6.   *primose . . . violet*: cf. 'To the Small Celandine', i. 4-5.
26.   *familiar*: closely related.
30.   Like Milton after the Restoration (*Paradise Lost* (*P.L.*) vii. 25-6).
47.   *left*: having been left (ablative absolute construction).
53.   *They . . . not*: his hopes do not need his sanction nor his foes his condemnation.
56.   *overlive*: survive.

To the Lord Chancellor.   Probably written in March or April 1817. Published posthumously (1839). After the suicide of Harriet, Shelley was refused custody of his two children in a celebrated hearing before Lord Eldon, on the alleged grounds of immorality and atheism (*Queen Mab* was cited to show that he 'blasphemously derided the Truth of the Christian revelation'). Shelley was confirmed in the view that he was on a trial as a critic of the contemporary power-structure. He even suspected that he might be forbidden the custody of his son by Mary. He did not publish the poem: as Mary said, it was 'not written to exhibit the pangs of distress to the public' but was 'the spontaneous outburst of a man who brooded over his wrongs and woes'. This fluent example of the flyting may have been influenced by the curse in *Manfred* (Act I) which Shelley particularly admired (*L.* ii. 283).
4.   *Masked*: cf. *M.A.* in which Eldon also appears. *a buried Form*: the Star Chamber.
19.   *prove*: feel, experience.
28.   The crux of the case was the children's education.

33ff. *hireling*: the children were to be looked after by specially appointed guardians, who would instruct them in the religious faith which Shelley had so passionately criticized in *Queen Mab*.

43. *which must be their error*: which will inevitably cause them to form false opinions.

51-2. Eldon was famous for weeping on the bench (cf. *M.A.*).

Ozymandias. Written late 1817. Published in *The Examiner* (11 January 1818) under the name *Glirastes* (dormouse or dormouse as preacher). Ozymandias is the Greek name for Rameses II (1301-1234 B.C.).

1. *a traveller*: conceivably Walter Coulson, editor of *The Traveller*, who visited the Shelleys in late 1817, but more probably a reference to Robert Pococke's *A Description of the East* (1743) which portrays several statues of Rameses and of Memnon in various stages of disintegration.

6-8. The passions depicted in the statue survive both the sculptor's hand and the heart of the pharaoh who gave them life. *mocked*: imitated (perhaps with a hint of silent irony).

10-11. This inscription is usually traced back to Diodorus Siculus; in fact, it was a historical commonplace.

Stanzas Written in Dejection, near Naples. Written December 1818. Published posthumously (1824). In a letter of the same month Shelley recorded that he had 'depression enough of spirits & not good health'; the main causes were the death of his daughter in September and the subsequent estrangement from Mary — but dejection was a recurrent condition with the Romantic poets.

4. orig. *The purple atmosphere of light*; the colour is recorded by Shelley in his letters and by Turner in his water-colours.

10-11. Cf. 'We set off an hour after sunrise one radiant morning in a little boat, there was not a cloud in the sky nor a wave upon the sea which was so translucent that you could see the hollow caverns clothed with the glaucous sea-moss, & the leaves & branches of those delicate weeds that pave the unequal bottom of the water' (*L.* ii. 61).

22. *the sage*: possibly Socrates or Diogenes (since 23 was originally *Who lived alone and called it pleasure*).

Julian and Maddalo. Begun probably in September 1818 and finished by 15 August 1819, when it was sent to Hunt for anonymous publication. Published posthumously (1824). The poem had its origins in a meeting and conversation between Shelley and Byron at Venice on 23 August 1818. Julian is based on Shelley, Maddalo on Byron, while the madman 'is also in some degree a painting from nature, but, with respect to time and place, ideal'. It has been variously suggested that the madman was based on Tasso (the subject of an unfinished play by Shelley) or even on Shelley himself, whose recent marital disagreements may be alluded to covertly in the enigmatic monologue. Yet this is irrelevant to an understanding of the poem since Shelley deliberately avoids specificity. Indeed, although there is a sense in which the poem can be seen as an argument between the authors of two very different poems on the subject of Prometheus, there is also a sense in which Shelley is arguing against himself. He instructed his publisher not to print *J.M.* with *Prometheus* because, 'It is an attempt in a different style, in which I am not yet sure of myself, *a sermo pedestris* way of treating human nature quite opposed to the idealism of that drama.' (Cf. *L.* ii. 108.)

Preface.   *concentered*: Byron's Prometheus, who is more selfish and less hopeful than Shelley's, finds in his defiant resistance his own *concentered recompense.*

48-52.   Cf. Shelley's critique of the Fourth Canto of *Childe Harold*, which he regarded as the product of Byronic self-contempt rather than misanthropy (*L.* ii. 58). *eagle spirit*: according to legend, the eagle can look directly at the sun without being blinded. Byron is too narrowly concerned with self and, like Coleridge in the *Letter to Maria Gisborne*, is blinded by his own 'internal lightning'.

88.   'The gondolas themselves are things of a most romantic & picturesque appearance; I can only compare them to moths of which a coffin might have been the chrysalis. They are hung with black, & painted black, & carpeted with grey . . .' (*L.* ii. 42.)

92.   Cf. *The Tempest*, IV. i. 151.

117.   Shelley could not swim, as Byron would have known since they were together in a boat during a storm on Lake Geneva in 1816.

170-6.   The basic premise of *P. U.* where regenerated man emerges 'free from guilt or pain, / Which were, for his will made or suffered them' (III. iv. 198-9). See also *O.L.*, 241-5.

173.   The punctuation is intended (similar constructions are common in Shelley). The sense is: We might be as happy, high, majestical as in our wildest dreams.

188.   *those . . . philosophy*: the Greek philosophers, who dispassionately analysed the great problems of existence before the Christian Church inhibited philosophical and theological speculation.

204.   Cf. 'there is some soul of goodness in things evil, / Would men observingly distil it out' (*Henry V*, IV. i. 3-4).

238.   *peculiar*: personal, relating exclusively to himself. Cf. 449-50.

244.   *humourist*: a man subject to humours; fantastical, whimsical.

320.   See the interrogation in *P. U.*, II. iv.

354-7.   Another premise which is central to *P. U.*

433.   *cearedst*: sealed, shut up (like a corpse in a coffin). Cf. 614; *Adonais*, 453-5. *my memory*: the memory of me.

471.   He has been changed not by his own inconstancy but by her reluctance to love him in return.

516.   *in his society*: in company with him.

536.   *nice*: refined. *gentleness*: although the Maniac *is* an inoffensive creature, gentleness here specifically implies the behaviour of a gentleman.

542.   *in measure*: in metrical form.

544-6.   Though this applies to a number of Shelley's own poems, he believed that 'Poetry is the record of the best and happiest moments of the happiest and best minds'.

555-6.   Literature and art are both products of the poetical faculty and often flourish simultaneously, as in classical Athens and Renaissance Italy.

561.   *know myself*: the famous Greek ideal of self-knowledge.

Prometheus Unbound.   Written autumn 1818 (Act I), spring 1819 (Acts II and III), autumn 1819 (Act IV). Published 1820. Shelley's play takes as its starting point the *Prometheus Bound* of Aeschylus but, in spite of incidental debts, is a highly original and independent creation. The first Act of Shelley's play comes closest to Aeschylus: it focuses on Prometheus, the benefactor of mankind and founder of human civilization, who has stolen fire from Heaven for which offence he has been nailed to a rock in the Caucasus and tortured physically and mentally. Aeschylus' play was part of a trilogy of which the other plays have not survived; however, we do know that in the final play Prometheus came to terms with Jupiter. Shelley could not accept such a compromise and provided his own version since Aeschylus had 'left the tale untold', that is, had failed to realize the best potential of his subject. In Shelley's version, heroic resistance is not sufficient; Prometheus is fortified by the love of Asia, who is the central figure of Act II. *P.U.* is a response to the grim political realities of the years between the failure of the French Revolution and the passing of the Reform Bill; like its predecessor, *Laon and Cythna*, it is a deliberate 'experiment on the temper of the public mind as to how far a thirst for a happier condition of moral and political society survives ... the tempests which have shaken the age in which we live'. Shelley's shrewd and carefully argued pamphlet *A Philosophical View of Reform* shows that he was well aware of 'the difficult and unbending realities of actual life'; the 'beautiful idealism' of his play was dictated by the needs of the situation, and by his artistic conscience. Shelley's great achievement was to translate politics into moral and psychological terms; while his play obviously deals with the external world of politics and public events, there is a sense in which it can be regarded as taking place in the mind of Prometheus. Jupiter, for example, is a typical tyrant but he is also a projection of the darker forces within Prometheus himself. When Prometheus has achieved a proper moral and psychological equilibrium, Jupiter disappears.

Epigraph.   'Do you hear these things, Amphiaraus, hidden under the earth?' (a line from *Epigoni*, a lost play by Aeschylus quoted by Cicero). Amphiaraus was a seer who became an oracular god; the context of the story concerns attitudes towards suffering. Here the question is directed towards Aeschylus.

Preface.   pernicious casuistry: cf. Preface to *The Cenci. a Scotch philosopher*: Robert Forsyth in *The Principles of Moral Science* (1805). *Paley and Malthus*: authors respectively of *The Principles of Moral and Political Philosophy* (1785) and of *An Essay on the Principle of Population* (1798). *systematical history*: such as *A Philosophical View of Reform*.

Act I. Stage directions. Indian Caucasus: Indian is Shelley's addition, because the Hindu Kush mountains were thought to have been the cradle of civilization. *morning slowly breaks*: The setting is similar to the bleak Alpine world of 'Mont Blanc'. As the revolutionary day dawns gradually, man's environment is reclaimed from the snows and ice and becomes a paradise on earth.

1. *Daemons*: spirits intermediary between man and God.
2. *One*: Prometheus (or possible Demogorgon).
6-8. Jupiter is here associated with the vindictive God of Christianity who rules over men's hearts and minds by a system of rewards and punishments based on expectation of an after-life. *hecatombs*: large sacrifices. *self-contempt*: a failure to acknowledge one's own true human dignity.
9. *eyeless in hate*: the syntax is ambiguous — rightly so, since when Prometheus responds to Jupiter with hatred they become identified.
59. *recall*: remember *and* revoke. Prometheus chooses to undergo a process of psychotherapy whereby he can relive the past and then cast out hatred.
65. *burning without beams*: 'Beyond our atmosphere the sun would appear a rayless orb of fire in the midst of a black concave' (Note to *Queen Mab*).
83. Colour is not inherent in objects but is a property of light.
121. *frore*: frozen.
124. *informs*: which gives you characteristic life and shape.
135. *inorganic*: associated with mortality and therefore incomprehensible to an immortal, like Prometheus.
137. *And love*: almost certainly means *And lovest*.
141. *wheel of pain*: the earth's axis, oblique until man achieves his harmonious paradise; here suggesting the wheel on which Ixion was tortured in Hades.
192. *Zoroaster*: Persian sage (Magus) whose religious philosophy posited a world divided between the powers of light and darkness. Much of the mythological framework and symbolism of *P.U.* has Zoroastrian associations (see Curran). To meet one's double is traditionally a sign of impending death: no such incident has been discovered in the life of Zoroaster himself but the strange spiritual manifestation is close to his philosophy, which posited the existence of Fravashis or daemonic forces similar to guardian spirits.
207. *Demogorgon*: a crucial figure in this play. Notoriously hard to define, he seems to represent the 'voiceless and invisible Consequence' (Aeschylus), an amoral force which links cause with effect.
212. *Hades*: lord of the underworld. *Typhon*: a monster.
216. *shades*: the ghosts who people the underworld.
229ff. *sweet sister's*: Ione and Panthea are the sisters of Asia, intermediaries between her and Prometheus.
262ff. It is important to remember that these are the words of Prometheus

spoken by the phantasm of Jupiter. What is involved is more than a dramatic irony: in his hating mood, Prometheus is identified with Jupiter.

273-4.   Man imposes tyrannies on himself, and may revoke them.

289.   Like the poisoned tunic given to Hercules by Nessus' wife.

292-3.   Like Satan in *P.L.* (i. 210-11).

306-11.   The Earth has failed to recognize that the true victory is to abstain from perpetuating the cycle of violence.

345.   Probably a word-play on Phlegethon and Cocytus, two streams in Hades (though Shelley's punctuation is ambiguous).

347-9.   After delivering Thebes from the Sphinx, Oedipus unwittingly married his mother and cursed his sons, so that they killed one another.

371.   *a secret*: that if Jupiter has a son by Thetis, he will be greater than his father. This is a crucial factor in the Greek original. In Shelley Jupiter is brought down by other means, though Demogorgon, who activates his fall, could be seen as the inevitable offspring of his actions.

377.   *fane*: temple.

387.   *thought-executing*: probably those who execute his commands, though there may be implications of efficiency and of repressive ruthlessness.

398-9.   Damocles was compelled to dine under a sword suspended by a single hair to illustrate the insecurity of kingly power.

479.   *lidless*: unclosed, never sleeping.

492-4.   The tyranny of Jupiter is replaced by a properly constituted internal monarchy; Shelley never argues for anarchy or total freedom from controls. Cf. 'Sonnet to the Republic of Benevento'.

530-1.   Dealings at summit conferences such as the Congress of Vienna (1814-15).

539.   'The Furies having mingled in a strange dance divide, and in the background is seen a plain covered with burning cities' (stage direction in MS.).

546-63.   The wars of religion are a sad perversion of the humane and benevolent doctrines of Christ, with whom Prometheus is associated (563).

567-77.   The French Revolution, from its hopeful beginnings (*disenchanted*: delivered from evil spells) to the Terror and the consequent despair in the possibilities of democracy.

609.   *hooded ounces*: hunting leopards, hooded before they are unleashed.

618-31.   The point of this temptation is that it is a true report. However, the condition is not necessarily permanent; there is still hope because Prometheus can rise above apathy and despair. *ravin*: prey, spoil. *they do*: the words of Christ, asking forgiveness for his persecutors; here used insidiously as an argument for despair.

658-61.   The spirits rise like angels from within individual human minds and help to create a climate of opinion, a spirit of the age (cf. Preface). The first four present visions of hope, the fifth is transitional, and the sixth suggests those misgivings and relapses into melancholy which can waylay even the optimistic.

737-51. The Poet of 'beautiful idealisms' transcends the specific realities of the everyday world (e.g. as in 'To a Sky-lark'). This is the highest kind of poetry; the yellow bees have their place, too, in poems such as *J.M.*

765-6. Love (associated with the illuminating power of electricity) has the crest of Venus on his helmet.

772-9. Based on a passage in Plato's *Symposium* (195) which describes how Love 'dwells within, and treads on the softest of existing things'.

Act II Scene IV. This Act concentrates on Asia. In this scene she visits Demogorgon in what appears to be the crater of a volcano; later, at the appropriate moment, he will erupt and overthrow Jupiter. The location is traditional to the oracular earth-spirit; the visit to the underworld is a recurring feature in epic poetry.

19ff. The image is based on the sight of about 300 fettered criminals hoeing the weeds in St Peter's Square (*L.* ii. 93-4).

32ff. Based, with significant differences, on *Prometheus Bound*, 196-254 and 442-506.

33-4. Saturn presided over the Golden Age but, since he can also be identified with Time, this state of happiness is far from permanent. Shelley had little time for Golden Ages or noble savages because 'uncivilized man is the most pernicious and miserable of beings'.

52. *unseasonable*; because in the Golden Age there had been perpetual spring.

61. Homeric tranquillizer; antidote to Circe's potions; unfading flower.

78-9. Man's divinity is emphasized by his Christ-like ability to walk on the water.

80. *mocked*: created a superior version of (cf. I. 747-8).

126ff. Now that Asia has acknowledged the power of Love, the destined Hour has come. The two Spirits represent two aspects of the revolutionary change which is about to take place: the necessary harshness involved in the fall of Jupiter and the hope of a more radiant future.

157. *ivory shell*: Asia's chariot associates her with Venus.

Act III Scene IV. Jupiter has fallen and this Act is largely devoted to reports on the regenerated world, external effects described by the Spirit of the Earth, internal by the Spirit of the Hour.

22. *a sound*: From Scene III we know this sound was produced by the Spirit of the Hour who breathed into a shell given to Asia by Proteus. Cf. the trumpet of the Resurrection in *O.W.W.*

47-50. The nightshade is no longer poisonous and the halcyons, who are traditionally associated with calm weather, have turned vegetarian.

57. *glozed on*: commented on, glossed.

70. *those foul shapes*: evil takes on many forms, all of which are at odds with 'the overruling Spirit of the collective energy of the moral and material world' (*God*).

75-8. Some editors refer to executions for adultery but Shelley was probably thinking of the sacrifice of Iphigenia by her father Agamemnon; Lucretius had described the scene vividly, concluding with the bitter cry *Tantum religio potuit suadere malorum?* (*De Rerum Natura*, I. 80-101).

unreclaiming: unprotesting and, by their passivity, failing to assist in the reclamation of the earth from its present barrenness (Shelley had helped to reclaim land from the sea at Tremadoc in Wales).

80.   *the painted veil*: those ephemeral illusions which, like the curtain in a theatre, interpose between man and reality.

90-4.   Shelley's regenerated man is still subject to certain limitations (this realism should be compared to the Utopian visions of Godwin and Condorcet). By a continuous effort of will, man may transcend guilt or pain, though he is not exempt from them. *intense*: probably means very blue, though with a suggestion of eager aspiration. *inane*: empty space (as in Lucretius and Milton).

Act IV. In this final speech, which concludes the rejoicings in which the whole universe takes part, Demogorgon propagates the Shelleyan virtues, which owe much to the Sermon on the Mount but are subtly different.

2.   *Earth-born's*: Prometheus'. *Heaven's despotism*: Jupiter and his power.

14.   *serpent*: traditionally the *ouroboros* (a snake devouring its own tail) is associated with Eternity. Here the serpent is seen as a destructive force (like the Dragon of Revelation) which can be kept at bay only by the continuous exercise of the virtues listed by Demogorgon. Jupiter is always potential unless we can learn from the example of Prometheus.

The Mask of Anarchy.   Written September 1819 and sent for publication in *The Examiner* on the 23rd. Published posthumously (1832). On 16 August 1819 Henry Hunt was addressing a crowd of 60,000 working people in Manchester on the subject of parliamentary reform when the Yeomanry attempted to arrest him. In the ensuing confusion, they were joined by a detachment of regular cavalry who charged the crowd: the toll was fifteen dead and 500 injured (both approximate figures). Because it took place on St Peter's Fields this unhappy incident became known as 'Peterloo' (with ironical reference to Wellington's success on another field). Shelley first heard the news when he read the issues of *The Examiner* for 22 and 29 August: 'These are, as it were, the distant thunders of the terrible storm which is approaching. The tyrants here, as in the French Revolution, have first shed blood. May their execrable lessons be learnt with equal docility!' Here Shelley adumbrates the doctrine of passive resistance which is central to his poem: it is essential that the reformers should not become involved in the fruitless cycle of violence but that they can see 'in the frank & spirited union of the advocates for Liberty, an asylum against every form in which oppression can be brought to bear against them'. The *Mask* of the title refers to the allegorical pageant, the masquerade which gives the poem its basic shape; it also suggests the impostures and deceits of authority (in the first of his *Examiner* articles Leigh Hunt had referred to 'the Men in the Brazen Masks of power' while Shelley himself described the monarchy as 'merely the mask' of the power of the rich). *Anarchy* suggests that despotic power is allied to chaos rather than to true authority. This poem is 'of the exoteric species' and was specifically intended for *The Examiner*; Leigh

Hunt, who had suffered enough for his frankness, preferred not to publish it till after the Reform Bill had been passed.

1-4. Shelley is following the conventions of visionary poetry. Cf. the opening of *T.L.*

6. *Castlereagh*: Foreign Secretary, associated by the radicals with war and oppression, particularly in Ireland and in the Napoleonic Wars.

8. *Seven bloodhounds*: 'the seven states (Austria, Bourbon France, Portugal, Prussia, Russia, Spain, Sweden) which, with England, agreed in 1815 to postpone indefinitely the abolition of the slave trade' (Matthews).

15. The Lord Chancellor in his robes (ermine was a symbol of purity). Eldon was famous for weeping in public (he could 'outweep the crocodile') yet such displays were proved meaningless by his judgments in Chancery where, far from suffering the little children to come unto him, he outraged human feeling by separating them from their parents. In 1817 he had refused Shelley the custody of his two children by Harriet (see notes on 'To the Lord Chancellor').

24. *Sidmouth*: Home Secretary, who raised large sums of money to build churches for the industrial poor, whom he repressed through the activities of the police and a complex network of spies, informers and *agents provocateurs*.

29. *spies*: see note to 24 and to 'England in 1819'.

30-33. 'And I looked, and behold a pale horse; and his name that sat on him was Death, and Hell followed with him. And power was given unto them over the fourth part of the earth, to kill with sword, and with hunger, and with the beasts of the earth' (Revelation vi 6:8).

49. For the psychological effects of desolation, see *P.U.*, I. 772-9.

88. Hope and Despair can be hard to distinguish. One of the temptations facing reformers after the apparent failure of the French Revolution was to surrender their ideals; like Prometheus they had to learn 'To hope, till hope creates / From its own wreck the thing it contemplates'.

90. *Time*: In the course of history many hopes of political reform have been frustrated; short of bloody conflict, one is still left. Shelley concretizes his vision of history forever aspiring towards something better in the figure of one of the oppressed poor.

110. *a Shape*: this has been identified both as Liberty and as Public Enlightenment (Hunt) but Shelley deliberately avoids specificity. The Shape is associated with a snake (in Shelley the principle of good resisting evil) and with Venus (the planet of Love). It bears obvious similarities to the glorious phantom in 'England in 1819'.

145. *accent*: speech, utterance.

176ff. *the Ghost of Gold*: paper money (Banknotina in *Swellfoot the Tyrant*). Cf. *Peter Bell the Third*, 166-71.

180ff. A paper currency might eventually force the people (i) to lose control of their own will and (ii) to indulge the desire to fight back — two serious infringements of Shelley's ethical ideals.

197-208. 'The foxes have holes, and the birds of the air have nests; but the
Son of man hath not where to lay his head' (Matthew 8:20).

220. *Fame*: Rumour.

239. *damn for ever*: in a free and enlightened community nobody would
believe in the myth of eternal damnation. Shelley considered that religion
was 'intimately connected with politics' and that by threatening punish-
ment after death it diverted and frustrated attempts to alter the political
status quo.

245. Britain, Austria, Prussia, Holland, Spain and Sardinia formed a co-
alition against revolutionary France in 1793.

250-1. Perhaps like Mary Magdalen, as a sign of repentance and submission
(Luke 7:45). *like him following Christ*: Zacchaeus (Luke 19:1-10).

257-8. The sources of the power and privilege which was once theirs but
which they now seek to eliminate.

266. *a great Assembly*: as at Peterloo and the other great meetings held by
the reformers; Shelley may have had in mind also the Assemblies held in
the early days of the French Revolution.

320. *sphereless stars*: meteors, therefore phenomena which are merely
temporary.

344-63. Shelley discusses the merits of passive resistance in *A Philosophical
View of Reform* (1819). It is the best course 'not because active resistance
is not justifiable when all other means shall have failed, but because in this
instance temperance and courage would produce greater advantages than
the most decisive victory'. Regular soldiers (as opposed to the militia
engaged at Peterloo) might thus be brought to reflect on the realities of
their situation and to ally themselves with their fellow-countrymen.

Ode to the West Wind. Written late October 1819. Published with *P.U.*
(1820). This ode brings together nature, politics and Shelley's private life in a
richly complex fusion which transcends all three. The drafts show clearly that
Shelley wished to avoid a note which was specifically personal: instead, he
plays the role of the prophetic poet, an Isaiah looking forward to a regen-
erated society. Although the poem has the structure of a hymn and celebrates
a numinous force, Shelley's most compelling concern is political and he looks
to nature for confirmation that out of seeming death can come new life.
Formally, the ode is highly inventive: each stanza is a sonnet built out of four
groups of *terza rima* and a concluding couplet.

4. *hectic*: feverish.

9. *azure sister*: the gentle west wind of spring, usually masculine (Zephyrus
or Favonius).

10. There are suggestions here of the Resurrection which are taken up again
at the end of the poem. Cf. 'for the trumpet shall sound, and the dead shall
be raised incorruptible, and we shall be changed' (I Corinthians 15:52).

15-18. Fractocumulus or scud, 'clouds running beside thunderstorms,
which can be seen discharging water into the sea but which themselves are
composed of water evaporated from the sea' (Ludlam) — hence the
tangled boughs. Angels: heralds or messengers, because they indicate

thunderstorms; also there may be a hint here of angels who are more energetically destructive than usual.

20-3. *locks*: not to be confused with the loose clouds, these are 'the equally high but dense plume of fibrous cloud which reaches far ahead of the towering cloud columns at the heart of a thunderstorm' (Ludlam). *Maenads*: female followers of Bacchus, usually in a frenzy. Shelley's description may have been influenced by a relief depicting four Maenads, which he saw at Florence.

29-42. The Mediterranean phenomenon known to meteorologists as 'the autumn break'.

32. In 1818 Shelley took a boat trip in the Bay of Baiae and observed 'the ruins of its antique grandeur standing like rocks in the transparent sea under our boat'. Baiae had been a fashionable resort with the Romans; Eustace's popular guide-book recorded that 'Baiae, indeed, was not only the seat of voluptuousness, but sometimes also the theatre of cruelty'.

42. *despoil*: strip (of their leaves).

51. *striven*: perhaps as Jacob wrestled with the angel.

54. Here Shelley despairs not as a private individual but as a prophetic poet who is a vehicle of the spirit of inspiration. Cf. the Psalms.

63. *dead thoughts*: his unsuccessful poems (notably *Laon and Cythna*) which had not fulfilled their true social function.

70. The political implications are important (a similar metaphor was used, for example, by Thomas Paine). Shelley hoped that the new birth would not involve violence. In one of his notebooks he wrote: 'the spring rebels not against winter but it succeeds it — the dawn rebels not against night but it disperses it.'

Peter Bell the Third. Written late October 1819 and sent to Hunt on 2 November for publication. Published posthumously (1839). Shelley was inspired by two reviews in *The Examiner*: Keats' review of *Peter Bell, A Lyrical Ballad* by John Hamilton Reynolds (a spoof and parody of Wordsworth's *Peter Bell*, whose appearance it antedated by a week) and Hunt's review of Wordsworth's poem. Shelley asked that his *Peter Bell* be published anonymously: 'My motive in this is solely not to prejudge myself in the present moment, as I have only expended a few days on this party squib & of course taken little pains. The verse & language, I have let come as they would, & I am about to publish more serious things this winter.' Elsewhere Shelley referred to the poem as 'a joke' and 'a trifle unworthy of me seriously to acknowledge'. He had long been exercised by Wordsworth's defection from the ranks of the reformers. He continued to admire Wordsworth's great poetry but considered that the dullness of *The Excursion* and the later poetry was the direct result of Wordsworth's moral and political derelictions. In Shelley's fiction, Peter (Wordsworth) has been taken to Hell by the Devil, who has offered him 'a situation'. Cf. 'Verses . . . on Receiving a Celandine' and 'An Exhortation'.

6-7. With an alliterative gusto reminiscent of popular verse, Shelley links together four diverse characters: John Castle, informer and *agent pro-vocateur*; George Canning, liberal Tory; William Cobbett, journalist, pamphleteer and influential radical; Viscount Castlereagh, Foreign Sec-retary, hated alike by radical leaders and by the people.

9.   *cozening*: cheating, defrauding by deceit. *trepanning*: catching in a trap, luring into a course of action, swindling.

11.   The name Southey is cancelled in the fair copy.

16.   *Chancery Court*: the court presided over by the Lord Chancellor where in 1817 Shelley was deprived of the custody of his two children by Harriet.

18-19.   See *A Philosophical View of Reform*.

26-7.   'These . . . are awful times. The tremendous question is now agitat-ing, whether a military & judicial despotism is to be established by our present rulers, or some form of government less unfavourable to the real & permanent interests of all men is to arise from the conflict of passions now gathering to overturn them' (*L.* ii. 148).

37.   *amant miserè*: love miserably (that is, give voice to their love by caterwauling); pronounced with mock-gentility to rhyme with *chastity*.

40.   'What would this husk and excuse for a virtue be without its kernel prostitution, or the kernel prostitution without this husk of a virtue? I wonder the women of the town do not form an association, like the Society for the Suppression of Vice, for the support of what may be called the "King, Church, and Constitution" of their order. But this subject is almost too horrible for a joke' (Shelley's note).

56.   *levees*: assemblies held by a prince or person of distinction.

63.   *a Cretan-tonguèd panic*: a panic based on unreliable rumours; appre-hension in relation to financial and commercial matters.

71-5.   This stanza performs two main functions: (1) It alludes to a passage in Wordsworth's *Peter Bell* which Shelley employed as an epigraph to his own poem ('Is it a party in a parlour, / Crammed just as they on earth were crammed, / Some sipping punch — some sipping tea; / But, as you by their faces see, / All silent, and all — damned!'); (2) It is a parody of the naiveties of the Wordsworthian style.

76-85.   Shelley claims that damnation is not a sentence passed by a divine judge but a condition resulting from a free and deliberate choice. Hell is not a place so much as a state of mind which man imposes on himself. *flams*: humbug, deception.

92-3.   Shelley was frightened that Cobbett's demagoguery would incite the poor and the oppressed to violent revolution which would *not* lead them to the kingdom of Heaven promised to them in the Sermon on the Mount (Matthew 5).

96-100.   An ironical picture of Shelley the idealist. These lines sum up the whole of Shelley's poetic endeavour; cf. the faith of Julian and the sceptical response of Maddalo in *J.M.*, 159-211.

104-5.   Cf. *Macbeth*, III. ii. 50-1.

117.   *Peter . . . Square*: Wordsworth moving in polite society.

147-56. Shelley suggests a certain narrowness of perspective, an egotistical limitation in Wordsworth. The implications are best illustrated by a passage from *D.P.*: 'The great secret of morals is love; or a going out of our own nature, and an identification of ourselves with the beautiful which exists in thought, action, or person, not our own. A man, to be greatly good, must imagine intensely and comprehensively; he must put himself in the place of another and of many others; the pains and pleasures of his species must become his own. The great instrument of moral good is the imagination; and poetry administers to the effect by acting upon the cause.'

167ff. Shelley's own view of poetry is more explicitly sexual: 'it strips the veil of familiarity from the world, and lays bare the naked and sleeping beauty, which is the spirit of its forms' (*D.P.*).

173. *a sister's kiss*: this may be an ironical allusion to Wordsworth's relations with Dorothy. The fair copy includes these lines: 'Another — "Impious Libertine! / That commits i — t with his sister / In ruined Abbies — mighty fine / To write odes on it!" — I opine / Peter had never even kissed her'. *Diogenes*: a Cynic philosopher, famous for his contempt of the flesh and of bodily comforts.

179. *Burns*: in the draft Peter appears clad in the skirts of a Scotch puritan — Burns represents a different Scottish tradition.

182-4. 'Mouth for kisses was never the worse; rather, it renews as the moon does' (moral of *Decameron*, 2:7). Shelley, who approved of Boccaccio's 'more serious theories of love', remarked that the application of this lighter one 'might do some good to the common narrow-minded conceptions of love'.

229. *a man*: Coleridge.

237-41. A common criticism of Coleridge: see Peacock's portrayals of him as Flosky in *Nightmare Abbey* and as Moley Mystic of Cimmerian Hall in *Melincourt*. Cf. *Letter to Maria Gisborne*, 202-8.

242ff. This rhapsodic passage is probably based both on first-hand accounts of Coleridge's conversation and on Shelley's reading of *Biographia Literaria*. The poetic theory bears a close similarity to some of the most celebrated passages in *D.P.*

244-5. See John 3:8.

252ff. The influence of Coleridge on Wordsworth which was partly responsible for *Lyrical Ballads*.

261. Cf. 'the human heart by which we live' (Immortality Ode).

275. *rocks and trees*: characteristic Wordsworthian subject-matter (see especially, 'Rolled round in earth's diurnal course, / With rocks, and stones, and trees').

286. References to *The Excursion* and perhaps to *Lyrical Ballads*.

301. *pipkins*: earthenware pots or pans. *cotter*: peasant who occupies a cottage, usually with land attached.

Ode to Heaven. Written December 1819. Published with *P.U.* (1820). 'The creation — such as it was perceived by his mind — a unit in immensity, was slight and narrow compared with the interminable forms of thought that might exist beyond, to be perceived perhaps hereafter by his own mind; or which are perceptible to other minds that fill the universe, not of space in the material sense, but of infinity in the immaterial one' (Mrs Shelley). The First Spirit celebrates Heaven as an objective reality, seemingly eternal; the Second Spirit (*a Remoter Voice* in MS.) re-defines Heaven in subjective terms; the Third Spirit (*a louder and still remoter Voice* in MS.) accuses the first two speakers of presumption and suggests there is no distinction between subject and object, between the individual mind and external Heaven. The final lines stress both the limitations of human perception and human life (37-45) and their infinite possibilities as part of the universe (46-54). For the terms of the debate, cf. 'Mont Blanc'; for the dialectical method, cf. 'The Two Spirits'.

19-22.   Man has created God in his own likeness and located him in Heaven.
38.   *atom-born*: suggests the Epicurean theory as developed by Lucretius in *De Rerum Natura*; atoms are the component elements of everything that exists, including man, and the only ultimate reality.
48.   *eyed*: implies the perceiving powers of the mind.

England in 1819.   Written late 1819 and sent to Hunt for publication. Published posthumously (1839). Cf. Burdett's Election Address on 11 October 1812, published in *The Examiner*: 'an army of spies and informers . . . a Phantom for a king; a degraded aristocracy; an oppressed people . . . vague and sanguinary Laws. . . .'
1.   George III was soon to die (29 January 1820) at the age of eighty-one, sixty years after coming to the throne. He had been irremediably insane since 1811.
2.   *Princes*: the sons of George III, notorious for their coarse tastes, dissolute habits and ostentatious extravagance.
7.   See notes to *M.A.*: St Peter's Fields, where the demonstrators were stabbed by the militia, might have been cultivated to save them from starvation.
8-9.   Here (as in ll. 4-6) it is implied that this oppressive system contains the seed of its own destruction.
10.   A legal system based on violence (*sanguine*: bloody) and on mercenary considerations (*Golden*); *tempt and slay* refers to the Government's use of *agents provocateurs* who stimulated revolution in order that it might be put down *pour encourager les autres*.
11.   Followed originally by *A cloak of lies worn on Power's holiday* (cf. Fraud in *M.A.* who is *Clothed with the Bible, as with light*).
12.   The unreformed Parliament.
13-14.   Cf. *Address to the People* (1817), which draws a contrast between the public mourning for the young Princess Charlotte and the public failure to recognize the death of British Liberty, symbolized by the execution of the Derby rioters, who had been led on to insurrection by a Government agent: 'Let us follow the corpse of British Liberty slowly and

reverentially to its tomb; and if some glorious Phantom should appear and make its throne of broken swords and sceptres and royal crowns trampled in the dust, let us say that the Spirit of Liberty has arisen from its grave and left all that was gross and mortal there, and kneel down and worship it as our Queen.'

Lines to a Critic. Written 1819 or 1820. Published posthumously (1824). The critic may well be Robert Southey whom Shelley (incorrectly) believed to be the author of a highly personalized attack on his moral character in the *Quarterly Review* for April 1819. Reverberations continued and as late as June 1820 Shelley wrote to Southey to ask if he was responsible. The poem can probably be linked to 'Lines to a Reviewer' and to the fragmentary 'Satire on Satire' in which he comments: 'I will only say, / If any friend would take Southey some day, / And tell him, in a country walk alone, / Softening harsh words with friendship's gentle tone, / How incorrect his public conduct is, / And what men think of it, 'twere not amiss.' In all three poems Shelley renounces hate and turns the other cheek.

7-8.   Cf. 'Of your antipathy / If I am the Narcissus, you are free / To pine into a sound with hating me' ('Lines to a Reviewer'). Narcissus was not responsive to the love of Echo; likewise, Shelley does not reciprocate the critic's hatred.

13.   *prove*: feel, experience.

Ode to Liberty. Written early in 1820. Published with *P.U.* (1820). Shelley was inspired by the rising in Spain which began on 1 January and whose repercussions in Italy he was able to observe from closer range and to celebrate in the *Ode to Naples*. Although these stirrings may have seemed like an answer to his question at the end of *O.W.W.*, Shelley's revolutionary optimism is qualified by his awareness of the difficulties involved in making the potential permanently real (cf. 'Sonnet to the Republic of Benevento'). This formal ode owes debts not only to Pindar and the tradition of prophetic poetry but to eighteenth-century poems such as Gray's 'The Progress of Poesy' and Collins' 'Ode to Liberty'.

1.   *vibrated*: emitted the electric charge of revolution whose current links nation with nation.

5-15.   Many of these images are traditional to visionary or 'inspired' poetry; Shelley is deliberately adopting the conventions of the Ode. Pindar compares his poetry to an eagle dropping on its prey (*Nemeans*, 3.80-2), while both he and Dante use the image of the ship. The *rapid plumes of song* recall Shelley's translation of Plato's *Ion* where the souls of poets are *arrayed in the plumes of rapid imagination*. The *voice out of the deep*, later *the great voice* (283), suggests that Shelley was also placing himself in the line of the Biblical prophets: in particular it recalls the *great voice* of Revelation 16:17.

16ff.   A description of the Creation. *daedal*: complex, richly adorned and carefully wrought like the work of the master-craftsman Daedalus.

20.   The atmosphere of the earth which sustains human life.

22. *a chaos and a curse*: key words with Shelley to describe the state of unregenerated man. In *Epipsychidion* the curse is redeemed and the chaos ordered by love, in *D.P.* by poetic imagination.

23. *thou*: Liberty. *power . . . worst*: a process examined in the plays of Aeschylus.

28. *their violated nurse*: the earth.

31ff. Cf. Asia's account of the human condition before Prometheus (*P.U.*, II. iv. 49-58).

41. *The Sister-Pest*: Religion.

43. *Anarchs*: see introductory note to *M.A.*

45. *astonished*: dismayed, terrified, bewildered.

47. *dividuous*: which break up.

58. *Parian stone*: the favourite marble of the Greek sculptors.

60. *lidless*: unsleeping, unblinking, watchful.

61ff. Although he was aware of its political and moral limitations, Shelley regarded classical Athens as the most perfect example of human civilization; '. . . what we are and hope to be, is derived, as it were, from the influence and inspiration of these glorious generations'. More perfect than the visionary city of cloud, Athens was a reality based on Liberty (*For thou wert*) and on man's will and desire to improve his own world.

65. *pavilions*: makes a canopy for it.

69-71. The image is derived from the Acropolis, the Athenian hill (*mount*) on which stood the Parthenon and other public buildings.

73. *mock*: imitate (not deride; no Yeatsian ironies are intended). *the eternal dead*: perhaps the Athenian heroes or demigods.

75. *latest oracle*: probably refers to the recent stirrings in Greece; *oracle* perhaps because it conveyed the divine message of liberty to those who were prepared to consider its meaning.

76-9. Cf. *P.U.*, III. iii. 159ff. Athens is a civilizing idea, a mental reality of continuing relevance. Shelley is here concerned with an ideal; this makes an interesting contrast with the moral realism of Wordsworth's 'Elegiac Stanzas on Peele Castle' from which 79 is derived.

92-3. The wolf was the emblem of Rome; in Euripides' *Bacchae* the Maenads (followers of Dionysus) give suck to fawns and wolf-cubs while under the influence of the god. *Cadmaean*: from Thebes, which was ruled by Cadmus.

93-4. In the early years of the Roman republic, Athens was still great.

98. *Camillus*: L. Furius C., Roman leader who went into voluntary exile when accused of embezzling spoils but did not refuse his country's call and saved Rome from the Gauls in 387 B.C. *Attilius*: M. Attilius Regulus, who commanded the Roman armies against the Carthaginians. Captured and sent to Rome on parole to negotiate a treaty, he dissuaded the senate from accepting the Carthaginian terms and voluntarily returned to Carthage, where he was tortured to death. His virtues were celebrated by Horace (*Odes*, 3.5). Cf. *D.P.* (*Prose*, p. 287).

99ff. These lines chart the gradual decline of the Republic into an Empire.

103-4.   The first poets of the Empire, notably Horace and Virgil, were much influenced by Greek models.

106.   *Hyrcanian*: waste and uncultivated region south of the Caspian Sea.

111.   *Naiad*: water nymph.

115.   Liberty was not in evidence in the Scandinavian or Celtic countries, represented here by their most sensitive cultural and religious antennae. *Scald*: Scandinavian bard.

117.   *groan not weep*: a response of passive suffering and disgust rather than of redeeming pity; Prometheus transcends the first and achieves the second.

119.   *the Galilean serpent*: the Christian Church.

124-8.   The rise of the Italian city states is related to the imagery of volcanic action; their assertion of freedom from popes and emperors is intimately connected with their great artistic achievements. Cf. 'Love . . . has been celebrated by a chorus of the greatest writers of the renovated world; and the music has penetrated the caverns of society, and its echoes still drown the dissonance of arms and superstition'.

139.   *dissever*: dissolve, disperse, divide.

141-4.   The Reformation is here related both to the electrical charge of revolution (cf. 1-2) and to the Resurrection (cf. *O.W.W.*) *Luther's leaden lance*: 'Dante was the first religious reformer, and Luther surpassed him rather in the rudeness and acrimony than in the boldness of his censures of papal usurpation.'

145-7.   *prophets*: 'those mighty intellects of our own country that succeeded the Reformation, the translators of the Bible, Shakespeare, Spenser, the dramatists of the reign of Elizabeth, and Lord Bacon' (Preface to *Laon and Cythna*).

148-9.   Milton, 'a republican and a bold inquirer into morals and religion', alone illuminated the Restoration in which all forms of poetry became 'hymns to the triumph of kingly power over liberty and virtue'.

151-65.   The period between the Restoration and the end of the eighteenth century, when hopes of liberty were fulfilled in the American War of Independence.

151.   Cf. the Spirit of the Hour in *P.U.*

166.   Cf. 'O happy Earth! reality of Heaven!' (*Daemon of the World*, 292).

171-80.   The conservative (*sceptred and mitred*) powers of Europe allied themselves against the French revolutionaries. They were resisted by Napoleon, a freedom fighter who became a tyrant (175) and suffered the appropriate pangs of conscience (178-80).

185-6.   *Aeolian*: responsive to the influence of the wind (Aeolus), a precursor of earthquake. *from Pithecusa to Pelorus*: from the Bay of Naples to Sicily.

188.   *Be dim*: i.e. in comparison with this new light of ours (Locock).

189-91.   *Her chains*: England's. Compared to Spain with its long tradition of autocratic rule, England should have little trouble in breaking the power of the moneyed interests (*threads of gold*) which control her.

192ff.   The twins are Spain and England; since they share a destiny, England will presumably follow the example of the Spanish Revolution. Both countries are called on to make their mark on history, like engraved seals which leave an impression on wax (cf. *L.* ii. 276).

196.   *Arminius*: the father of German independence, conqueror of the Romans in A.D. 9.

199.   *Thy*: Germany's.

200.   *mysterious*: associated with religious ritual.

204.   *thou*: Italy.

218.   *gordian word*: The empire of Asia was promised by an oracle to him who could untie the complicated knot made by King Gordius of Phrygia; Alexander cut it with one stroke of his sword.

221.   The *fasces*, a bundle of rods with an axe in the middle, were carried before Roman magistrates as an emblem of their authority.

225.   *reluctant*: struggling, offering resistance.

231-40.   Shelley employs conventional religious imagery to describe the divinity in man, the 'Immortal Deity / Whose throne is in the depth of Human thought'. In 233 Shelley displays his usual unwillingness to be dogmatic as to whether the source of human inspiration is internal or external.

234-5.   For Shelley's distrust of language, see 'To a Sky-lark', *Epipsychidion* and 'These words are inefficient and metaphorical. Most words so. — No help —' (MS. note to *On Love*).

243-5.   Cf. the relations between Jupiter and Prometheus.

249.   *intercessor*: Art plays the role traditionally allotted to the saints and to the Blessed Virgin. *Diving*: *Driving* (1820).

254-5.   Wealth appropriates from the labouring classes a thousand gifts of Liberty and Nature for each one which it allows them to keep (cf. *A Philosophical View of Reform, Prose*, pp. 243-7).

258.   *Eoan*: eastern, pertaining to the dawn.

271-85.   Shelley is developing the traditional motif of failing inspiration. Cf. *D.P.*, especially 'the poet becomes a man, and is abandoned to the sudden reflux of the influences under which others habitually live'.

The Cloud.   Written probably in early 1820. Published with *P.U.* (1820). This poem is informed by Shelley's observation of cloud behaviour and by his scientific reading but its animation is derived from the central conception of the spirit of the cloud, which personifies the tantalizingly elusive principle of life.

17-30.   According to Adam Walker, 'water rises through the air, flying on the wings of electricity'. The *pilot* is the electricity which guides the cloud; there is a mutual attraction between this positive force and the negative electricity below (*the genii, The Spirit he loves*), which results in thunderstorms or rain. The informing principle of the cloud remains intact even though the cloud itself may disappear. *dissolving*: can be read as both transitive and intransitive.

58.   *these*: the stars.
71.   *sphere-fire*: the sun.
75.   *pores*: Erasmus Darwin referred to 'each nice pore of ocean, earth, and air' while Adam Walker described how rain 'sinks into the chinks and pores of the ground'. The cloud is mainly formed by 'sweat' drawn up by the sun from the sea, rivers and rivulets.
79.   *convex*: 'The earth's atmosphere bends a ray of sunlight into a curve ... convex to an observer in a cloud looking down' (King-Hele). The difference from the limited perspective of troubled humanity is tactfully suggested.
81-4.   The empty tomb (*cenotaph*) is unbuilt as the cloud fills the sky and the blue dome disappears.

The Sensitive Plant.   Written early 1820. Published with *P.U.* (1820). The Sensitive Plant is the mimosa, whose apparent sentiency provided writers of the eighteenth century and the Romantic period with a convenient image for the position of man in the natural world. The poem places the plant in an Eden-like garden presided over by a 'Lady, the wonder of her kind'. In the autumn she dies and, without her protection, the Sensitive Plant and the other flowers of the garden decay and rot. There is no vernal resurrection; in the spring only 'the mandrakes, and toadstools, and docks, and darnels, / Rose like the dead from their ruined charnels'. The Conclusion tries to make sense of this stark evidence of mortality.
23-4.   Cf. 'Perception, I believe, is, in some degree, in all sorts of animals; though in some possibly the avenues provided by nature for the reception of sensations are so few, and the perception they are received with so obscure and dull, that it comes extremely short of the quickness and variety of sensation which is in other animals ...' (Locke, *An Essay Concerning Human Understanding*, in a passage directly following his discussion of sensation in vegetables).

An Exhortation.   Written April 1820. Published with *P.U.* (1820). Shelley told Mrs Gisborne this was 'a kind of excuse for Wordsworth'. For Shelley, as for Keats, the chameleon's ability to grow 'like what it looks upon' usually suggested the poetic imagination; here it may suggest the turn-coat since Peter Bell (also based on Wordsworth) 'changes colours like a chameleon, and his coat like a snake. He is a Proteus of a Peter'. The *boon* in the final line is probably an ironic reference to Wordsworth's own lament, 'We have given our hearts away, a sordid boon' ('The world is too much with us').

Song.   Written May 1820. Published posthumously (1824).

To a Sky-lark.   Written summer 1820 (probably June). Published with *P.U.* (1820). 'It was on a beautiful summer evening, while wandering among the lanes whose myrtle hedges were the bowers of the fireflies, that we heard the carolling of the skylark ...' (Mrs Shelley). This poem has much in common with the stanzas on poetry and music in the Homeric *Hymn to Mercury* (translated in July) and with *D.P.* (1821). As usual with Shelley, it carefully exploits synaesthetic effects to evoke feelings which transcend the power of ordinary words; it also acknowledges openly the inadequacy of language and of image to capture the essence of the sky-lark's song. The unusual stanza form has been related both to the flight of the bird and to its song, whose extended trill is reproduced in 'the delicate hesitant poise of each stanza upon its prolonged floating last line' (K. Raine).

3.   *or near it*: as usual, Shelley qualifies his assertion.

5.   *unpremeditated*: Cf. *P.L.*, ix. 24.

8.   *a cloud of fire*: primarily, this means a cloud illuminated by the setting sun but it may also refer to the *nuée ardente* of a volcano (at Vesuvius in 1772 it 'appeared in the night tinged like clouds with the setting sun'). Cf. *P.U.*, I. 157-8.

22.   *silver sphere*: Venus (the morning star) which gradually disappears with the coming of daylight (cf. *T.L.*, 413-20).

37.   *in the light of thought*: the poet's personal identity is subsumed in the radiance of inspiration.

66.   *Hymeneal*: for a wedding.

86.   Cf. *Hamlet*, IV. iv. 37.

103. *harmonious madness*: 'For a poet is indeed a thing ethereally light, winged, and sacred, nor can he compose anything worth calling poetry until he becomes inspired and as it were mad; or whilst any reason remains in him' (Shelley's version of Plato's *Ion*). Plato's *Phaedrus*, which Shelley had read in May, may also have influenced both this phrase and the whole conception of the poem.

Letter to Maria Gisborne.   Written 1-7 July 1820. Published posthumously (1824). This verse epistle, which was not intended for publication, was written when the Shelleys were staying at Leghorn in the house of their friends, John and Maria Gisborne, who were on a visit to London. Maria had been a friend of the Godwins and had recently given Shelley lessons in Spanish; the fluent delight with which Shelley here develops his images may owe more than a little to these tutorials on Calderón. The workshop described in the poem belonged to Mrs Gisborne's son, Henry Reveley, a nautical engineer who had been engaged in designing a steamboat with Shelley's enthusiastic support.

10.   *that*: this decaying form. Like a caterpillar, Shelley will emerge from the cocoon gloriously resurrected.

12.   *asphodels*: immortal flowers in Elysium.

17.   *Archimedean*: like that of Archimedes, Sicilian mathematician and inventor, one of whose works was a treatise 'On Bodies floating in Fluids'.

20.   *force . . . spells*: mathematical calculations, which can tame the elements as if by magic.

23-4.   *Vulcan*: blacksmith and armourer to Jupiter (Zeus). *Ixion*: bound to a wheel in Hades for seducing Zeus's wife. *Titans*: the giant sons of Heaven and Earth who rebelled against Saturn; Shelley here fuses them with the giants whose later rebellion was suppressed by Zeus.

25. *St. Dominic*: founder of the Dominicans and a prominent figure in the Inquisition.

27ff. Philip II's Council authorized the Spanish Armada of 1588; their Catholic faith allowed them to presume that English Protestants were doomed to eternal damnation because they were outside the fold of the Church.

33-4. '. . . Ferdinand has proclaimed the Constitution of 1812, and called the Cortes. The Inquisition is abolished, the dungeons opened and the patriots pouring out' (Mary Shelley to Maria Gisborne, 26 March 1820). Shelley anticipated the event in 'An Ode to the Assertors of Liberty' (1819) and celebrated its place in the pattern of European revolutionary politics in *O.L.*

45. *Proteus*: the old man of the sea, who could assume any shape in order to elude capture.

51. *Tubal Cain*: according to Genesis (4:23) the first artificer in brass and iron.

53-4. '. . . the Boilers, & the Keel of the Boat, & the Cylinder, & all the other elements of that soul which is to guide our "Monstruo di fuego e agua" over the sea' (*L*. ii. 132).

75. A rough model in the form of a paper boat.

95. A famous mathematician and astronomer; the authors of textbooks on geometry and algebra.

98. *Baron de Tott*: author of the popular *Mémoires sur les Turcs* (1784).

103. *mo*: more.

106. *Archimage*: the great enchanter in Spenser's *Faerie Queene*.

114. *Libeccio*: the south-west wind. Cf. 'The Libecchio here howls like a chorus of fiends all day' (*L*. ii. 213).

119-20. Cf. *Epipsychidion*, 434.

142. *the sad enchantress*: Memory.

154-66. Memory's catalogue of *how* is interrupted here by a long parenthesis in which the *shroud of talk* is the subject of the infinitives *hide, blame, anatomize* and *guess*.

170-4. The image is probably that of an oasis (cf. *L*. ii. 150).

175-86. In the summer of 1819 Maria Gisborne (*wisest lady*) taught Shelley enough Spanish to read the plays of Calderón. *indued*: put on, perhaps also with the sense of *learnt*.

197-201. *Godwin*: William Godwin (1756-1836), author of *Political Justice*, once the inspiration of Shelley's Utopian radicalism but now a shrivelled and cautious shadow of his former self and an importunate and impecunious father-in-law. In spite of personal animosities, Shelley still acknowledged his essential greatness as we can tell from the implied parallel with Milton (*P.L.*, vii. 25-6).

202-8. Shelley suggests that Coleridge is the victim of his own extraordinary abilities; he has the eagle's capacity to look directly into the sun but he has blinded himself by the dazzle of his own brilliance.

209-25.   Leigh Hunt (1784-1859), poet, essayist and critic; editor of *The Examiner*; good friend and courageous and perceptive reviewer of the poetry of Keats and Shelley, whose true merits he was one of the first to recognize. Cf. the description by Keats in *Sleep and Poetry*.

213.   *Shout*: Robert Shout, statuary with a shop in High Holborn.

226-30.   Thomas Jefferson Hogg (1792-1862) was sent down from Oxford with Shelley for refusing to answer questions concerning *The Necessity of Atheism*. He remained a close friend, involved himself with Shelley's wives and women friends, and wrote a two-volume biography of the young Shelley which was unreliable but highly influential.

233-47.   Thomas Love Peacock (1785-1866) was another close friend of Shelley and greatly influenced his taste in Greek literature. He worked at the India House (*turns Hindoo*), and had recently married a Welsh girl (*Snowdonian Antelope*). *cameleopard*: giraffe.

243-7.   Cf. 8-14.

247-50.   Horace Smith (1779-1849), stockbroker and author with his brother of *Rejected Addresses*, a witty collection of parodies.

257.   *unpavilioned*: not covered with a canopy of clouds.

261.   *inverse deep*: the sky is an inverted image of the sea.

269-73.   The horrible reality of London prostitution is set against two manifestations of Italian night-life which are more agreeable — the serenade, and the amorous murmurings of Apollonia, the landlord's daughter.

286.   *Contadino*: Italian peasant.

292ff.   Cf. the invitation to Emilia at the end of *Epipsychidion*.

302.   Shelley remained a vegetarian and water-drinker on principle.

305.   *syllabubs*: dishes made of cream and wine.

308.   *the Grand Duke*: of Tuscany, in which Leghorn was situated.

316-7.   I won't need to dull my nerves with the opiate of poetic composition (Helicon is the home of the Muses) or of amorous involvement (Himeros, says Shelley, is 'a synonym of Love').

Hymn to Mercury.   Translated from the Greek in July 1820 (finished on the 14th). Published posthumously (1824). Shelley himself described this *Hymn* as 'infinitely comical' and claimed that he made his translation 'for want of spirit to invent'. Yet the poem touches on his deepest concerns: the passages on poetry and song bear obvious affinities to *D.P.* and 'To a Sky-lark' and Mercury (Hermes), who discovers fire, is a comic version of Prometheus. Shelley was also intrigued by the figure of the capricious child-god who seemed to embody a mysterious, energetic and ultimately positive force (cf. the Spirit of the Earth in *P.U.*, the informing spirit of 'The Cloud', and *The Witch of Atlas*). To capture the tone of the original in a 'legible' translation, Shelley employs *ottava rima*. A suitably archaic flavour is obtained by the occasional use of Spenserian diction.

8.   Jupiter's wife was happily unaware of her husband's behaviour.

29.   *despasturing*: cropping (a Spenserian word).

65.   *division*: a rapid melodic passage, a run; variations.

69.   *unpremeditated*: cf. *P.L.*, ix. 24.
73.   *not quite legitimate*: Shelley adds this to the original.
143.   *delve*: pit, hollow (another Spenserian touch).
189.   *thin*: so he can pass through the keyhole (Shelley's addition).

Two Songs for Midas.   Written 1820 for Mary Shelley's play, *Midas*. Published posthumously (1824). The sun-god Apollo and the goat-god Pan compete in a singing contest before Tmolus, the official adjudicator, who votes for Apollo, and Midas, king of Phrygia, who supports Pan — for which he is given asses ears. The songs represent not only two kinds of poetry but the respective possibilities of supra-mortal and mortal existence.
Apollo.
19-20.   Colour is not inherent in things but a property of light.
21-2.   Most stars obtain their energy, like the sun, by transmuting hydrogen into helium (King-Hele) but Shelley's main concern is with the sun as a symbol of light and energy.
31-2.   Cf. *Mundi oculus* (Ovid); 'Thou Sun, of this great world both eye and soul' (*P.L.*, v. 171). This Narcissistic self-satisfaction is appropriate to the divine nature, which has no self-doubts or hesitations.
33-4.   Apollo was the god of music, poetry, prophecy and medicine.
Pan.   Pan is the animating spirit of the whole natural world (Pan means whole): cf. 'that universal Pan who may be a God or man' (*Essay on Christianity*).
14.   *Tempe*: a valley in Thessaly; 'the poets describe it as the most delightful spot on the earth' (Lempriére).
18ff.   See note to choruses from *Hellas*, i. 34.
26.   *daedal*: see note to *O.L.*, 16.
27.   *giant wars*: wars of the Giants against Zeus, which involved piling Pelion on Ossa.
31.   The nymph Syrinx was changed by the gods into a reed of which Pan made himself a pipe; his music, unlike that of Apollo, is closely connected with his unhappiness.
34.   *both ye*: Apollo (affected by envy) and Tmolus (affected by age).

The Two Spirits: An Allegory.   Written 1820. Published posthumously (1824). The two Spirits may be associated respectively with pessimistic and optimistic philosophies. The Second Spirit is dedicated to hope, love and infinite possibility; the First is cautious, limited and sceptical. This dialogue represents a characteristic feature of Shelley's intellectual world, the perpetual balancing of hypothesis against hypothesis, the guarded approach to the ultimately unknowable truth. The narrator's conclusion (33-48) devotes one stanza to each pole of the dialectic, though it is probably significant that the final words are on the side of hope rather than despair. The setting of these stanzas should be compared to those of 'Mont Blanc' and *P.U.*, the dialectical method to that of *J.M.*
10.   *shade of night*: the conical shadow cast by the earth in space.

Sonnet to the Republic of Benevento. Probably written at the end of summer 1820 (with *Ode to Naples*). Published posthumously (1824) under title 'Political Greatness'. This sonnet was written in the context of the rising of the Carbonari against Ferdinand of Naples in 1820 (see notes to *O.L.*). Benevento was a small papal state situated in the midst of Neapolitan territory. In July 1820 Benevento and Ponte-Corvo 'drove out the Roman garrisons, disclaimed their allegiance to the Pope, and sent to request admission to the rights of Neapolitan citizenship and fraternity'. This request was unsuccessful. 'The principalities then fought to obtain the concession of certain privileges and reform from their own government; but the papal court insisted upon their unconditional submission, and the two cities then formed themselves into an independent republic, and took measures for the defence of their independence' (*Annual Register*). The poem suggests that political revolutions are of little value unless they are accompanied or preceded by an interior, psychological revolution.

6.   *pageant*: as shown in the glass (orig. *mirror*) of Art.

6-7.   Cf. *T.L.*

8-9.   Staining the potential Heaven of Art with their ugly reality.

9-10.   *What . . . custom*: ultimately neither physical force nor habit are significant (when compared to the power of individual man).

10-14.   Cf. the triumph of Prometheus over Jupiter, and *T.L.*, 211-13. 'He [Diogenes] said, It is in the power of each individual to level the inequality which is the topic of the complaint of mankind. Let him be aware of his own worth and the station which he really occupies in the scale of moral beings . . . Each man possesses the power in this respect to legislate for himself' (*Essay on Christianity*).

Goodnight. Written in 1820. Published in *The Literary Pocket-Book* (1822). A slightly different version was presented to Sophia Stacey on 29 December 1820. This poem is a translation from Shelley's own 'Buona Notte'.

Fragment: To the Moon. Written 1820 or 1821. Published posthumously (1824). After a gap, the manuscript continues 'Thou chosen sister of the spirit / That gazes on thee till it pities'. This suggests that Shelley may have intended to relate this symbol of alienation to a specific human context (cf. opening invocation of 'Lines Written in the Bay of Lerici').

Epipsychidion. Written after December 1820; finished 16 February 1821. Published anonymously (1821). The title has been interpreted variously as 'soul out of my soul', 'soul within the soul' and 'a little additional soul': all of these interpretations are based on the false assumption that there is such a thing as an *epipsyche*. It seems much more likely that the title means 'little soul song', on the analogy of *epithalamion* to which it provides a more liberated alternative. The poem charts a personal history of love, false and true, making use of an idealized framework largely derived from the first Canzone of

Dante's *Convito* (which Shelley translated) and from his *Vita Nuova*: the Song of Songs also contributes to the central conjunction of sister and bride. The climax is the appearance of Emilia (the Sun to Mary's Moon), an idealized version of Emilia Viviani, daughter of the governor of Pisa, who had been imprisoned in a convent to await the selection of a suitable husband. Though the poem is undeniably based on biographical realities, Shelley took pains to alchemize it. He told his publisher: 'it is to be published simply for the esoteric few [only one hundred copies] ; and I make its author a secret, to avoid the malignity of those who turn sweet food into poison. . . .'

Epigraph: . . . 'The soul that loves is hurled forth from the created world and creates in the infinite a world for itself and for itself alone, most different from this present dark and dismal pit.'

Advertisement: . . . The Italian means 'it would be a great disgrace to him who should rhyme anything under the garb of a figure or of rhetorical colouring, if afterwards, being asked, he should not be able to denude his words of this garb, in such wise that they should have a true meaning'.

1.   *that orphan one*: Shelley's presiding Spirit.

15.   Cf. Plato's description of the souls of poets 'arrayed in the plumes of rapid imagination' (Shelley's translation of the *Ion*).

21-6.   Cf. the description of Asia (*P.U.*, II. v. 48-71).

33.   The inadequacy of language is one of the poem's main themes.

38.   *lights*: eyes.

43-4.   The world will misinterpret and disapprove of our relationship.

46.   *another*: his wife.

60-1.   *A Star*: the North Star.

89-90.   Cf. 'the deep truth is imageless' (*P.U.*, II. iv. 116).

91 ff.   This passage seems to combine the language of science with that of religious devotion. Diffusion is 'the spontaneous molecular mixing or inter-penetration of two fluids without chemical combination', hence the inter-mixture is *unentangled*. Cf. 'This whiteness is produced by a successive intermixture of the colours, without their being assimilated' (Newton). *Stains*: colours. *unintermitted*: continuous.

100.   Shelley's draft is very confused but it appears that he may have intended a plural and omitted to make the necessary changes.

117.   *third sphere*: the sphere of Venus or love (*il terzo ciel*).

121-2.   April is made flesh, Frost is a skeleton.

145-6.   Cf. 'The slow, soft stroke of a continuous wind / In which the leaves tremblingly were / All bent' (Shelley's translation of *Purgatorio*, xxviii. 9-11).

161 ff.   *True Love* (ideal love) was originally *Free Love* but Shelley abandoned this because its connotations are misleading. For the general idea, see *Purgatorio*, xv. 46-75.

185-9.   This paradox represents the potential paradise which lies behind the unredeemed world.

190.   The autobiographical narrative begins here. *a Being*: an idealized female figure (a characteristic feature of Shelley's mental world).

199-200.   Cf. Dante's Beatrice in Paradise and Asia in *P.U.*

211-12.   *that Storm*: those disturbing contemporary influences which separate us from our past.

221-2.   *owlet light*: twilight. *Hesper*: the evening star (cf. 'the desire of the moth for the star').

228.   *the dreary cone*: the earth's shadow in space (the 'pyramid of night', *P.U.*, IV. 444).

240.   *sightless*: probably invisible but Destiny is also blind ('the world's eyeless charioteer'). Cf. *H.I.B.*, 27-31.

243-5.   The world of thoughts (*mine*) is created out of and within the chaos of the poet himself (*me*). Cf. 'All things exist as they are perceived; at least in relation to the percipient. "The mind is its own place, and of itself can make a heaven of hell, a hell of heaven." . . . It [Poetry] makes us the inhabitant of a world to which the familiar world is a chaos' (*D.P.*).

249.   *wintry forest*: an image derived from *Inferno*, i.

256-66.   A reference to Shelley's cousin Harriet Grove or to a prostitute at Oxford who infected him with venereal disease. Shelley avoids specifics: both the setting and the woman's attributes suggest the traditional enchantress who offers the poet a false love.

268.   *idol*: image. Cf. 'Every human mind has what Lord Bacon calls *idola specus*, peculiar images which reside in the inner cave of thought'.

271.   *One*: perhaps Shelley's cousin Harriet Grove.

272-4.   Cf. *Adonais*, 276-9.

277.   *One*: Shelley's wife, Mary Godwin (for a more flattering version of Mary's influence see the Dedication to *Laon and Cythna*).

294.   *Endymion*: a shepherd loved by the Moon (Diana).

300-6.   A living death (cf. Life-in-Death in *The Ancient Mariner*).

308ff.   Though this could refer to later disturbances in the pattern of Shelley's married life, it probably refers to the suicide of Shelley's first wife Harriet (*She*) and perhaps of Fanny Godwin, and to the subsequent seizure of his children. The Tempest may be Harriet's sister Eliza whom Shelley held responsible for the suicide and who instituted the Chancery proceedings against him.

334.   *frore*: frozen, frosty.

345.   *Twin Spheres*: Emilia (sun) and Mary (moon).

368ff.   Claire Clairmont, Mary's half-sister and the mother of Byron's daughter Allegra, who accompanied the Shelleys to Italy. She had a close relationship with Shelley emotionally as well as intellectually and there was constant friction between her and Mary. At this time she was living in Florence; 373 is, in the literal sense, an invitation to return, more generally a plea to repair the estrangement.

374.   *Love's folding-star*: Venus as Hesperus (the evening star).

400.   *continents*: those things which contain it.

412.   *halcyons*: legendary birds which charmed the winds and waves into calm, while brooding on their floating nests.

445.   *peopled . . . airs*: cf. *The Tempest*, III. ii. 134.

454. Synaesthesia is characteristic of Shelley's attempts to convey the essence of mystical experience. Cf. 'the divinest odour ... produces a sensation of voluptuous faintness like the combinations of sweet music' (*L*. ii. 85).
456. *antenatal*: previous to birth.
459. *Lucifer*: Venus as morning star.
482. *their ... interstices*: spaces between them.
494. *Titanic*: built by the Titans, the giant sons of Heaven and Earth.
506. *serene*: expanse of blue sky.
507. *Parian*: made of white marble from the Greek island, Paros.
581. *unimbued*: pure, unstained, not impregnated by any foreign substance.
587ff. A conventional collapse of poetic inspiration (cf. *O.L.*).

Lines Written on Hearing the News of the Death of Napoleon. Written 1821. Published with *Hellas* (1822). Napoleon died on 5 May 1821. As early as 1812 Shelley had written: 'Excepting Lord Castlereagh you could not have mentioned any character but Buonaparte whom I contemn and abhor more vehemently'. In 1815 he expressed 'Feelings of a Republican on the Fall of Bonaparte' and Napoleon featured briefly in later poems such as *O.L.* and *T.L.* Shelley once planned to base a play on his career.
3-4. This energy is characteristic of Shelley's planets; here it has a Biblical flavour (cf. 'when morning stars sang together', Job 38:7).
8. *Napoleon*: originally *thy Napoleon*.
30. Cf. 'The mists in their eastern caves uprolled' ('Boat on the Serchio', 16).
40. *hopes ... fled*: orig. *fair shapes he obliterated*. Napoleon had disappointed the supporters of Liberty by assuming despotic power for himself.

Adonais. Written between mid-April and early July 1821. Published July 1821. The title is probably derived from Bion's *Lament for Adonis*, a Hellenistic elegy part of which he translated and which with Moschus' *Lament for Bion* provided the main structural influence for his own lament. The poem mourns the recent death of Keats whom Shelley did not know well but whom he had invited to recuperate in his house at Pisa. For the purposes of the poem Shelley assumes that Keats' demise had been accelerated by the harsh treatment received by *Endymion* in the *Quarterly Review* for April 1818. Like the preface, the elegy is in part an attack on the Tory reviewers, for whom Shelley 'dipped my pen in consuming fire'. The animus of this attack is fuelled by his personal sense of neglect and his long-standing indignation against critics like Southey. Shelley described *Adonais* as 'a highly-wrought piece of *art*' and 'in spite of its mysticism, ... the least imperfect of my compositions'. He originally planned to precede the poem by a critical essay on *Hyperion* to justify the claim to greatness which he had made for Keats.

Epigraph. 'Thou wert the morning-star among the living, / Ere thy fair light had fled; / Now, having died, thou art as Hesperus, giving / New splendour to the dead' (Shelley's translation).

Preface. The Greek means: 'poison came to thy lips, Bion; poison didst thou eat. To such lips could it approach and not be sweetened? What human was so brutal as to mix the drug for thee, or give it at thy bidding? He escapes my song' (trans. A. S. F. Gow).

3.   *so dear a head*: a classical formulation (cf. Horace's *tam cari capitis*).

5.   *thy obscure compeers*: hours which have not been selected for such prominent duties.

11-12.   *shaft . . . darkness*: the anonymous review in the *Quarterly* (cf. Psalms 91:5–6).

12.   *Urania*: the Muse of Poetry (invoked by Milton, *P.L.*, vii. 1-39) and therefore the mother of Adonais/Keats. She takes over the function of the mourning Aphrodite, the lover of Adonis in the original myth.

14.   *Paradise*: park or pleasure-garden; also Heaven, since Urania is a Heavenly Muse.

29-36.   The disillusionment of 'republican' Milton who died only eight years after the Restoration. *third among the sons of light*: the third great epic poet in succession to Homer and Dante. There may be a heterodox implication here: Milton's light is not that of the New Testament but the light of prophetic poetry. He faced death not with the terror proper to a Christian who believes in Hell but with a calm and self-content worthy of the *kings of thought*.

39-43.   Successful minor poets have known more happiness than greater spirits whose potential was thwarted or never realized.

48-9.   Cf. Keats' *Isabella*, which Shelley had seen by the end of October 1820.

51.   *extreme*: last, latest.

55.   *that high Capital*: Rome.

63.   *liquid*: pure, free from harshness or discord.

69.   *the eternal Hunger*: decomposition.

73-81.   Here and in later stanzas (notably 12) Shelley transforms the traditional mourning Loves into a gathering of mental presences more suitable to a poet.

94.   *anadem*: headband, chaplet, garland.

99.   *the barbèd fire*: the fire of love's arrows.

107.   *clips*: embraces.

120-3.   The clouds of early morning obscured the last stars instead of falling as dew. In many societies, particularly in the East, unbound hair is a sign of mourning.

127.   Echo has abandoned her usual functions.

133-4.   Narcissus rejected the advances of Echo, who pined away till she was only a voice.

141-4.   Hyacinth was loved by Phoebus Apollo, who killed him by accident. Narcissus fell in love with his own reflection. After death both became flowers who now exhale sighs of compassion (*ruth*) rather than sweet scents.

145-51.   *spirit's sister*: Keats had written 'Ode to a Nightingale'. *scale Heaven*: in epic poems like that about the sun-god Hyperion of which Shelley wrote: 'if "Hyperion" be not grand poetry, none has been produced by our contemporaries.'

158.   The spring is imaged as the funeral of the winter, like the rituals of Adonis a paradoxical mixture of joy and grief, whose ultimate implications will turn out to be positive.

159-60.   *brake*: thicket. *brere*: bush or shrub.

174-6.   The flowers illuminate death by their fragrance, as the stars illumine night by their splendour (light). Shelley's synaesthetic boldness is held in check by the cautious precision of his own explication.

177-9.   *that . . . knows*: the mind of man. For the image in 178, cf. Byron's 'So we'll go no more a roving'. *sightless*: invisible.

185-9.   Since death is our creditor, the condition on which we enjoy the beauties of nature is the inevitability of time, change, sorrow.

195.   *their sister*: the Echo who had recited Adonais' poems.

202.   *ghost*: soul, principle of life.

204-6.   *So*: in this way.

208-16.   This passage owes something both to Venus' quest for Adonais and to Plato's description of the influence of Love (see note to *P.U.*, I. 772-9); here the spirit of Poetry meets with unsympathetic reactions.

219.   *Blushed to annihilation*: since a blush brings blood to the face it negates the pallor of death.

227.   This detail is derived from Bion.

228.   *heartless*: disheartened, dejected.

234.   *I am chained to Time*: because she is the Muse of mortal poets.

235-43.   In his immaturity, Keats departed from the paths of poetic convention before he had acquired either the mental resilience to respond appropriately to his critics or the mature achievements which could have dispersed them. The *unpastured dragon* may include suggestions of the *Quarterly* but is not so narrowly specific. *the mirrored shield*: like that used by Perseus against the Medusa. *crescent*: increasing.

249-52.   Byron smote and silenced his critics with *English Bards and Scotch Reviewers* (1809) as Apollo killed the dragon Python.

253-61.   The great poet reveals the truth and obscures his lesser contemporaries as the sun the stars; when he dies, those lesser figures who dimmed his work by criticism or misunderstanding, or who shared in his glory by imitation or by association, will disappear also.

262.   *mountain shepherds*: the pastoral mode is used to introduce a procession of contemporary poets.

264.   *Pilgrim of Eternity*: Byron, author of *Childe Harold's Pilgrimage*.

268-70.   Thomas Moore, fashionably successful Irish poet, liberal and friend of Byron, gave voice to the sad condition of Ireland (*Ierne*) in his *Irish Melodies*.

271. *one frail Form*: Shelley himself in mythological guise.
275. *Actaeon-like*: Actaeon saw Artemis (Diana) naked, for which he was changed into a stag and then devoured by his own dogs.
280. *pardlike*: like the leopard, which was sacred to Dionysus.
283. *superincumbent*: which lies or presses on him.
291-2. The *thyrsus* was a staff traditionally carried by Dionysus and his Bacchantes (cypress for mourning here replacing the original pine-cone). In Plato's *Ion*, which Shelley translated, poets are compared to the Bacchantes who 'when possessed by the God, draw honey and milk from the rivers in which, when they come to their senses, they find nothing but simple water'.
297. Cf. Cowper's self-portrait, 'I was a stricken deer, that left the herd / Long since'.
298. *partial*: prejudiced, for reasons explained in 300.
300-1. In *On Love* Shelley recorded that when he had assumed that he could appeal to something in common with other men 'and unburden my inmost soul to them, I have found my language misunderstood like one in a distant and savage land'.
306. *Cain's or Christ's*: 'The introduction of the name of *Christ* as an antithesis to *Cain* is surely any thing but irreverence or sarcasm' (*L.* ii. 306). This is neither a simple equation nor a blasphemous conjunction. Both Cain and Christ were outcasts but the horrible irony is that while one killed his brother, the other was the harmless benefactor of humanity.
307-15. Leigh Hunt was one of the first to recognize the promise of Keats.
316. *drunk poison*: a detail mentioned in the second epigraph. In the course of the poem the death of Adonis is accounted for in a variety of ways.
319. *nameless worm*: the anonymous reviewer in the *Quarterly*.
327. *noteless*: of no note, undistinguished.
336. *wakes or sleeps*: Shelley's affirmation is qualified by a characteristic fastidiousness of definition.
338. A reference to the Burial of the Dead.
381-5. *plastic stress*: shaping, moulding, creative principle. According to the Greek philosophers, 'God in creating the world, made not the best that he, or even inferior intelligence could conceive; but . . . he moulded the reluctant and stubborn materials ready to his hand into the nearest arrangement possible to the perfect archetype existing in his contemplation' (*On the Devil and Devils*).
395-6 The great minds of the past are a vital influence.
397. A list of poets who were cut off before maturity, like Keats. Chatterton who poisoned himself at seventeen was an emblem of unrecognized genius to the Romantics; Sir Philip Sidney died heroically at thirty-two; Lucan (one of Shelley's favourite Roman poets) betrayed his fellow-conspirators against Nero but committed suicide with redeeming dignity at twenty-six.
414. *Vesper*: Hesperus, the evening star (see epigraph).

415-23. Learn to acknowledge the vastness of the universe and the minuteness of the individual and moderate your misgivings and fear of death.

417. *pendulous*: suspended (in space).

439-50. 'The English burying place is a green slope near the walls, under the pyramidal tomb of Cestius [a Roman tribune] and is I think the most beautiful and solemn cemetery I ever beheld. To see the sun shining on its bright grass . . . and to mark the tombs, mostly of women and young people who were buried there, one might, if one were to die, desire the sleep they seem to sleep' (*L.* ii. 60). Shelley's young son William was buried there (440, 453-5).

463. *Stains*: enriches by colouring (as in stained glass); but see 356.

466-8. Cf. *O.L.*, 234-5.

477. Perhaps a reference to the Wedding Service.

484. *are mirrors*: more correctly *is a mirror*, but Shelley is thinking of the multiplicity of the web of being.

487-95. Images of poetic inspiration (cf. *O.L.* and *Epipsychidion*).

The Aziola. Written 1821 (probably at the Baths of San Giuliano, near Pisa, between May and the end of October). Published posthumously (1829). Mary remembered: 'the cicale at noon-day kept up their hum; the aziola cooed in the quiet evening.' The aziola is a small owl (*assiolo*).

7-9. Shelley anticipates the answer; perhaps this would have been changed if he had lived to revise the MS. draft.

Two Choruses from Hellas. Written autumn 1821. Published 1822. *Hellas* (Greece) celebrates the Greek rising against the Turks of which the Shelleys first heard news from their Greek friend Prince Mavrocordato who was to play a prominent part in its later stages. Taking its cue from the *Persae* of Aeschylus, *Hellas* focuses on the court of the defeated Emperor at Constantinople; it is suffused by a deep melancholy and world-weariness which qualifies Shelley's delight in the rebirth of Greek liberty. Both choruses are spoken by Greek women, captives at the court of Mahmud. The second chorus concludes the play on a note of prophetic doubt.

I.

5. *they*: living and thinking beings who 'to use a common and inadequate phrase, *clothe themselves in matter*' and whose immortality, through reincarnation, is contrasted with 'the transience of the noblest manifestations of the external world' (Shelley's note).

11-14. Shelley is conjecturing 'a progressive state of more or less exalted existence, according to the degree of perfection which every distinct intelligence may have attained' (Shelley's note).

15. *Power*: Christ who, like Prometheus, came to liberate humanity but was tortured for his good intentions.

24. Institutional Christianity became an oppressive force after the death of Christ, whose teachings it traduced.

25-8.   Islam (symbolized by the crescent moon) is a later development than Christianity and will disappear first.

30.   *one*: like Mahmud at the beginning of the play.

34ff.   Shelley is careful to record in a note that he does not endorse the Christian point of view ostensibly expressed in this chorus (e.g. the identification of Truth and Christianity). Like Milton in 'On the Morning of Christ's Nativity', whose metre he has adopted, he regrets the passing of the ancient mythology (*dreams*). 'The sylvans and fauns with their leader, the great Pan, were most poetical personages and were connected in the imagination of the Pagans with all that could enliven and delight. They were supposed to be innocent beings not greatly different in habits from the shepherds and herdsmen of which they were the patron saints. But the Christians contrived to turn the wrecks of the Greek mythology, as well as the little they understood of their philosophy, to purposes of deformity and falsehood' (*On the Devil and Devils*).

II.   Shelley comments: 'The final chorus is indistinct and obscure, as the event of the living drama whose arrival it foretells.' In particular, he was afraid that the Holy Alliance would help the Turks to crush the rising. To prophesy happiness rather than wars is 'a more hazardous exercise of the faculty which bards possess or feign' yet with the authority and excuse of Isaiah and Virgil (Fourth Eclogue) he anticipates 'the possible and perhaps approaching state of society'.

4.   *weeds*: garments usually associated with mourning.

9-12.   For the geography, see 'Song of Pan'. *Cyclads*: a group of islands in the Aegean Sea.

13.   *Argo*: ship in which Jason recovered the Golden Fleece (*prize*).

17-18.   Ulysses was seduced by Calypso on his way home from the Trojan War.

21-4.   By solving the Sphinx's riddle, Oedipus liberated Thebes from the plague; but he also murdered his father Laius, with tragic consequences ('Unnatural love, and more unnatural hate', *P.U.*, I. 349).

31-4.   *Saturn and Love*: 'among the deities of a real or imaginary state of innocence and happiness' (*The golden years*); *All* those *who fell*: 'The Gods of Greece, Asia, and Egypt', superseded by Christ (*One who rose*); *many unsubdued*: 'the monstrous objects of the idolatry of China, India, the Antarctic islands, and the native tribes of America' (Shelley's note).

35-6.   This religion will not be based on blood sacrifices or on mercenary considerations.

37.   *cease*: the chorus is horrified by the sudden thought of what may lie in store.

39-40.   Cf. 'Yet shall some few traces of olden sin lurk behind . . . a second warfare, too, shall there be, and again shall a great Achilles be sent to Troy' (Virgil, Fourth Eclogue, trans. H. Fairclough).

The flower that smiles today.   Written 1821. Published posthumously (1824). Geoffrey Matthews has suggested that this lyric was intended for the opening of *Hellas*, where it was to be sung by a favourite slave to the sleeping Mahmud, whose empire is collapsing as he sleeps.

12.   *these*: Virtue, Friendship and Love, like all human attributes do not disappear when they decline from their original purity but continue to exist in a debased and joyless form.

20.   *thou*: probably the sleeping Emperor.

To Night.   Written 1821. Published posthumously (1824).

Fragment: Rose leaves when the rose is dead.   Dated 1821 by Mrs Shelley. Published posthumously (1824). This text reproduces the order of the stanzas in the MS. draft. Mary Shelley reversed this order and most editors have followed her. The evidence is unclear: the two stanzas are followed by several abortive lines which might represent an attempt to rewrite 3-4 or might be the beginning of a new stanza.

2.   *the beloved's*: originally *a Sultana's*.

3.   *thoughts*: perhaps poetic thoughts (=poems, like the *dead thoughts* in *O.W.W.*). This may refer to the poetry of Emilia Viviani, since drafts of *Epipsychidion* appear in the same notebook as this fragment.

O World, O Life, O Time.   Dated 1821 by Mrs Shelley. Published posthumously (1824).

8.   Shelley left a gap for an adjective to describe summer.

When passion's trance is overpast.   Written in 1821. Published posthumously (1824).

One word is too often profaned.   Dated 1821 by Mrs Shelley. Published posthumously (1824).

To Edward Williams.   Written 26 January 1822. Published posthumously (1834). Edward Ellerker Williams and his wife Jane (to whom most of Shelley's last poems were addressed) were close friends and neighbours of the Shelleys in 1821 and 1822: at this time they lived in the same building in Pisa. Williams was an old Etonian, a retired army officer with artistic leanings; he shared Shelley's taste for boating and they went down together in the *Don Juan*. The poem was accompanied by a cautionary note: 'If any of the stanzas should please you, you may read them to Jane, but to no one else, — and yet on second thoughts I had rather you would not.' Shelley himself would not have published this poem which refers so plainly to his growing estrangement from Mary.

1.   An allusion may be intended to Shelley's nickname (see note on *Prologue in Heaven*).

16.   *its evil, good*: like Satan (*P.L.*, iv. 110).

35.   The final verdict was always in the negative.

41-8. 'The foxes have holes, and the birds of the air have nests; but the Son of man hath not where to lay his head' (Matthew 8:20).

To Jane: The Recollection. Written spring 1822, probably February. Published posthumously (1824; 1839). This poem and 'To Jane: The Invitation', which were originally published as one piece, are centred on a walk made on 2 February 1822 by Shelley, Jane Williams and Mary, which took them through the pine forest of the Cascine near Pisa to the sea.

83. *too faithful*: cf. *with more than truth* (80). Also perhaps a reference to Shelley's allegiance to Mary, who was on the walk and who must have been associated with the *unwelcome thought.*

Prologue in Heaven. Translated from Goethe's *Faust* early 1822. Published posthumously (1824). Shelley intended this and his version of the *Walpurgisnacht* for a paper in *The Liberal*, a new journal founded by Leigh Hunt, Byron and himself. He also translated three scenes from Calderón's *El mágico prodigioso*, a play which 'evidently furnished the *germ* of Faust'. His paper would probably have explored the role of the Devil in both of these plays and might have been a sequel to his unfinished essay *On the Devil and Devils.* The *Prologue in Heaven* had not been translated into English before, largely because it was considered blasphemous. Even Byron, who knew it was based on the Book of Job, referred to 'the daring language of the prologue, which no one will ever venture to translate'.

7. *unwithered*: Shelley's substitution for *unbegreiflich* (incomprehensible).

21. *desolation*: lightning.

28. Shelley provides a literal prose translation of 'this astonishing chorus' in a footnote, because 'it is impossible to represent in another language the melody of the versification; even the volatile strength and delicacy of the ideas escape in the crucible of translation, and the reader is surprised to find a *caput mortuum*' (the worthless residue from an alchemical experiment).

96. 'Muhme is literally aunt, and in the same sense as we find it employed in the old English play's Paramour' (Shelley's note). When Shelley translated this passage to Byron, Byron nicknamed him *The Snake*.

99. *who rebelled*: Shelley's version of *die verneinen* (who deny), perhaps intentional since he translated the words correctly in an earlier prose version.

105. *create*: cause trouble.

107. In Goethe this is specified as *Das Werdende* (the Becoming).

109-10. Cf. *H.I.B.*

Fragment: The Triumph of Life. Probably written between late May and the end of June 1822. Published posthumously from very rough drafts in 1824. This was Shelley's last major poem and was left unfinished and unrevised at his death. The Life of the title is life seen as conqueror and destroyer of man and his ideals, a grim and relentless process which only a heroic few can honourably resist. The poem is based on Petrarch's *Trionfi*, a sequence of triumphal processions involving Love, Chastity, Death, Fame, Time and Eternity, each of which triumphs over its predecessor; there is no indication as to whether Shelley intended a similar sequence nor as to how he would have resolved the unfinished action of his own *Triumph*. He was also influenced by the Arches of Titus and Constantine at Rome, which provided compelling images of 'that mixure of energy & error which is called a Triumph', by Beaumont and Fletcher, by accounts of a masque given by the Inns of Court in honour of Charles I, and perhaps by the Jubilees of 1809 and 1814. Another major influence was Dante: the role of guide and interpreter played by Rousseau is obviously modelled on the role played by Virgil in the *Divine Comedy*.

3. *Rejoicing in his splendour*: unlike man, the powers of nature are self-confident and unashamed to acknowledge their own splendour (cf. 'The Cloud').

5. *smokeless altars*: as opposed to the altars of human religion with their offerings of sacrifice.

7. *orison*: prayer.

21. *But I*: the narrator is out of tune with the processes of nature; he is awake through the night and turns his back to the sunrise.

23. *cone of night*: earth's shadow in space.

29. *strange trance*: the prelude to a visionary poem (cf. *M.A.*).

30-3. Cf. *P.U.*, IV. 211-12; a paradoxical natural phenomenon.

79-85. Cf. 'For lo! the new moon winter-bright! / And overspread with phantom light, / . . . I see the old moon in her lap, foretelling / The coming-on of rain and squally blast' (Coleridge, 'Dejection: An Ode'). *its*: the sleeping tempest's.

91. *cloud like crape*: orig. *a widow's veil of crape*.

94. *Janus-visaged*: with faces at back and front. Harold Bloom sees this Shape as 'a parody of the cherubim or guiding angels of the divine chariot in Ezekiel, Revelation, Dante, and Milton'.

103. *banded*: blindfolded.

111-16. A typical triumph under the Roman empire (cf. *O.L.*, 99-103).

121. *their age*: probably their period in history.

126. *the great winter*: the end of the world.

132. *diadem*: crown.

134. *they . . . Jerusalem*: Socrates and Jesus, in Shelley's view the greatest figures in human history.

137ff. The dance of sexual attraction (*that fierce Spirit*).

175. Impotence destroys the old (*these*), sensuality the young (*those*).

190. *grim Feature*: cf. *P.L.*, x. 279.

210. *wreaths*: haloes, signs of intellectual rather than spiritual achievement.

211-15. They failed to acquire self-knowledge and so were unable to achieve the necessary internal equilibrium. For the importance of psychological politics, see 'Sonnet to the Republic of Benevento'.

217-19. *child . . . destroyed*: Napoleon (cf. *O.L.*, 174–80).

235-6. Two sages (Voltaire and Kant) and three benevolent rulers (Frederick the Great of Prussia, Catherine the Great of Russia, Leopold II of Austria). It is likely that *demagogue* does not refer to any of these but to Pitt whose name was replaced by that of Kant.

240-3. Unlike the others who were conquered by the temptations of the external world, Rousseau was led astray by his own better qualities: 'But from those first acts of goodness, poured out with effusions of heart, were born chains of successive engagements that I had not foreseen, and of which I could no longer shake off the yoke' (*The Reveries of a Solitary*).

254-9. Unlike Socrates whose restraint is recorded in the *Symposium*, Plato succumbed to sexual temptations. The *star* (256) is probably the subject of his epigram tactfully translated by Shelley as 'To Stella' but in reality addressed to a youth.

261. *the tutor and his pupil*: Aristotle and Alexander.

269-73. Bacon's inductive approach to scientific fact broke with the Aristotelian tradition and caused nature to yield up its secrets. Proteus was the old man of the sea who could assume any shape to elude capture; Bacon interpreted this myth as an allegory of nature in *The Wisdom of the Ancients*.

274-9. *the great bards*: originally *Homer and his brethren*. The artistic control of great poets provides an antidote to the potentially harmful passions which they portray; Rousseau was not sufficiently insulated from his subject-matter and so he infected his readers.

283-4. The Roman emperors after the death of liberty (*Caesar's crime*) to the establishment of Christianity as the state religion under Constantine.

288-92. Popes and theologians who imposed on the world their own false notions of divinity (cf. *Laon and Cythna*, 3244ff.). Shelley associated 'the tremendous Gregory' (the Great) with the imposition of 'the opinion of the world'. John may be the XXII, who made notorious use of the Inquisition.

308ff. A symbolic landscape to represent Rousseau's birth into this world.

314-16. Cf. Shelley's translation from the *Purgatorio*, 25-31.

335-9. Cf. Wordsworth's Immortality Ode.

348ff. Because of the fragmentary nature of the poem, the meaning of this Shape is not clear. Although she is beautiful, she has a devastating effect on the observer which is associated with the threatening radiance of the day (382-92). She seems to have all the ambivalence of nature and of life.

357. *Iris*: the rainbow.

359. *Nepenthe*: a drug or potion which banishes grief or trouble.

361. *palms*: soles of the feet.

392. *Heaven's living eyes*: the stars.

414-18. *Lucifer*: Venus as the morning star (cf. 'To a Sky-lark', 18-25). *chrysolite*: yellowish green.

419-23. Characteristic synaesthesia to evoke a preternatural experience.

421-2. 'The favourite song, *Stanco di pascolar le pecorelle*, is a Brescian national air' (Mrs Shelley).

427. *day-appearing dream*: translates a phrase from Aeschylus' *Agamemnon*.

439-41. For the triumphal arch of the rainbow, cf. 'The Cloud', 67-70.

471-6. Dante in the *Divine Comedy*; the love is his for Beatrice.

479. *the sphere*: Venus.

499. Possibly specific references to Napoleon's infant son who was declared King of Rome in 1811, and to George III whose insanity became total in the same year.

500. *anatomies*: skeletons, withered lifeless forms.

To Jane (The keen stars were twinkling). Written in June 1822. Published posthumously (1832; 1839). 'I sate down to write some words for an ariette which might be profane — but it was in vain to struggle with the ruling spirit, who compelled me to speak of things sacred to yours & Wilhelmeister's indulgence — I commit them to your secrecy & your mercy & will try & do better another time.' By his own admission, Shelley's ideas of music were 'gross' and he was always susceptible to feminine music-makers (see 'To Constantia, Singing'). He was particularly delighted by the talents of Jane Williams: 'Williams is captain, and we drive along this delightful bay in the evening wind, under the summer moon, until earth appears another world. Jane brings her guitar, and if the past and future could be obliterated, the present would content me so well that I could say with Faust to the passing moment, "Remain, thou, thou art so beautiful" ' (*L*. ii. 435-6).

17. *dews*: in the sense of the adjective *liquid* (pure and clear in tone). Cf. the imagery of 'To a Sky-lark'.

Fragment: Lines Written in the Bay of Lerici. Written late June 1822. Published posthumously (1862). These roughly drafted lines, which refer to Shelley's friendship with Jane Williams, were found in the MS. of *T.L*.

1-14. The opening invocation to the moon was added at a later stage of composition but it provides an important objective correlative for the poet's feelings about his beloved. After the invocation, the moon is referred to in the third person.

10-12. Albatrosses are reputed to sleep on the wing.

21-4. Jane had hypnotic powers (see 'The Magnetic Lady to her Patient').

39-44. The ships are associated with daemons, those spirits intermediary between man and god who are the good angels of Shelley's universe. For the sea as purveyor of medicine, see 'Sonnet: On Launching some bottles filled with Knowledge into the Bristol Channel', which begins, 'Vessels of Heavenly medicine'.

55-8. (Unlike man), the fish are single-mindedly devoted to the pursuit of pleasure and oblivious of its fatal consequences. *Too happy* expresses this ambivalence (cf. Keats' responses to the nightingale). These paradoxes are explored at greater length in another late lyric 'We meet not as then we parted'.

58.   Though we cannot be certain, it seems possible that the poem was intended to finish with this generalized reflection. Shelley first wrote 'Destroying life not peace' and then cancelled the first word; it is not clear whether 'alone' is an alternative to 'not peace' or whether it should be retained in the text.

INDEX OF FIRST LINES

A glorious people vibrated again   91
An old, mad, blind, despised and dying King   90
Art thou pale for weariness   124
As I lay asleep in Italy   65

Bright wanderer, fair coquette of Heaven   189

Chameleons feed on light and air   101

'Do you not hear the aziola cry?'   158

From the forests and highlands   121

Goodnight? ah! no; the night is ill   124

Hail to thee, blithe Spirit!   104
Hell is a city much like London   79
Honey from silkworms who can gather   90

I bring fresh showers for the thirsting flowers   98
I met a traveller from an antique land   11
I rode one evening with Count Maddalo   13
I thought of thee, fair Celandine   7
I weep for Adonais — he is dead!   144

Monarch of Gods and Daemons, and all Spirits   33
Mother, I am grown wiser, though a child   61

Nor happiness, nor majesty, nor fame   123
Now the last day of many days   166

O thou, who plumed with strong desire   122
O wild West Wind, thou breath of Autumn's being   76
O World, O Life, O Time   163
One word is too often profaned   164

Palace-roof of cloudless nights!   88

Rarely, rarely, comest thou   102
Rose leaves, when the rose is dead   162

Sing, Muse, the son of Maia and of Jove   115
Sweet Spirit! Sister of that orphan one   126
Swift as a spirit hastening to his task   171
Swiftly walk o'er the western wave   161

The awful shadow of some unseen Power   1
The everlasting universe of things   3
The flower that smiles to-day   161
The keen stars were twinkling   188
The serpent is shut out from Paradise   164
The sleepless Hours who watch me as I lie   120
The spider spreads her webs, whether she be   107
The Sun is warm, the sky is clear   11
The Sun makes music as of old   168
The world's great age begins anew   159
This is the Day, which down the void abysm   64
Thy country's curse, is on thee, darkest crest   9

What! alive and so bold, O Earth?   141
What veiled form sits on that ebon throne?   57
When passion's trance is overpast   163
Whether the Sensitive Plant, or that   100
Worlds on worlds are rolling ever   158